Journal of a Country Lawyer

XMAS 1995
GIVEN TO ME BY MY
DAUGHTER - DIANNA
SON-IN LAW CLIEN.

Gerald S Leeler.

Journal of a
Country Lawyer

Wonderful Gift

Crime, Sin and Damn Good Fun

E. C. Burton

hancock

house

ISBN 0-88839-364-4
Copyright © 1995 E. C. Burton

Cataloging in Publication Data
Burton, Edward C. (Edward Cherry), 1931-
  Journal of a country lawyer
  Crime, sin, and damn good fun

  ISBN 0-88839-364-4

  1. Burton, Edward C. (Edward Cherry), 1931-
2. Country lawyers—Canada—Biography. I. Title.
KE416.B87A3 1995   349.71'092   C95-910645-6
KF373.B87A3 1995

Editing: Colin Lamont
Production: Myron Shutty, Nancy Kerr, and Sandi Miller
Cover Design: Karen Whitman
Cover Photo: E. C. Burton

Published simultaneously in Canada and the United States by

HANCOCK HOUSE PUBLISHERS LTD.
19313 Zero Avenue, Surrey, B.C. V4P 1M7
(604) 538-1114   Fax (604) 538-2262

HANCOCK HOUSE PUBLISHERS
1431 Harrison Avenue, Blaine, WA 98230-5005
(604) 538-1114   Fax (604) 538-2262

Contents

Foreword 7

Preface 9

Introduction 11

One: Trials I Remember 25
    The Case of Dalton Barber 28
    An Unspeakable Crime 33
    The Baby Snatcher 43
    What's In a Name 48
    The Bear and Grace Keesic 55
    The Killing of Carl Rae 58
    A Delayed Trial 61

Two: Coroner's Cases 67
    Justice for Caleb 68
    Death in the O.R. 70
    Dead Trapper 74
    The Runaway, Charlie Wenjack 75
    Werner Lake 76
    Confederation Lake 78
    Drinking the Cargo 78
    A Primitive Postmortem 80
    An Aircraft Fatality 82

Three: Behind the Scenes 87
    Death of the King 88
    The Redditt Train Wreck: Whiskey Galore 90
    The Art and Science of Highgrading Explained 114
    The Girl in the Boat 119

Sinbad The Police Dog 120
The Rifleman 122
Deadman's Run 123
Hiding the Nitro 126
Night of Terror 127
A Survivor 130
Crazies I Have Known 131

Four: Sex and the Thinking Crown Attorney 139
Abuses of the Clergy 140
A Perspective on Rape 147
Whores 155
Collecting the Evidence 164
The Transvestite 166

Five: Unfinished Business 169
Bomber, Mad 170
Who Was Maggoty Maisie? 184

Six: Cultural Divide 189
A Long, Hot Summer 191
On the Coast of Hudson Bay 227

Appendix 237

Foreword

*I do not care to speak ill of a man behind his back, but I
believe the man is an attorney.*

Samuel Johnson 1709-1784

I wouldn't say I've made a career out of slamming lawyers, but I've
taken my shots whenever I got the chance.

After all, lawyers have always done as much for me.

I remember the lawyer who charged me a week's pay (my week,
not his week)—to glance for a nanosecond at one of my book contracts.
Said contract later turned out to be full of more holes than Bonnie and
Clyde's Model T.

I didn't get my lawyer's fee back.

I remember my yard sale in Thunder Bay and looking up to see my
ex-wife's divorce lawyer pawing over a rack of my old jackets.

My ex-wife's lawyer! This reptile had just fleeced me in court for
everything but the gotchies I stood in—and now he was in my back
yard, looking for bargains???

I ran away from my own yard sale. It was either that or succumb to
the temptation to commit homicide with a weed whacker.

And I remember too well, the august members of the Vancouver
Bar Association. They invited me to be guest speaker at their annual
convention a few years back. Little did I know that there was an
unspoken, but nonetheless sacred, Convention convention known to
initiates as Driving the Guest Speaker from the Stage.

They heaved buns. They yelled obscenities. They hooted. They
howled. I'm pretty sure they foamed at the mouth. They chuggalugged

bottles of rare vintage wines and whistled and stomped and generally acted like a high school mud wrestling team on a victory bus.

So you can imagine when one E.C. Burton Q.C., asked me to write an introduction to his memoirs, a veritable kaleidoscope of reactions flickered through my mind, hardly any of them printable.

But he sent me the manuscript. I glanced at it. Then I looked again. Then I started leafing through a page or two.

I was hooked. The next time I looked up it was 3:00 A.M. and I was only halfway through a chapter called *The Redditt Train Wreck: Whiskey Galore.*

What can you say about a legal tome that includes chapters such as *Hiding the Nitro, The Transvestite, Who Was Maggoty Maisie,* and *Crazies I Have Known.*

What can I say but read *Journal of a Country Lawyer.* If you don't enjoy it as much as I did, then check your pulse. You might be dead.

Or my ex-wife's divorce lawyer.

ARTHUR BLACK

Preface

Frequently, people ask me why I wrote this book. English teachers everywhere will be greatly disappointed, but the truth is, I am not sure why I wrote it. Authors write because they feel a need to teach, or for ego gratification, or for money, or because they are natural storytellers, and some combination of these factors no doubt motivated me, too. But that is not the complete answer. Upon searching my soul I have to admit that I feel an irresistible compulsion to tell the rest of the world that I did not lead an ordinary, humdrum life. Perhaps I am really trying to justify my existence as a lawyer for the last thirty-five years.

So far, I have been successful at avoiding boredom in life. While it could not be said that evading the ordinary and escaping from ennui have been cornerstones of my existence, I freely admit they have been part of the foundation. This journal, if you read just beneath the surface, tells how I managed to do it in my professional life. The reader should look at the book not merely as a collection of stories, but as a record defined by points along the way.

In writing about how things were in the old days, I hope it isn't perceived that I advocate doing things the same way today, although some beneficial practices and attitudes might well be brought back, notably a commonsense perspective on just what it is the prosecution is trying to achieve.

Personal hero stories have been kept to a minimum, as I am disinclined to write an autobiography. Even so, when I read my own ink, it is plain that some reflection of myself shows through in many of the stories, even in the ones in which I do not appear. I am therefore forced to concede that I have injected some of my own personality into the stories, and to that extent, the book is indeed autobiographical. So much for objectivity in writing. Everything in the book is basically true, give or take latitude in such matters as names and places, many of which have been changed to protect the sensibilities of people still living, even some of the villains themselves. But everything I write about actually happened.

The Old Inspector, who appears in many places in this book, was very real, as was the Young Crown attorney, whom I knew well.

The title of this book, *Journal of a Country Lawyer; Crime, Sin and Damn Good Fun* is taken from the chapter dealing with ladies of easy virtue, but the concept really has a much wider application. At the age of sixty-three, I still possess a modest fervor to save the world, and it is my thesis that if society and its law makers would only make the appropriate distinctions between crime, sin and damn good fun, the administration of justice would be greatly simplified.

In the writing of this book I am indebted to everyone I ever met, particularly to Erica, who has been by my side for thirty-five years, and to Charlie Wilkins who has given invaluable literary advice, and Annette O'Brien for her constructive criticism.

E. C. B.

Introduction

The Making of a Crown Attorney or a brief autobiography wherein the author tells just enough of the truth to instruct the reader without scandalizing him.

Getting appointed to be a Crown attorney was not difficult, but learning to do the job was a fascinating and never-ending process. I was privileged to take part in a changing era, and to come through it with my integrity more or less intact.

I now realize that preparation for the job began back in my childhood and in my youth, but of course I had no understanding of that during those times. As the only child of a bush pilot and a newspaper woman, our family was frequently on the move. I got to know many places and people and had adventures that had profound effects on me. My formative years could not possibly be duplicated in this age of sanitized government control of just about everything.

I was too young to remember much about the depression, but my parents were significantly affected by it. Pop was a doughty Englishman with a streak of adventure in his makeup, the type of person who exported to the rest of the world what people have come to think of as British civilization. Mom was the type of American girl they used to make movies about, a bit of a flapper in her lighter moments, but competent in her field and confident in her own abilities. The family went from good flying jobs (the air mail when I was born in 1931) to lesser flying jobs (flying training and flying jobs in northern Quebec's fur trade) to ground jobs (running a mine store at the Perron Mines in Quebec) to farming (running an orange grove in Florida). When the Second World War came along, Pop went back to flying, this time to

11

the Ontario Provincial Air Service, a branch of what is now known as the Ministry of Natural Resources. I became a forestry brat and had a great time minding fire towers, working in tourist camps, and bumming rides in old aircraft, some of which, like the Vickers Vedette, were relics of the 1920s.

An uncountable number of elementary schools in Quebec, Ontario, and North Florida, which was my mother's home, had me on their rolls for periods ranging from a few days to a few months. It was a great contrast from the one room schoolhouse in a small mining community in remote northern Quebec, complete with a broken-down and dissipated old teacher who actually lived in the classroom and cooked on a woodstove in the corner while conducting classes, to a small country school in North Florida where, after school, my pals would retrieve their hunting rifles from the teacher to go coon hunting, to a brief stint at upscale Seabreeze High in Daytona Beach. On occasion I took correspondence courses or just read books. High school was mostly in Sault Ste. Marie, Ontario, with brief time outs in Kenora, Ontario, and Soo, Michigan. My higher education was at Michigan College of Mining and Technology and the University of Western Ontario, and eventually at Osgoode Hall Law School. Somewhere along the way I took a couple of years out and prospected, mined, railroaded, and did so many odd jobs I can't even remember them. Once I was even on pogey for two weeks.

Eventually I settled in Kenora, simply because that's where my parents were living when it was time for me to put down some roots. I always liked my parents, who were unfailingly good-natured and supportive. I never went through a phase, so common in the later decades of the century, in which I was alienated from my parents.

Legal education was carried on much differently in Ontario in the 1950s. We went to lectures for two years, we articled for one year, and then returned to Toronto for a fourth year of mixed lectures and articles. My principal during my year under articles in Kenora was Jack K. Doner, a fugitive from Saskatchewan's flatlands and one of the most generous and openhearted people I have ever known. He confined himself to a solicitor's practice and never went to court—if he could help it. After the first week Jack told me I would never make a solicitor, but he nevertheless kept on paying me to go to court with his friend, Tom Brett, in the hope that I would learn something from him. Jack even raised me to forty dollars a week by the end of the year, at a time when the average student was only making thirty dollars. Perhaps the extra ten dollars was for doing odd chores like running into Winnipeg for a truckload of pop when he needed it for the business which he ran on the side. Jack let me have space in his office when I came back from law school in the spring of 1959 until I was ready to open my own chambers. Later he did the same for other young lawyers.

When I returned to Kenora, a most delightful and unforseen prospect awaited me. I met my future wife, Erica, who was working in the Magistrate's Office, just back after several years of living in Montreal and California. I had never met anyone quite so wonderful. We hit it off immediately, and were married the following summer. My roots in Kenora were now very firmly established. In due course we had two sons and a daughter.

Kenora was a good place to live and raise a family. A picturesque small town, it is situated on the north shore of Lake of the Woods, which extends down into northern Minnesota and is one of the most beautiful, scenic areas in the country. Our island camp thirteen miles south remains our favorite place to spend the summers, though we have managed to see a good bit of the world through the years.

My efforts at private practice in Kenora were woefully unsuccessful, as the only action I ever had was in magistrate's court, and then as now, most people who got into trouble didn't have much money. I had great difficulty with most of the estates and land transactions sent to me by friends and other lawyers, and towards the end of my unhappy one and a half years in private practice, I got a knot in the bottom of my stomach every time I went near the office, even though I had transformed it into a rather pleasant place. Deeds and mortgages still make me want to puke. If my part-time bookkeeper, Helen Doran, hadn't taken it upon herself to bill clients I would have starved. A Model A Ford half ton, several rifles, numerous trout, and the odd piece of moose or deer meat were satisfactory while I was living with my folks, but after getting married, I needed to have an income to contribute to my own household—not a lot, but more than I was making at the practice of law. I came to the disheartening conclusion that I would never make a living at a profession for which I was temperamentally unsuited.

Most of my success in Magistrate's Court resulted in self-esteem, but not in financial status. There was no legal aid in those days as Papa State had not yet inflicted the citizenry with total welfare. Nothing I was exposed to in law school really prepared me for criminal defense work,

13

unless it was the impromptu debates, but we weren't accorded official marks for these. I credit the impromptu debates and the kind tutelage of Tom Brett, a Kenora lawyer of great forensic skill, for whatever success I had in criminal court. Tom would have been a Queen's Counsel(QC) if he had not been a Liberal in the time of a Conservative government.

I always had a soft spot for Tom because he once publicly chastised a magistrate who was greatly exceeding the bounds of good taste in tearing strips off me for some inconsequential mistake. For the next fifteen years, until he retired, that magistrate was the very soul of congeniality to me, although he regularly ate up other lawyers for anything he considered a slight infraction.

Most of the money I made came out of Red Lake. Twice a month Magistrate Joe Fregeau held court up there, invariably on a Thursday. I would drive up Wednesday afternoon or evening after attending court in Dryden, and park myself in a room at the Red Lake Inn, and sure enough, before long the friendly desk clerk, Joe Falvo, would begin to send clients up to the room. I would see them all whether or not they had money. I was a lot happier if they had money, but I usually took them on even if they were stony broke. During a lull in the action, I would walk over to the police detachment and talk to the Ontario Provincial Police (OPP) Corporal, Dick Bender, who at the first meeting invariably intimidated young policemen and young lawyers. He was a big man with a kink in his nose that contributed to what one might call an "interesting" face, if one did not want to stretch the truth by calling him handsome. If you troubled to look beyond the nose you found a pair of permanently twinkling eyes. The conversation would go something like this:

"Hello, Burton, what the hell do you want in here this evening?"

"Well now. I thought I might find someone in here to share this jug with."

"What do you mean share it? We're having a police social on Friday, so you can just leave it on the desk over there."

This process was the very original form of disclosure in the Province of Ontario. They make more of a fuss about it today, and it is not as effective as it was in 1959. After the initial sparring I would get down to business.

"You got anyone unjustly locked up who is clamoring for a good lawyer?"

14

"Yeah, we got half the goddamned town locked up, and if you're the only lawyer in town you'll have to do."

A pregnant pause, while the all-powerful corporal decided how much he was going to tell me.

"Larry Keesic is in cell number one. He's charged with breaking and entering Fergie's General Store over on McKenzie island, but we haven't got much on him. The magistrate is probably going to let him go, so you might as well defend him and get the credit for an acquittal. He's so dumb that he won't know that he would get off even without you. He's got twenty-four dollars and sixty-one cents in his prisoner's bag and he owes Fergie about five dollars, and you can have the rest. I've already got a signed release for the money in his bag."

This may not sound like much but in those days a bottle of whiskey was only four dollars and fifty cents at the liquor store, or ten dollars at a bootlegger's. In any event I held myself out as a practitioner of criminal law, and I felt I had to extend my services to anyone who wanted them regardless of their ability to pay.

There would be another pause while Dick frowned at my briefcase, the six-bottle one that I used all through law school, the one my daughter used thirty-five years later in law school. I had to promise not to subvert his men by offering them a drink in the office before he would continue.

"George Kusevich is locked up in number four. He kicked the snot out of his old lady last week and Dr. Hay says she may abort because of it. I suppose bastards like him are entitled to a defense, but if you get him off I'll personally break your neck." You had to look the corporal in the eye to determine just how serious he was, and even so you couldn't be sure.

He went on more slowly, carefully avoiding my eyes. "He's got about one hundred dollars in his kitty, but if he's convicted I want you to give his wife half so she can eat while he's doing his time."

The corporal was really a notorious softie underneath his gruff exterior.

Another pause, unbearable. Like as not we would go upstairs to one of the police apartments where it was acceptable practice to have a drink or two. Out of old faithful would come another jug. I would fire the cap into the garbage, drawing scowls from the policeman's wife. The sound was like a magnet, and policemen would materialize from their living quarters. The contents of the jug would dematerialize and tongues would loosen. Someone would take up where the corporal left off.

15

"Old Kusevich isn't such a bad shit. I went out and got him a steak for supper and he volunteered (a snicker here) five dollars to little league baseball. Anyway, that lump in Mrs. K's belly isn't George's, it is courtesy of the nightshift out at the Madsen Mine. Doc Hay just made up that crap about how she might abort to scare George into behaving."

Appreciative smiles here. Kids' baseball was a favorite with the police. But I could see my hundred dollars shrinking. It was now down to forty-five dollars. However, there was a ray of hope in that at least one policeman figured Kusevich wasn't all that bad of a fellow. Perhaps I could build a defense on this, and if successful, bill George for a reasonable fee later. But right now I had to think of something to divert the group's attention from George Kusevich before some other mischief maker whittled the poke down even further.

Probably I would say, "Let's have a little snort here, and someone tell me what you've got on a fella named Albert Johnson." Some thirsty policeman would produce the details on Albert Johnson, and, by and by, I would see all my clients. If they were not security risks I would see them downstairs in the office. If they were bad dudes I had to see them right in the cells, risking uncomplimentary speculations concerning my physical attributes as I passed the women's section.

Late in the evening I might seek out witnesses who would be able to help me with trials on the next day.

The following day we would embark on trials, almost never asking for adjournments or electing trial by a higher court. Bail was difficult to obtain and accused persons wanted to get it over with; win, lose, or draw. Today, after bail reform and the Charter, people think much differently.

Frequently I would defend Tom Brett's cases, too, if he couldn't make the 172 dusty, potholed miles from Kenora in time for court. When I got back to Kenora, Mr. Brett and I would divvy up the take. One glorious day my share came to $500.00, probably as much as I made all the rest of the month. It was at about this time that I began to call him Tom, not Mr. Brett.

I tried not to defend hopeless cases. Where a case might have really serious consequences to a morally guilty client, I would throw myself into it with gusto, but in most instances I tried to dicker with my friend and tormentor, Corporal Bender, or perhaps with the Crown, or I might even throw my client on the mercy of the court, as they used to say. For that matter, it's still a good expression. At any rate, I had a fairly high incidence of success and I managed it without antagonizing the police or resorting to sleazy tactics.

There are two basic philosophies in the legal profession about how one should service clients who are before a court. At the one end of the spectrum is the lawyer who "takes instructions" from his client. At the other end is the lawyer who "gives advice" to his client. The distinction between the two is very real. The lawyer who takes instructions is apt to plead the most futile case not guilty and consume the time of the court and considerable public funds in so doing. Of course he may get lucky once in a while, but more frequently the court is bored, the Crown is irritated, and the client's interests may not be well served. This type of lawyer considers it his primary duty to service the action, and of course it is a legitimate stance if not carried to unreasonable lengths, but a lawyer may lose credibility if he carries it too far.

I rather preferred the other school of thought—if my clients were smart enough to give me instructions they wouldn't need my services, so I advised them to the best of my ability, and if we had any strong disagreement they would have to find another lawyer. I have often observed that when a lawyer starts out an apologetic speech with "My client has instructed me..." he may really mean that he is just a mouthpiece who doesn't have the courage of his convictions. Perhaps I have overstated the case, but after many years of courtroom practice I have come to easily recognize the lawyer who, at all costs, places his duty to the client above his duty to the court. He may win a few cases that way, but all his clients ever after will suffer from his lack of credibility with the court and his fellow lawyers.

So went my time as an articled student and my year and a half in private practice. I look back on it as a time of apprenticeship, or dues paying. It was a time of beginning.

For years there had been two half-time Crown attorneys in the District of Kenora, that huge, underpopulated tract of land in the northwest part of Ontario, an area of 150,000 square miles. T.A. O'Flaherty spent more than half his time prosecuting in Kenora, and Norm McAulay, or later his young partner, Bob Gibson, spent about half their time servicing the Magistrate's courts in the Dryden end of the district. The vast hinterland to the north received no service at all. The half-time Crowns were paid $3,600 annually in 1960, a miserly sum even by the standards of the day, plus an additional fifty dollars a month towards the

17

salary of a secretary. They asked for more and were turned down. T.A. O'Flaherty and Bob Gibson resigned and that's where I came in.

I made an appointment to meet the Honorable Kelso Roberts, who was then the attorney general, in Red Lake, to see about the job. Because of the nasty November weather, his aircraft could not land, but diverted instead to Sioux Lookout. Inspector T.G. Corsie and Constable Eric "Towel Rack" Miller (so named because of a remarkable appendage, which when tumescent, could support a wet bath towel) drove me the 200 miles to Sioux Lookout, where I met with Kelso Roberts in a cheap hotel room the next morning.

The Honorable Attorney General was monumentally hungover, and as his toilet was the only one not frozen up in the hotel, the room was like a public highway. The interview was highly unorthodox and most unsatisfactory, as in addition to people trooping in to use the toilet, the Honorable Mr. Roberts and his deputy, Bill Common, were huddled fully dressed in the double bed, shivering from the cold.

Inspector Corsie was a man of highly-developed perceptions, and the first thing he did after meeting the boss (the OPP came under the umbrella of the attorney general at the time) was to send Const. Miller out to a bootlegger for a bottle of whiskey. "Just tell her it's for me and she won't charge you anything." The Towel Rack was back within minutes, and being the junior person present, he was the last to have a pull at the bottle.

In between snorts the attorney general and I talked about mining (he was a mining lawyer away back) and politics (I was a Liberal and he, of course, was a Conservative) and spent a very few minutes talking about my qualifications for the job. He must have liked me, for I got the job in spite of my politics. I promised never to use my position to cut the Conservative throat behind its back, and he promised to keep the local Conservative party organization off my back. I didn't and he did, at least until I grew enough whiskers to look after myself.

It was only later that I found out that Kelso Roberts and my dad had been partners in a little mining syndicate in the Territories, many years previously. Kelso did the legal work and my dad did the flying, and neither of them made a nickel out of it. I don't think Mr. Roberts remembered my dad, or he would have mentioned it.

When I took the job in February, 1961, I really thought it was going to be temporary, until I could find something else to put bread and butter on the table. I had tried prospecting, mining, railroading, millwrighting, and a host of other jobs in the two years and many summer vacations when I was not in school. I certainly wasn't going to waste three years of university and four years of law school to go back to that sort of thing, even though it had been fun at the time. I had always felt an inner compulsion to write, but had never actually done any of it, and I now thought of newspaper work. The problem eventually solved itself, because much to my surprise I found that I actually liked being a Crown attorney, and I stayed. I continued to be the Crown attorney for Kenora for almost twenty-five years, and the Crown attorney in Thunder Bay for three years, and my last two years as director of Crown attorneys for Northwest Ontario.

The first years were tough, really tough, but the experience was great. Kenora was so far from Toronto it might as well have been on the other side of the moon as far as my bosses were concerned, and they encouraged me to make my own decisions. I had some big cases and some little cases, but usually no time to prepare them. Any guidance I got was from my fellow lawyers or the police and not from Toronto. Dick Bender, whom I still saw occasionally until he died in 1994, eventually retired as a superintendent. For years he continued to tell me how to run my cases, and if he thought I was going soft in the plea-bargaining process he would say, "Darn it Burton, you are letting that Winnipeg lawyer bamboozle you. You are trading a horse for a rabbit."

The worst part of it was the driving—some 25,000 miles a year in addition to full days in court. I serviced two full-time magistrates (They call them provincial judges now. The title was given to them in lieu of a raise in the hopes that they would rise to their upgraded status. They did.) with regular courts in Kenora and Dryden and satellite courts in Red Lake and Sioux Lookout. Before long, other satellite courts and fly-in courts were established. It was some years before I was afforded the luxury of an assistant Crown.

Being interested in numerous causes related and unrelated to the justice system, and sometimes out of a sense of duty, I involved myself in several worthy causes which I felt needed my input and support. On those evenings when I wasn't on the road or attending meetings of one sort or another, I often collapsed into bed right after supper. Eventually, I became wiser and cut back on this sort of activity, and to no one's surprise but my own, I found that the worthy causes carried on quite well without me.

One association to which I continued to devote my time was the local flying club. A fledgling club when I joined, it had some good, dedicated people who were also interesting characters with whom I enjoyed associating. It provided excellent flying training with a hands-on approach to trouble-shooting and maintenance. Given the type of aircraft available, which were anything but state-of-the-art, and the desolate and inhospitable terrain which comprises much of the area, the training proved invaluable on more than one occasion, when difficulties arose and no ground crew was on hand. I spent as much time as I could afford hanging around the club and getting my wings. When I finally got my land-plane and seaplane endorsements, suddenly court trips to places like Red Lake and Sioux Lookout took on a whole new dimension. Occasionally I would take along a companion who could be persuaded to wait out the court session in return for a promised touchdown on a remote lake for a spot of fishing on the way home. There were times, when the weather was against me, that I found the old maxim to be true "when there's time to spare, go by air." I arrived late on occasion, but had learned to gauge weather conditions well enough so that I always got where I was going.

Life was good, and I was on a roll.

Crown attorneys as a breed were not exceptionally well regarded in the 1960s. Indeed, Kelso Roberts told me on that morning in Sioux Lookout that if there was any broken-down party hack in the province who wanted the job, he would have had to give it to him. I wasn't quite sure what he was trying to tell me, but it didn't take me long to learn. There were a number of incompetent people on the rolls; some were strictly patronage appointments; and all were certainly underpaid. One night after particularly offensive carryings-on by several of my new colleagues, at a conference in a big hotel on the Niagara Peninsula, Erica and I found ourselves wondering what kind of a bunch of people I had gotten myself involved with. There were a number of really fine people in the group, but we had more than our share of members who did not come up to the mark.

The situation improved within a few years. The Crown Attorneys Association obtained money for educational purposes, the government improved its hiring practices, and eventually we got better raises. The raises did a great deal for our self-esteem, and I believe that we all, including the clods, made an effort to merit our improved status. Attrition took care of some of the old-timers and the rest either pulled up their socks or quit. By the 1970s, the Crown attorney's system in

Ontario boasted really first-class lawyers, but still no women. That was to come later.

All things change with time. Crown attorneys were once expected to be first-rate prosecutors, but very little else. Every day was spent in the courtroom. However, by 1975 most Crown attorneys were doing a great deal more—advising Toronto on policy, working more closely with the police, lecturing, teaching, and advising various government ministries on enforcement problems. It wasn't so much that the nature of these non-prosecutorial duties changed, but that the time consumed by them increased substantially. The young assistants still spend most of their time in the courtroom, but they are now considered to be budding agents of the attorney general, not merely technical prosecutors. The kind of assistant I liked was one who felt he was in training for my job.

After many years in the courtroom I became battle weary, an affliction common to many Crown attorneys. Prisoners, victims, and witnesses seemed to have become a continuous stream of misery, all of a breed, and I became conscious that I was not seeing them as individual humans but only as cases, and every case was a drag. Periodically I thought of leaving to go to—what? The idea of entering politics was alluring; I felt a need to become less depersonalized in my dealings with humanity, to get at some understanding and possible alleviation of the conditions in society in which this misery flourished, rather than just deal with the end results. Fortunately, my political masters allowed me time and funds to indulge my interest in the plight of the Ojibway and Cree Indians of northwest Ontario, who were having problems meeting the larger world on its own terms, and their run-ins with the law were appalling. I like to think I was of assistance to them in the process of coping with modern society. Without this challenge and a few other projects normally outside the scope of a Crown attorney, I couldn't have stayed with it. Crowns are poor actuarial risks (as are all trial lawyers) and at one time, if they didn't go back to private practice or to the bench, their chances of living to retirement were poor. I had already had my fling with private practice, and I had no wish to go to the bench. Eventually I went to Thunder Bay as Crown attorney, and I spent the last two years of my career as Director of Crown Attorneys for the Northwest Region. But long before this, the fun had gone out of the game.

Becoming a Crown attorney was a sink or swim proposition. I

21

swam. I have always been thankful I wasn't under the watchful eye of a big city newspaper in the beginning years. Toronto was twenty-six hours away by train, or two days drive to the south and east. Winnipeg was two hours away to the west, but the two big dailies paid little attention to Kenora, and in any event, my bosses in Toronto did not read the Winnipeg papers. Fortunately *The Kenora Miner and News* and *The Dryden Observer* were tolerant papers. Small town papers don't dump on local public officials if they are doing their best. By the time Kenora and Dryden got daily air service to Toronto I had learned my job well enough to avoid public censure. Looking back at my many years on the job, I was quite successful at it, at least partly because of an uncanny ability for avoiding the consequences of my own follies.

Murders and violence I had aplenty, but the district was quite free of white-collar crime and anything smacking of professional or organized crime, although that crept in during the 1980s. I think that the reason for the violence was that northwestern Ontario has always had a boom or bust economy and seasonal workers. The per capita consumption of alcohol has always been high. When people have time on their hands they drink, and when they drink, they fight. It's that simple. People who do that sort of thing also steal, though often not very successfully. The majority of lawbreakers in these parts are stupid or unfortunate, and with the exception of dope pushers everywhere, and a certain core of would-be criminal apprentices in Thunder Bay, there are very few professionals. The law manages to cope with the heavy-duty dudes in a fairly efficient manner, and most of them spend a lot of time in durance vile. Anonymity, the shield of the criminal, can only be achieved in a city, and Thunder Bay, the only city of any size between Sault Ste. Marie and Winnipeg, is really a very small city.

The anonymity granted by today's system to young offenders by shielding them from public exposure seems to me to be an undeserved protection, and defeats the purpose of steering young people away from criminal activity by removing a very potent deterrent: the disapproval by society of unacceptable behavior.

The practical consequence of small-time criminal work was that the Crown attorneys seldom got their teeth into a good solid case against some rotter who was truly a public enemy, where they could do the knight in shining armor bit, decimating the bad guys for the benefit of society. Crown attorneys seldom get good ink, but are prosecutors of the mindless violence that human beings do to each other. Still, the Crown attorneys serve a high purpose, and together with the other people involved in the administration of justice, they keep the lid on crime.

Speaking of keeping the lid on crime, I want to say that in a civilized society we do not aim to stamp out crime absolutely, as that can only happen in a totalitarian or police state, which Canada emphatically is not. In the interests of individual freedom and civil rights, society maintains a certain tolerance for deviant behavior (i.e. crime) and therefore checks and balances are put on activities of the police and the courts, and inevitably a percentage of guilty people go free.

Everyone has an image of himself, or a world view. My self-image is that I am a reasonably laid-back sort of a person, probably more so than most people involved in prosecutions. Nevertheless, I have the uneasy feeling that the Canadian Charter of Rights, which began to take effect in 1982, is having a detrimental effect on the quality of life in Canada. The bad guys are getting ahead of us, and unfortunately this includes many young miscreants we euphemistically call young offenders. The courts have been far, far too liberal in interpreting what was intended only to be a check on the power of the state to interfere in the lives of citizens. The Charter was supposed to be a shield against unjust oppression as opposed to a bludgeon to be used against legitimate authority. It was my duty as a Crown attorney to see to the enforcement of this charter and this I did, but with less enthusiasm as time went by.

When I retired in 1991, I was freed from an indefinable obligation to refrain from being publicly critical of the law. I am quite frankly pleased to be able to take potshots at the Charter and the Young Offenders Act in the hope of persuading the public to demand amendments that will once again enable the people in white hats to keep the lid on crime. If the public is made aware of the problems created by these well-intended public laws, perhaps the politicians will take heart and undo some of the mischief they did when they helped to create such a permissive society.

Some of the incidents in this book have nothing directly to do with the development of my career as a Crown attorney and they aren't necessarily in chronological order, but I include them because they had something to do with preparing me for what was to come. They are about episodes in which I, or someone I knew, participated, and which impressed me.

One

Trials I Remember

Some cases stand out in the memory more vividly than others, and the following seven stories are among them. Most cases that I will relate are ones I had something to do with, which does not necessarily mean that the stories are about me at all. In fact the "Dalton Barber" story and the story I call "A Delayed Trial" featured other Crown attorneys.

Even though the Barber case was not mine, I recall it well, partly because my friend Bob MacGarva was the investigating officer, but more so because it was not the usual mindless stomping, shooting, or beating I had become accustomed to prosecuting.

Another reason for my interest was that I had been slightly acquainted with Dalton Barber as a kid.

The second case in this section, "The Unspeakable Crime" will live forever in my memory because I wanted to win it very badly, but I lost it. They say that the Crown never wins and that the Crown never loses. Don't you believe it. When you get a really evil person in your sights, it becomes a keen disappointment if he walks. It is different, of course, if the main players are on a level playing field by their own choice, and one of them ends up dead. In such a case the loser, be it Crown attorney or defense, merely shrugs his shoulders and accepts the outcome, chalking it up to bad luck. But when the victim is a twelve-year-old girl and you know you have the right man in the prisoners box you try very, very hard to gain a conviction.

A word about racial slurs, prompted by the case of Glen Anderson, "The Baby Snatcher." It is difficult to write about anyone who belongs to a racial minority. Even a casual mention of a person's race is apt to cause someone to claim to be offended. It is not my wish to offend sensibilities in this story or elsewhere, but it is a fact that cultural factors enter into our legitimate considerations all the time. It is also a fact that the judge and jury had to try to understand the motivating factors in the behavior of the parties, not only of Glen, but also of Maggie, the young woman who bore his child and then rejected him.

I have called Maggie a Metis, because present conventions seem to require it. Until the 1960s, she would have been called a half-breed, with no pejorative overtones intended. But she was really just a young woman who mourned for her baby as would any young woman.

Now consider the "Tommy Hawk" case, the fourth in this section. I enjoyed handling the case because it was quite different from the usual to which I had become accustomed. The trial itself was arduous work, truly exhausting, for both myself and my frequent opponent Greg Brodsky, of Winnipeg. Greg was a hardworking guy, who, for years, was involved as defense counsel in most of the major cases in Manitoba, Saskatchewan, and Northwestern Ontario. He was amiable both in and out of the courtroom, and had the capacity to get by on very little sleep. We worked long and hard on the Hawk case and even spent one night sleeping on a cot and a reclining chair in my office. The truth is I only spent twenty-five hours in preparation. If I had had the time I might have spent seventy-five hours, but even so I was really fairly well prepared. The jury brought in a verdict of guilty to manslaughter.

For the second trial (ordered after an appeal) I brought in two heavy hitters and a student from the big city. They docketed their time spent in preparation. It totaled a whopping 750 hours, thirty times more than I had spent. The facts and issues were the same as when I did the first trial. The verdict was again manslaughter.

It probably isn't necessary to explain why I included the story called "The Bear" but the case sticks in my mind because of my friend's remarkable competence in examining the Crown witness with no more than a few minutes preparation. Perhaps the fact that the accused was such an especially rotten bastard is further reason to remember it. He beat a beautiful child until she was dead, and I felt good when he went to prison, wishing only that it had been for a longer time.

It was never my intention to emphasize hero stories that described my part in events. Nevertheless, I had to include the story of how I obtained the conviction of Zacharias Netamageesic for bum stomping Carl Rae to death, because I'm entitled to toot my whistle a little. I really did a fine job on the prosecution, and I want the world to know it.

The last case in this section is "A Delayed Trial" but it is really about insanity, or mental disorder. I was in on the case in the beginning, as a student of the lawyer who was defending, but at the trial the prosecution was by Bill Saranchuck. I remember it well because everyone noticed that there was "something funny" about the accused's eyes. No one has ever told me if there is any truth to the folklore to the effect that you can always see insanity in the eyes of mentally disabled people. But you could sure see it in the eyes of Wilf MacIntosh.

The Case of Dalton Barber

Dalton Barber was a thoroughly decent guy, as far as I knew when I was growing up. He was an executive with Algoma Steel and he had a big boat tied up to his dock near the golf club on the Saint Mary's River. When I would come alongside in my borrowed putt putt he would slip me a bottle of cold beer, even though I was far from the legal drinking age. When you are sixteen and a man treats you like a fellow human being, you are apt to think of him kindly. But, truthfully, I didn't have a lot to do with him, and I more or less forgot about his existence for the next nineteen years.

On a winter day in 1966, Erica and I found ourselves passing through Sault Ste. Marie, and of course we had to drive around and see the school I went to, our old home, my friend's old home, and other places of nostalgic interest to me. We stopped at a local hotel for dinner, and I was astonished to see Inspector Bob MacGarva of the Criminal Investigation Branch of the OPP at a nearby table. Of course we had a grand reunion with much back slapping and telling of tall tales.

I had known Bob for a long time. After the war he was a young policeman working under the Old Inspector in Kenora when I was still in my teens, and he investigated many of the murders in OPP District Seventeen. Frequently my father flew him about on his investigations. Bob was soon promoted to corporal because of his investigative abilities, and was an occasional visitor at our table.

Our friendship was sealed one day in about 1954 when my mother and I were out duck hunting on Lake of the Woods, and the OPP boat arrived on the scene, driven by none other than Corporal Bob MacGarva. His passenger was the much feared game warden, Sven Flostrand, who was just a hair's breadth away from seriously embarrassing us, the more so because we were in a boat owned by the Forestry Branch.

Bob was highly perceptive, and as Sven stretched a leg over to our boat he opened the throttle slightly, thereby widening the gap between the boats. "What the hell are you doing, Bob?" wailed the game warden, as he hung precariously between the two boats.

"The wind caught me. I'll have to go around and try again. Get back aboard before you fall in the water," said Bob. He took his time about coming around, and I managed to drift into some weeds where we put our hunting gear in more or less legal order. Is it any wonder that I revered the man?

As a student and later as a defense lawyer I had more to do with Bob. He had been in and out of my life for fifteen years or so by the time I met him in the hotel dining room in the Soo.

Bob was in a state of high dudgeon. He had been ordered to go up to the Soo from general headquarters in Toronto just a day or two before to investigate a highly suspicious death, and was being stonewalled by some of the local justice officials. An inference hung in the air that a few of these officials might be protecting the prominent Dalton Barber, the death of his wife being the subject of the investigation. Bob complained bitterly to his superiors, and even as we were eating dinner a call came telling him that an outside Crown attorney had been appointed to assist and advise, and to carry out any resulting prosecution. The new man was Sam Caldbick, QC, of Timmins, one of the most highly esteemed prosecutors in Canada. Bob was greatly relieved, but even a trip to the movies to see Inspector Clousseau couldn't make him laugh that evening.

The Barber case was as fascinating as any of the great crimes of the century, and if it had happened in a big city anywhere in the world it would have been written up and talked about for decades. Imaginative sleuthing by the police and dedicated scientists, coupled with brilliant legal work by both lawyers and the judge, resulted in a case which no tale of fiction could match. I followed the case over the next few months, and in the years to come I discussed it with Doug Lucas of the Center of Forensic Sciences, and Robert Barber, Dalton's young cousin, now a lawyer in Marathon and Thunder Bay. Robert has a family perspective on the case, as another cousin who was Dalton's brother, also at that time an executive with Algoma Steel, played a part in the ultimate resolution of the matter.

This is the story as I have pieced it together.

In the small hours of December 3, 1965, William Dalton Barber telephoned his doctor to say that he had found his wife dead in a Pontiac Acadian station wagon parked in their house garage. The doctor came immediately, first trying the bell and then walking into the house, which he found to be full of fumes. Dalton Barber was lying across the foot of the bed, apparently unconscious. In a very few minutes he made a remarkable recovery, even asking for his pipe before they took him to the emergency room at one of the local hospitals. One of the hospital nurses noted that the backs of his hands were covered with a dark stain of some sort, but attached no particular importance to it at the time.

Mrs. Barber was dead, but still warm, in the bed. The sheet and mattress were stained with urine, not quite what one would expect if she had died elsewhere. Soot was observed in various places in the room, and in particular just under a window sill. The Acadian was in the garage with a cold motor, giving rise to an inference that if Mrs. Barber had in fact died of carbon monoxide poisoning from the exhaust it must have been some time ago.

On the other hand the police had noted on the way in that the motor of the Vanguard parked in the driveway was warm.

Smoke from a recent fire lingered in the fireplace downstairs.

No hose was found which could have been used to transmit carbon monoxide upstairs, and neither vehicle parked by itself in the garage could have done it.

Barber said the cars had been parked right where the police had found them. He and his wife had "the usual argument" after dinner, and he went to bed early. At some time in the night, fumes awakened him and he got up to look for his wife. He found her asleep in the Acadian, the vehicle with the cold motor in the garage. He dragged his wife up to the bedroom, phoned the doctor, and collapsed.

It seemed to the Sault Ste. Marie police force that something about the facts just didn't ring true, but there was no real proof of foul play by Dalton Barber or anyone else. There was the urine stain on the bed, and there was the fact that Dalton seemed to be confused about which car he found his wife in, but these things were not proof of wrongdoing. The local officials were not interested in pursuing the case.

Matters might have rested like that if friends of Mrs. Barber's had not noticed there was a woman staying in the house with Dalton, and because of their insistence the case was reopened and Bob MacGarva was put to work on it.

Bob MacGarva and Inspector Bob McEwan of the Soo police force began to dig.

McEwan's grapevine told him that Barber had asked several acquaintances to procure knockout drops for him. In the meantime, MacGarva had asked his wife Evelyn to read a number of unpublished manuscripts Dalton had written, just to see if they offered clues to any course of activity Dalton might have pursued. Evelyn found from her reading that Dalton focused on knockout drops, which is a common chemical compound available at many drugstores. Detective novels of the thirties and forties often featured knockout drops, which are well known to medical people as a primitive anesthetic.

Bob went looking in drug stores for evidence of knockout drops sold at a time close to the death of Mrs. Barber, to no avail. No pharmacy between the Soo and Sudbury had sold such a thing for a very long time. Eventually his search took him to a small town on the Upper Peninsula of Michigan and to an old fashioned drug store.

The old pharmacist chewed on the problem for a few minutes, then answered "Yes, I sold such a compound to a man just a few months ago." Bob's search had taken him in ever widening circles and he had all but lost hope. Nevertheless he showed the pharmacist his book of mug shots, and the old man unhesitatingly asserted that he had sold some to the fella in one of the pictures only last fall. The picture he selected was that of Dalton Barber.

The Center of Forensic Sciences was in on the case from the beginning, and they tried very hard to identify chloral hydrate, better known as knockout drops, in Mrs. Barber's body, but success eluded them because of the residues from embalming fluid that remained in the body, which had been exhumed for further examination. Nevertheless the evidence of Barber's quest for knockout drops was valuable in explaining how Mrs. Barber might have been controlled prior to her death.

When the trial opened on May 3, 1966, it was obvious that there was a weakness in the Crown's case, in that the Crown could not show how the carbon monoxide had been introduced into the bedroom. The fact that Barber had been caught out in several inconsistencies was suspicious, but even coupled with the purchase of knockout drops did not mean that he had murdered his wife, or so defense counsel Terry Murphy, QC, was prepared to argue. It was a pretty good argument, too, and MacGarva said that he and Crown attorney Sam Caldbick felt pessimistic going into the case.

The Crown was rescued by the Barbers' former cleaning lady, who was fired by Dalton shortly after the death of Mrs. Barber.

She had, as one might expect, been following the case in the local newspaper, and she came forward literally at the courtroom door with a remarkable story that changed the fortunes of the Crown. She told Bob MacGarva and Doug Lucas that on the day after Mrs. Barber's death she found some burned pieces of garden hose in the fireplace, and threw them out on the ash pile behind the house, thus illustrating perfectly the old maxim that "the police are the people and the people are the police," a concept which was enunciated by the British statesman Sir Robert Peel early in the nineteenth century.

The police made an immediate search, and did indeed retrieve pieces of partly burned hose from under the receding spring snows.

No one was quite sure what to do about this new find. The judge finally ruled that if it could be scientifically proved that the hose could have been used to introduce the carbon monoxide into the bedroom, the evidence would be admissible at the trial. The problem was that the end of the trial was at hand, and Doug Lucas had not brought suitable test equipment to the Soo from Toronto.

Dalton Barber's family was very close, and they stood behind him. He steadfastly maintained his innocence and they acted upon that premise. They were decent, law-abiding people, and had no reason to think Dalton was a murderer. Dalton's brother Jack, a vice president of Algoma Steel, felt quite safe in offering the facilities of the steel plant laboratory to Doug Lucas for analysis of the hose, and the offer was accepted. It was obvious to everyone concerned that Jack and his cousin James, also a senior executive with Algoma Steel, still believed in the innocence of Dalton, the offer of lab facilities having been made in perfectly good faith.

A series of midnight tests now took place, both at Barber's home and at the steel plant laboratory.

Under the direction of Doug Lucas, the Vanguard was placed in the driveway and a piece of ordinary hose like that found on the ash pile was connected to the exhaust and the other end was run into the bedroom window and air samples were taken from the vicinity of the pillows on the bed. The fumes in the bedroom became so overpowering after fifteen minutes that the experiment was discontinued.

Upon tidying up after the experiment it was noted by those present, including Sam Caldbick and Terry Murphy, that as the hose was pulled back out through the window, the end of the hose sprayed soot particles over the sill under the window, explaining why similar particles had

32

been noted by the police at the time of the first investigation. Another interesting discovery on that last night before the end of the trial was that when one pulled the hose out of the end of the exhaust pipe, one's hands became sticky with guck, and when one washed the guck off, the effect was to transfer some of the guck to the backs of the hands.

The final discovery of the night was made back at the lab, where it was shown that the air samples taken earlier from the head of the bed were more than high enough in carbon monoxide to cause death.

Family members and defense counsel both admitted to losing confidence in Dalton Barber's innocence at this stage.

In the morning the new evidence was placed before the jury, which had no trouble finding Dalton Barber guilty of non-capital murder.

Dalton Barber served seven years of a life sentence before being paroled. He lived out his life in relative obscurity in southern Ontario, and just before he died of cancer, he married the lady who came to live with him after he murdered his wife.

While Barber was serving time his wife's sister made an application to prevent him disposing of his deceased wife's share of the jointly owned property. The case has won a place in legal history as *Schobelt v Barber* [1967] 1 O.R. 349. It follows the doctrine that a man shall not be allowed to profit by his own wrong, and resulted in a declaration that...the defendant in his personal capacity holds the property on trust, one half for himself and the other one half for the next of kin of Marjorie Sophia Barber deceased.

An Unspeakable Crime

If anyone ever had the right to be a rotten son-of-a-bitch I suppose it was Joe Bluewater. Not really, of course, because nobody ever can be justified in raping and strangling his own twelve-year-old half sister by standing on her throat. A dreadful background will only go so far towards explaining a horrifying crime and does not excuse it. But when I tell you what happened to him as a child it will help you to understand how he did it without suffering from pangs of conscience.

33

I don't intend to identify Joe by his real name or by location, because, as is the case with many of the stories I have set down on paper, there are many people still around who could be hurt by the unvarnished truth.

Let us look at his background, and you will see what I mean. The facts that follow are lifted right out of the brief that was prepared by Inspector MacGarva of the Criminal Investigation Branch of the OPP—the same Bob MacGarva who appears elsewhere in this book as a corporal, a superintendent, and a chief superintendent. In important cases a detailed brief is always prepared by the police for the Crown attorney. I rediscovered this one in the possession of Jack Murray, who, by 1993, was the chief of the Fort Frances Municipal Police, but in 1964 was a young OPP constable who assisted in the investigation of the murder of Lois Marie Redwater. Jack uses the brief as an instruction aid with his younger constables. The brief contains truth.

Joe Bluewater was eighteen years old the summer he killed. He was born to Noreen Bluewater and Alfred Redwater in 1946, but registered as Bluewater. If this sounds complicated, it is, and it becomes more so. When Joe was one year old, his biological father went to jail, and his mother took up with Albert Paypompay, who was murdered in 1953. It was while Noreen was living with Paypompay that she abandoned Joe in his moss bag in a driving rain. A band councilor found him and took him to the home of Absalom and Daisy Redwater, Absalom being the brother of Joe's father Alfred, and therefore Joe's biological uncle. Absalom and Daisy adopted him by native custom, but never got around to a formal adoption according to the laws of the Province of Ontario. Joe Bluewater regarded them as his parents, and so shall we for the purpose of this story.

Because of the haphazard lifestyle into which he was born Joe did not get much of an education, although it was available to him. He went to an Indian residential school for one and a half years, and to a railroad sponsored day school for a period of time, but could do little more than write his name as a young adult.

At the age of five, Joe fell into a lake and was under water for at least five minutes before being rescued and revived. One wonders if there was any brain damage from this episode.

In 1954 Joe watched his biological mother, Noreen, murder his half sister, who was aged three at the time, and he gave evidence at her trial. He was nine when he took the stand to tell how his sister died. I speculate that this traumatic event and the telling of it must have had a terrible influence on the boy. It is of course significant that Noreen was charged with several other violent offenses, including another baby murder, during this period of time. Most certainly Joe must have been enured to death and violence before he was in his teens.

Joe was considered a prime suspect in the Maggoty Maisie case which I have described elsewhere, because of the similarity of the modus operandi with that of the murder of Lois Marie Redwater which I am about to describe, but nothing concrete was ever proven. Joe Bluewater was not liked by his neighbors, and was considered to be a chronic liar. He broke into numerous cottages in the area, and any time something happened that attracted the attention of the police they made enquiries as to Joe's whereabouts.

When he was fifteen, Joe fathered a son by his biological cousin. This baby, whom I will call Jason, was also taken by Absalom and Daisy as a customary adoption, a commendable practice that is part of native tradition. I mention it because I want the reader to know that even in the deprived circumstances in which Joe's people lived they were not all bad. Twenty-nine years later Absalom and Daisy were still taking in foster children.

The two Redwater families lived some distance from each other on a conspicuously beautiful chain of lakes near a village accessible by road from Kenora. Sparkling blue water alive with game fish, storybook pine trees and rocky islets made for an entrancing setting that should have shaped their lives differently, but I have never heard a positive or pleasant story to indicate that any member of this family ever rose above its squalor and misery.

The two brothers, Alfred and Absalom, made a living of sorts by sporadically guiding for a nearby tourist camp in the summer, and trapping in the spring and early winter. When they had money they spent it, most frequently on booze. Hunger was a constant companion in the crude log shacks.

On Wednesday afternoon, August 5, 1964, the brothers had empty pockets, but had worked up a goodly summer thirst. Together with Joe, they bummed a ride into the village, as I will call it, the little community the families related to, where one of the brothers pawned his chain saw. It yielded enough money to buy them a few beers in the local pub, twelve bottles of cheap domestic sherry (rot gut, but a good buy from the standpoint of alcohol content) and two cases of beer. They got a ride back to the lake, hid half the wine and a case of beer in the bush, and crossed the bay in a small boat to Absolom Redwater's shack.

And then the men drank. Prodigiously. You have to understand what I mean by prodigiously. In another case, a few years earlier, both brothers were shown by irrefutable evidence to have been on their feet and functioning, (after a fashion) with a blood alcohol content of six point zero parts per thousand. Most people are dead with a blood alcohol content of four point five parts per thousand. They slept briefly, then got up and went at it again. I mean these boys were drinkers! In thirty years of prosecuting I came across only two other cases of blood alcohol readings of that level, and both of those people were dead before dawn.

On this occasion no doubt Joe and the women and children dipped in too, and by midevening they sent Joe back across the bay to pick up the other case of beer.

Around midnight everyone was asleep but Joe and a ten-year-old half sister. Joe decided to leave, and he tried to take the young girl with him by force, but she was like an eel and he couldn't hold her. She was probably very fortunate to get away.

Joe took his father's twelve-foot skiff with a fifteen-horse power outboard and went over to Alfred's home. There were six children there, including his half sisters Serena, age thirteen, and Lois Marie, age twelve. Joe came in smelling of liquor, saying his father had sent him to fetch the remaining wine, and the two older girls could go with him for the ride. If this sounds improbable, just bear in mind that this whole scenario is most improbable by the standards of most of us. This family was not like anyone you've ever known.

On the other side of the lake one of the girls tied the boat to a twig while Joe went looking for the wine. He found four full bottles, one half full bottle and one almost empty bottle. No doubt the men had opened the bottles on the way back from the village, before hiding them.

Without lingering, the party set off on a wild ride through the chain of lakes, which all three of them knew like other children know the street they live on. Even though it was pitch dark they managed to avoid reefs, floating logs, and all the obstacles to be found in inland lakes. After a while they stopped to sleep on an island.

Joe and Serena had to help Lois Marie up to a rock, no doubt because she was drunk. Joe sent Serena back to the boat on a pretext, and when she returned she found Lois Marie sleeping and Joe lying on top of her. They may or may not have been having intercourse. Serena went to sleep on the other side of the rock.

When she awoke to the sound of a motor in the morning it was to see the boat circling at high speed, with Joe and Lois Marie sitting side by side on the back seat, laughing as they went. They disappeared up a creek towards the next lake in the chain, leaving Serena to be picked up by passing tourists more than a day later.

Lois Marie was never seen alive again.

From this point on the story has to be pieced together by deduction and by filtering Joe's numerous statements for what little truth they contain. Only Joe's very last statement contained the truth, but this was not admissible at trial for reasons we will see later in the narrative.

Serena set up a hue and cry for her sister, and a fruitless search resulted. Neither Lois Marie nor Joe were to be found, but the boat was found at a landing within walking distance of the village where the wine was purchased.

All through the fall of 1964, Constable Murray followed up leads. He talked to several people who had seen Joe behaving suspiciously at about the time Lois Marie disappeared, but no one knew where either she or Joe could be found.

In early autumn Constable Murray heard that Joe was in jail in Kenora, and passed the information on to Detective Sergeant Ken Wilson. On the following day, Wilson interviewed Joe Bluewater, who had been charged and convicted of theft since last heard of. He said he had left Lois Marie near the bus stop at the foot of the road leading to the village on the early morning of August 6. Detective Sergeant Wilson was reasonably sure Joe was lying, and as is policy in homicide cases, the Criminal Investigation Branch was called in. That is how Inspector Bob MacGarva came into the picture.

Bob MacGarva and Jack Murray spent four and a half hours with Joe on October 16. This time he claimed Lois Marie had left him at the bus stop, saying she was going to walk to the home of an old lady, to whom she was related, in the village. Joe caught the bus to Ignace, a little town more than a hundred miles to the east, arriving there on the morning of August 7.

Bob interviewed Joe again on October 20. As before, Joe said nothing inculpatory.

Again on October 21, there was a fruitless interview in which Joe insisted all his previous stories were true. At the end of the interview he asked to be taken to where he had left some clothing, just outside of Kenora. On the way back to town he said he wanted to tell the truth about what happened. This time the police officers scented the quarry, so they took him to the police office and gave him the official warning. It has changed but little over the years, and all common-law countries require that it be given to suspects who appear to be about to make a confession.

"You may be charged in connection with the death of your sister Lois Marie Redwater. Do you wish to say anything in answer to the charge? You are not obliged to say anything unless you wish to do so, but anything you do say will be taken down in writing and may be given in evidence."

Joe proceeded to tell his version of what had happened on the early morning of August 6. Every word of it was taken down by the police. As suspects usually do in cases like this, Joe started off by laying a foundation tending to show he was drunk, and therefore, in his mind at least, not responsible for what happened. He said he and Lois Marie had left the island in a drunken condition, and that she had told him that they had taken Serena home. Joe and Lois Marie careened around in the boat, still drinking. Later he modified the part about the drinking, saying he only gave her one shot. In his own words:

"I drink the whole bottle and I ran around the lake and that is when she fell out of the boat. I was going full speed that time. By the time I turned back and looked for her. I didn't see her any place. I stopped the motor and hollered at her but there was no answer. I didn't know what to do. Either jump in the lake to look for her but I was in too bad condition. I stayed there for about a half hour and couldn't see her at all. After that I took off to the village...." and he goes on to say how he had a drink with someone, and hung around for a couple of days, eventually taking the bus to Ignace.

Joe was a good-looking lad, in the pouty Elvis Presleyish fashion, and he had no trouble finding work at a tourist camp in the Ignace area until he was picked up in early October.

Now it is a fact that bodies usually come to the surface of the water in August in this part of the world, even slender young bodies like Lois Marie. Yet she did not float up. The conclusion is that she wasn't in the water. She never showed up at home or at the village or at any of the places a twelve-year-old girl might be expected to. The inevitable conclusion was that Lois Marie was somewhere on the shores of the chain of lakes, dead. They searched and searched, but couldn't find the slightest trace of her. They even took Joe to the lake and had him show them where Lois Marie was supposed to have drowned, however a search of the lake bottom and shoreline revealed nothing.

On November 9 Bob MacGarva and Detective Sergeant Alex Forster, who was new to the case, interviewed Joe Bluewater at the Fort William Industrial Farm, which is where Kenora prisoners went to serve time in excess of a month in those days. They took with them a letter from Absalom Redwater asking Joe to tell the truth, and saying that Corporal MacGarva would help him. How on earth he figured Corporal MacGarva would help Joe I do not know, but the fact is that Bob was well known to the Redwater clan through previous investigations, and they may have looked on him as a sort of necessary irritant in their lives, something like paying insurance or taxes would be to anyone else. MacGarva had, of course, asked Absalom to write the letter.

After reading the letter Joe stated that when Lois Marie fell out of the boat she was hit and killed by the motor. He towed her into shore and pulled her into the bush and left her there. He drew a map showing the location.

On the following day, November 10, the badly decomposed nude body of Lois Marie Redwater was found seventy-five feet from the shoreline, covered by moss, twigs, and rotten logs. There was no sign of injury to the skull or skeleton.

The police still were not satisfied they had the truth of the matter, because Joe had contradicted himself or changed his story so many times. As a prime example, there should have been a skull injury from the propeller of the boat if Joe's last statement were to be believed, but there was none. They made a decision to interview him again, in the full knowledge that even if he did break down and tell the truth it probably would not be admissible at trial.

To put the legalities at their simplest, the law is more concerned with fair play than it is with getting at the truth, or with salting criminals away. While the law may be an ass in many respects, and in fact people concerned with the administration of justice chafe at this restriction, it makes sense if you think about it. If it were otherwise a venal police authority would be able to do anything it wished in the quest for evidence, including all the wicked things we read about occurring in the middle ages and even today in the banana republics. Sure, they extract confessions and catch criminals that way, but at what cost to individual rights and the dignity of the nation! Anyway, Bob MacGarva was concerned that one more step in the interrogation process would be one step too many, and he turned out to be right. He nevertheless hoped that Joe would say something that would lead to the finding of further evidence, even if what he said was not itself admissible. In those pre-Charter days, Canadian courts did not espouse the doctrine of "the fruit of the poisoned tree" which would prevent such evidence from being admissible.

Bob and Alex went back to Joe on November 12, and cautioned him about the murder in very specific terms. Joe sparred for a few minutes, then said he had nothing to say. The officers were about to stow their papers in the brief case when Joe started talking. He indicated that he would write a statement himself, but after one paragraph it became apparent that he could not. He asked Bob MacGarva to write for him. It went like this:

...I rember Stoping at the Shore didin Know Where I Was...

Continued by Inspector MacGarva at Bluewater's request:

...where I was. But I guess we both started this crazy deal of going on top of her all the time screwing her and we still had a bottle left at the time and I was pretty drunk. We drink that bottle and I was pretty drunk. I didn't know anything actually and the next thing I knew Lois Marie was dead. There was just me and her there all alone and I knew that there would be trouble. Before we start here you couldn't find her clothes. I was laying about ten feet from where she was laying. I left my shirt there and I got up and went to where she was laying and that is when I found out she was dead. She had some blood on her head I do not know from she got it. Then I started covering her up when I found out she was dead and how it happened I do not know. There was just me and her there. When she got off at the shore she fell in the boat and had a little bit of blood on her head and before that when I found out she was dead she had more blood on her head at the middle on the back. I guess there is no one else to blame but me. We were all alone. That is all I guess.
(signed) Joe Bluewater

On November 26 Bob MacGarva and Alex Forster again attended at the Industrial Farm to ask Joe to direct them to Lois Marie's clothing. They chatted at some length. During the course of the conversation (concerning which there had been no further caution) Joe stated that he had killed Lois Marie by placing his foot on her throat and holding it there until she quit breathing. They cautioned Joe at that point, and he gave the statement which follows:

> I do not know what to say. I will have to think about it. That point where I left Serena. Lois Marie was in pretty bad condition when we left there. I guess you know what I mean there must have been a fight there, me and her. She was laying in the boat and we took off to where you found her body. Then when we got off there I dragged her off the boat and she was half dead already. I did not know what to do when she was half dead whether to leave her there or not so I thought to myself I might as well finish her off. That is all I know. Then I cover her up with sticks.
> What do you mean by, I finished her off?
> I choked her I guess because she was half dead. She wouldn't have been living anyway. She would have died anyway.
> (signed) J. Bluewater

On December 3, we held an inquest into the death of Lois Marie Redwater at Dryden. Joe Bluewater again stated that he had killed Lois Marie by choking her to death with his foot. I didn't really know what to do about the admission made at the inquest. The law of Ontario at the time was that you couldn't hold an inquest in a matter in which criminal charges had been laid, and indeed no charges had yet been laid, as Joe was still serving time on the theft charge. Nevertheless, I decided I would not bring into the trial the admission given at the inquest on the grounds that it would certainly be against the spirit of the law if not the letter of the law. In the years since I have wondered if it was the right decision. It would have been good to put Joe Bluewater away for the rest of his life, but I have to say that I had a higher duty to the abstract entity we know as "the Law."

One other facet of the investigation is worth mentioning. I dearly wanted to have Lois Marie's clothes examined by the Center of Forensic Sciences, but the clothing had never been found. Bob MacGarva sweet talked Joe into going to look for the clothing on a day in early winter, and I went along for the ride.

It started out to be a beautiful sunny day, but as we walked across the lake from the landing it began to turn cold. Bitter, bone biting cold. Brass monkeys cold, as the saying goes. We had put Joe on the end of a sixteen foot chain, and we attached a brand-new, long legged constable named Andy Maksymchuk to the other end. The two of them hared out a full 200 yards ahead of Bob MacGarva and myself, sometimes running and sometimes sliding on the new ice. There was no snow on the ground in the search area, but we found nothing of significance. We abandoned our bonfire without making tea.

Joe had on a light windbreaker, but he didn't seem to feel the cold. Andy was somewhat better dressed but he appeared to be half frozen. Bob and I were well dressed, and we were chilled to the bone. As we passed within sight of Absalom Redwater's residence Joe put on a burst of speed, thinking, as he told us back in the car, that one of his relatives might just take a shot at him with a 30-30 rifle. I will always remember the sight of Joe hoofing it across the glare ice taking ten feet at a stride, pulling Andy along on the end of the chain, their shadows dancing ahead of them. Andy was unable to catch up to him and shouted, "Slow down you son of a bitch, I'm supposed to be leading you." Even Joe had to smile at that. Neither Bob nor Andy had bothered to bring a gun, but fortunately no one was home at the Redwater shack.

And that was about the only laugh there was in the whole case. There was nothing funny about the facts, and the trial was a disaster.

Harry Walsh, QC, of Winnipeg was for the defense, and he was a formidable opponent. I learned a lot from him in my early days as a Crown attorney, one of the most important things being that you put away personal grievances at the end of a trial. Harry served notice on me that he was going to eat me alive because of the irregularities in the taking of the many statements, and because of the inquest, but he didn't have to do it because the inculpatory statements were not admitted, and they were really all I had. Harry wasn't even required to present a defense.

The irregularities Harry referred to were, of course, the pressures put on Joe by relays of police officers in numerous interviews. It was successfully argued by the defense that these tactics eventually wore him down and forced him to give an inculpatory statement. The concept is somewhat artificial, in my view, but that is the way the courts see it.

Joe Bluewater walked out of the court room a free man, and went right back to the village. It was widely predicted by the police and by lawyers who were familiar with the Redwater clan that someone would bump him off before long, but it didn't happen. I can't really think why not.

Today Joe lives on a faraway reserve, but returns regularly to the village to visit his son Jason, now a grown man, who until recently still lived with Absalom and Daisy Redwater. Joe is presently charged with obstructing justice, in that he deliberately transported Jason back to the village after undertaking to a bail court that he would take him somewhere else. Jason has since been convicted of two separate counts of attempted murder, one of them being an attempt on the life of a young foster child living with Absalom and Daisy. He is serving four and a half years in the penitentiary for this episode.

Life apparently still goes on at the village. But death is never very far away. The legacy of violence of Noreen Bluewater, Joe's mother, is being carried on through the generations.

The Baby Snatcher

Glen Anderson learned to hate at an early age, because as the son of a white father and a mixed black and Indian mother he was treated with disdain by both Indians and whites. Members of other races never accepted Glen or his clan, and he had a bad time of it growing up in the Kenora area. That's the way it was when he met Maggie Black, a Metis (mixed Indian and white) girl in Kenora. She was sixteen and he was eighteen.

Before long Maggie became pregnant, and at about the same time, Glen went to jail for something unconnected with this story. Maggie was not in love with Glen, and she returned to her family in a Metis village, east of Dryden, on the Trans-Canada Highway and continued to live with them after her baby was born. After the fashion of their people, the family accepted the baby whole-heartedly.

When Glen got out of jail he went straight back to Kenora and acquired a handgun in a poolroom. Why he wanted a gun was never made clear, but perhaps as a member of the prison subculture he didn't need a reason. With his last few dollars he purchased a one-way bus ticket to Borup's Corners, arriving there on a cold, rainy day in the spring. By asking a few questions he found out where Maggie lived, and he presented himself at the door, a cold, wet, bedraggled figure.

Maggie Black and her family didn't make Glen welcome, but they didn't kick him out either, because of the gun. In any event it would not have been in their nature to eject Glen or anyone else on such a miserable day. Glen wanted to live with Maggie, but she wanted nothing to do with him. They argued bitterly all afternoon about the baby. At dinner time Maggie's mother wordlessly put a plate before him, and he wolfed it down.

The evening hours were a time of tension and strain, and they all sat around by the light of a kerosene lamp with nothing much to say to each other. Occasionally Glen would flash his gun. He was allowed to sleep on a couch.

In the wee hours of the night the family was awakened by a lot of noise in the house, and much crashing about in the dark. The door slammed and someone ran out into the pitch black night. The family milled about until a candle was lit, and it became apparent that Glen had snatched the baby from its crib, and run off into the freezing rain.

Members of the family tried to give chase, but Glen had a good start on them, and they were unable to follow without light. Someone went to a neighbor's phone to call the OPP in Dryden. Everyone knew that Glen would have to be found very quickly or the baby would perish of exposure. The police, who only had an abbreviated and garbled version of what had happened, immediately sped eastwards towards Borup's Corners.

When Glen ran out with the baby he had to pick his way very carefully down the lane to the highway, for he could see nothing. He had one dollar and eighty cents in his pocket, and not the faintest idea of where he was going or what he was going to do with the crying infant. He reached the highway and turned west, towards Dryden, and ran down the center of the road where the yellow line was occasionally visible in the lightning flashes, and the lights of the few vehicles that were abroad.

It began to sink in that he had committed an enormous crime, and that things were going to get worse before they got better.

By the time Glen reached Melgund Creek some twenty minutes had elapsed, and the baby was no longer crying. Glen ran on over the short bridge, and when he got to the other side he no longer had the baby. Baby Black was in the frigid waters of the rain swollen creek, which still had chunks of winter ice floating in it.

Glen stumbled through the darkness for another mile until he came to the Half Moon Inn, really an old-time country service station operated by an elderly couple. Glen pounded on the door and gave them a confused story about a baby which they relayed to the Dryden detachment. There was no sign of the baby and they made Glen wait on the porch.

Moments later the police wheeled up to ask directions to the Black residence, and Glen stepped off the porch and into the back seat of the cruiser. He may have told them the baby was in the creek, but he did not tell them how it got there. Nevertheless, that was where they found the tiny body at first light, caught up in some branches just downstream from the bridge.

I built my case on the theory that for some perverse reason of his own Glen deliberately threw the baby over the bridge rail, which made it murder in the eyes of the law. It may be that Glen threw the baby over to spite poor Maggie, or perhaps he knew the jig was up when the baby stopped crying, and he just wanted to get rid of it. As a matter of law I did not have to be able to point to a specific motive; and in my heart I suspected that perhaps, Glen did not even have a specific motive, just as I understood that Glen did not necessarily have a specific use for the gun in his pocket in order to justify buying it. Kenora juries were always good at bypassing unexplainable phenomena that weren't relevant. My task was merely to prove that Glen meant to throw the baby over the bridge.

Peter Burns of Dryden defended Anderson, and as this was his first big case he had T.A. O'Flaherty, by now a QC, of Kenora assist him. Peter and T.A. sweat blood preparing the defense, and their hard work paid off.

At the trial I put in the case just about the way I have described it here, and Peter was forced to call Glen to the stand in an attempt to rebut some of the Crown evidence. The dilemma faced by the defense was that if the defense failed to call any rebuttal a murder conviction would surely result. On the other hand, if the defense put the accused on the stand he might make the situation even worse, but it was a chance they had to take.

Glen turned out to be a surprisingly good witness, really much better than I thought he would be. T.A. O'Flaherty had put Glen through his paces, making him tell his story over and over again in private, until he was fairly articulate. T.A. had learned previously by bitter experience that you can't simply shove a witness on the stand and say, "Okay, now tell your story." As I saw it Glen's story was quite incredible, but it was enough to establish a reasonable doubt in the minds of the jury.

Glen admitted he had no idea of how to care for or feed the baby, but he said he loved it with all his heart. The only other person he had ever loved was Maggie, the baby's mother, and she had rebuffed him. Given Glen's background the story so far was believable.

Glen said he was determined to take the baby and damn the consequences. He waited for the family to go to sleep, then sneaked into the darkness of Maggie's room, blundered about noisily, snatched the baby, and ran out into the night. When Glen got to the road he could see nothing, not even the center line, but he managed to pick his way down the highway with the aid of lightning flashes. On arriving at the bridge over Melgund Creek he suddenly realized he was right close to the railing. He swerved and slipped, and the now silent baby flew out of his frozen hands, under the low railing, and into the creek. Glen was horrified, and he ran on to the Half Moon Inn where he met up with the police.

That was his story, and I made very few inroads on it in cross-examination.

Pundits in the law have spoken about "the purifying crucible of cross examination" and I have often wished I were as effective a cross examiner as are the lawyer heroes in the television shows, like Perry Mason, or Matlock. Good old Perry won every case by dint of his abilities as a cross examiner. But I made no miles with Glen Anderson.

I didn't believe Glen's version of baby Black's death and I didn't think the jury would either, although I have mellowed with age and experience, and with the passing of time I think that Glen's story was, after all, just barely plausible. The jury saw it that way and acquitted Glen of murder but brought in a verdict of manslaughter, because even taking Glen's story at its best what he did was criminal negligence, that being one way of arriving at a verdict of manslaughter. His whole course of action spoke of wanton and reckless disregard for the safety of the baby. The negligence was not confined to the act of letting the baby slip through the railing. In fact, or so the jury probably reasoned, the death of baby Black from some unnatural cause was foreseeable from the time Glen made up his mind to steal the child.

Glen drew two years in the penitentiary. This was definitely a big win for Peter Burns because it was still theoretically possible to be hanged for murder at that time, and I considered it a loss.

Glen did his time and returned to Kenora several years later, older, smarter, and more vicious than ever. He found himself a girl and resolved to take her home with him. The Crown alleged that she resisted and he forcibly dragged her over the railroad tracks to where he lived on the outskirts of Keewatin, cracking her head on the way and causing her death. The charge was murder.

Glen, on the other hand, said she had hurt herself in the bush, and he was carrying her home to get first aid when she slipped from his arms and hit her head on the tracks. In other words he was being a good samaritan and the girl died of an unforeseeable accident. Assistant Crown attorney Stan Nottingham cross-examined vigorously, but the jury bought the accident story and acquitted outright.

When I say "...the jury bought the story..." I mean they felt there was a reasonable doubt about the issue, and they resolved it in Glen's favor as the law requires.

In the Keewatin case it was an all or nothing situation. If the jury had accepted the theory of the Crown it could have convicted of murder, but there was no lesser but included offense to fall back on as there was in the Melgund Creek case. There was nothing intermediate that the jury could find between murder and an outright acquittal. The point of comparison with the Melgund Creek incident is that the jury found, or at least was in reasonable doubt, that Glen did not have the specific intention to kill baby Black, and it was therefore not murder, but there was a large body of facts to support the included offense of criminal negligence.

It is worth noting that Canadian juries are not allowed to hear about previous misdeeds of an accused person, and are (usually) required to judge a case on its individual merits. One wonders what the result of the Keewatin incident would have been if the jury had known about the Melgund Creek case.

Glen Anderson walked away from the Keewatin incident but almost immediately he was in trouble in Winnipeg on a weapons charge of some sort. He drew pen time, again, and that was the last I heard of him.

What's In a Name

Some people believe that giving a child a descriptive name will tend to influence his or her outlook throughout life. Thus, if your name is Oh Be Joyful you will tend to be just that—a happy, cheerful person. If your name is Running Deer you are apt to be alert and quick to action.

In addition to their anglicized names, many native people in Northern Ontario are still given descriptive names, although these names may not be widely used or known outside native circles. In western Canada some native people may have only descriptive given names, and not anglicized names at all. These names are often imaginative and beautiful, and one finds with some frequency that they describe accurately the person to whom they are attached. It is a native Canadian custom which I find particularly attractive. My old friend Charlie Fisher, who spends much of his time explaining whites to Indians, and vice versa, thinks that these names have a subtle influence on their holders, because people try to live up to their names. Perhaps it is so.

Tommy Hawk (not Thomas or Tom) was born in 1952, at the south end of Lake of the Woods. He was a member of the Manitou Rapids band of Indians, a part of the Fort Frances Indian Agency. His parents and brothers and sisters were apparently all normal.

But whatever possessed them to name him Tommy? Tommy Hawk, the traditional instrument of death among the North American Indians. They should have named him Dicky, or Harry, or Sue, or anything but Tommy. Now don't waste time by speculating that Tommy Hawk is not spelled the same as tomahawk, and no connection exists. The white man's spelling of Indian words has always varied from place to place depending on the ear of the listener, and "Tommy" is close enough to "toma" in the native ear to make connection a certainty.

Tommy was only fifteen when he killed first, on November 11, 1967. He and his fourteen-year-old chum George Nanie walked along the tracks to Emo, a pleasant, law-abiding farmers' village a few miles east of the reserve. During the evening they stole .22 caliber rifles from a hardware store and booze from the local Legion Hall. The beer made them brave, so they plodded back over the ties, beyond the reserve to the farm operated by Tommy's part-time employer, John Wappel.

Who knows what they talked about on the way back through the dark? Was it kid stuff like school, girls, and pulling their wires? Or was it man stuff, like what a rotten life they had in comparison to the neighboring white people, and how the Indians were getting a dirty deal that forced them into second-class status, and how one son-of-a-bitchin' white man was going to get what he had coming that night? I suspect it was simply that Tommy thought his farmer benefactor had some money lying about, and they talked about how they were going to get it, and how they were going to spend it. George Nanie said they intended to steal Wappel's car.

Would Tommy have had the guts to carry it off if his vision of himself were not somehow associated with the tomahawk, the weapon of war? Of course the booze must have given him some courage, but then lots of kids get into the sauce and do stupid things; but they don't murder because of it.

Tommy and his young companion were rummaging the farmhouse when the farmer unexpectedly appeared on the scene. An exchange of words took place, and Tommy shot him through the heart. The boys stumbled from the house in a state of confusion, rushing away from their terrible deed. On their way back to the reserve they discarded their guns, a knife, and an Indian feather headdress.

The two lads finked on each other, of course. They always do. Contrary to popular opinion the police don't have to extract confessions by improper means. They just set the stage, use a little practical psychology, and it often results in the offender spilling his guts. (At any rate that's the way it was before the Young Offenders' Act and the Charter of Rights intervened to protect the darlings.) If there is more than one offender there is that much more chance of someone talking. Perhaps there is, after all, such a thing as conscience. Often these spontaneous utterances and formal confessions are not used at trial, because there is such a hassle about getting them admitted into evidence, but they are frequently useful because they lead the police to solid evidence they would not have found without the cooperation of the accused.

Very shortly after the case broke Tommy was recognized to be the ringleader, and the Crown bent its efforts towards convicting him. The first step was to move him into adult court from juvenile court, with the usual legal bickering. Then there was a preliminary hearing, and at long last a trial. Crown counsel Jack "Bathtub" Smith, QC, of Fort Frances, was determined that the only proper verdict was guilty of murder. Defense counsel Charlie McCormack, also of Fort Frances, was equally determined that the only proper verdict was an acquittal. A classic case of the irresistible force and the immovable object.

The jury brought in a verdict of murder.

McCormack appealed to the Ontario Court of Appeal on a point of law, and was successful in obtaining an order for a new trial, I suspect largely on the non-legal ground that there is something abhorrent about convicting children of murder. Surely children don't have the capacity to form the deliberate intention to kill!

Now I have always admired Smith and McCormack for what they did at this point. There had been bitterness between them, and McCormack had lost fifteen pounds with concern for his client. Smith as a naturally compassionate man was filled with self-doubts about his role in the prosecution of the young Indian boy. They both quite independently doubted their own objectivity, swallowed their pride, and retained outside counsel. They made a lot of noise about instructing the Toronto men (Bob Carter, QC, for the defense and Herb Langdon, QC, for the Crown) to go for an acquittal and a murder conviction respectively.

When Carter and Langdon met in Fort Frances they closeted themselves in a hotel room for fifteen minutes, excluding the Fort Frances lawyers, then came out and announced that they had agreed that the defense would offer and the Crown would accept a plea to manslaughter. Friends of the law profession will recognize this as plea bargaining, without which the business of the criminal courts in North America could not be accomplished. This sudden end to the controversy caused consternation at first, but when the smoke cleared the two original opposing lawyers were vastly relieved.

Justice Edson Haines of the Ontario Supreme Court Trial Bench gave Tommy five years for his part in the killing of farmer John Wappel. Tommy was then sixteen years old.

Before I lose my train of thought, I want to say that Smith and McCormack put in uncounted hours of sweat and study and soul-searching in the course of the Tommy Hawk case. They labored for high principle and the love of justice, and not for money. If McCormack, who was blind, got anything, it was a fixed fee pittance from the Department of Indian Affairs, as this was before the days of legal aid, and Smith only got a salary from the Ministry of the Attorney General of the Province of Ontario for his duties—nothing for all the extra effort he put into the case. They were both embarked upon the serious business of dragon slaying, and it took a lot of professional integrity to back off and let two other lawyers take the case over. The egos of many lawyers I know simply wouldn't have permitted them to take the objective view.

Pretty soon everyone forgot about Tommy. Except for Charlie McCormack and his wife Hilda, who had worked just as hard as he had, no one cared. Tommy sent them the occasional plaintive letter, and Charlie would write off a letter to the Parole Board or whoever on his behalf.

Tommy spent a period of time in a provincial institution for young offenders, and was eventually transferred to the penitentiary. He was solitary, moody, and unpredictable, and was not popular with his fellow inmates. He got paroled, but was back in the slammer shortly thereafter for breaking and entering. He had to serve a sentence for that, plus the unexpired portion of his original sentence. Somewhere along the way he got involved in a prison riot at Kingston Penitentiary, resulting in his being called as a Crown witness against his fellow inmates. This made him more than ever unpopular, and for his own protection he was confined alone for long periods of time. If he had a kink it was bound to be intensified in this atmosphere. It was at about this time that the prison authorities began to realize that Tommy, who had grown into a husky young man, was not only dangerous but highly intelligent.

In the spring of 1971, Tommy was transferred to Stoney Mountain Penitentiary near Winnipeg, in Manitoba. The reasons for this were never made clear, but it may have been for his own protection, or it may have been to be closer to his family at Manitou Rapids, which is at the western end of Ontario, only a few hours' drive from Stoney Mountain. Here he was again put by himself to protect him from the prison population.

What does a man do when he is by himself all the time? He thinks. He hates. He fantasizes and loses touch with reality. He plots to be a big man, and make a mark for himself when he gets out. Perhaps Tommy also contemplated his name, and all that it signified. Probably he dreamed of violence.

The remarkable thing is that he also read deeply in electronics and mathematics, to the extent that his keepers were eventually persuaded to let him out every day to pursue his studies at a community college in nearby Winnipeg. Until this education program began he had spent a full year in what was virtually solitary confinement. One is constrained to wonder about the lack of common sense of administrators who would lock a dangerous man away for a year, and then turn him loose on society. In any event, they did, and it worked out not too badly as long as Tommy was on day passes. It should be said on behalf of the authorities that it made sense to release Tommy a little bit at a time rather than ejecting him into society all at once.

The trouble came when he got his first weekend pass, on September 29, 1972. He was supposed to go to a designated responsible home, and the people there were supposed to immediately contact the authorities if he didn't show, or if there was any problem. He didn't show, and they didn't call. Instead Tommy went to downtown Winnipeg and met Marlene Richard, a girl who was a sometime inmate of mental institutions, and who had wandered her way to Winnipeg from Toronto. Birds of a feather! They had a few beers, probably Tommy's first since he shot old man Wappel some five years earlier, and they spent the night in a downtown hostel. The next day they hitchhiked east on the Trans-Canada Highway, spending the night in the bush near Kenora. They may have been heading east to visit Marlene's mother in Toronto, or perhaps they intended to head south from Kenora to Manitou Rapids. Most likely they had no clear cut plans and were just larking and to hell with the consequences.

After a miserable night in the bush they hit the road again. Enter Victor Anson, sixty-four, an elderly local bachelor who had always minded his own business.

Victor had just undergone a prostate operation a few weeks before, and was taking advantage of a beautiful fall day to go out to his camp (cottage, to everyone outside Northern Ontario).

Just as he was about to turn off the highway west of Kenora onto the bush road he got a flat. As he was fixing it, Tommy and Marlene came walking along, and spied Victor and his case of beer. Perhaps Victor spied Marlene and felt primeval stirrings in his britches. In any event there was instant rapport, and they drove off up the bush road to Trout Lake.

We have only the word of Marlene and Tommy about what happened next, because when Victor Anson came back down the road it was feet first and toes up.

Marlene said they drank some beer, Victor paid Tommy two dollars for her favors (that's inflation for you - it used to be two bits in stories about sleazy affairs), Tommy became annoyed when the old fellow wanted a second helping, and an argument ensued with Tommy demanding the car keys, ending when Tommy slugged the old man with a baseball bat. Anson fell across the door in a pool of blood, and the two young people fled through a window. Neither of them knew how to drive, and they bushed the car within a mile. Both fled on foot, in different directions.

Tommy's story varied not so much in detail as in the complexion he put on the affair. He said he was drunk and defending himself and perhaps Marlene, and that's why he slugged the old man. It was really a mixed defense of drunkenness which would eradicate the specific intention necessary to make it murder as opposed to manslaughter; provocation, which would have somewhat the same effect; and self-defense, which if accepted would be grounds for an outright acquittal. At one time there was even an ungentlemanly hint by Tommy that Marlene might have done Victor Anson in herself. If there is any lesson to be learned by defense lawyers, it is that when you are in a jam you shouldn't try to ride too many horses at the same time.

In due course the police arrived at the cabin, and the investigation commenced. Usually the identification officer goes in and takes photos, exhibits, measurements and the like, and then disappears back to his darkroom. However, in this case, Corporal Jack Medland happened also to have been associated with the first Tommy Hawk case, down near Emo. It was an alert piece of police work when a drawing of a tomahawk on the inside of the cover of an electronics textbook left at the scene happened to catch his eye.

The next morning Corporal Medland picked up Tommy as he was walking on the highway near Kenora.

When Marlene left Tommy at the stranded car she found her way into Kenora, and spent the night in a sleeping bag with a young man in a park. The police caught up to the young man before they caught up to Marlene, and were understandably anxious that he should tell them what he knew of her movements. He was reluctant to cooperate until someone slipped him the word that Marlene was passing out a bad social disease,

53

and if he would only tell them where Marlene was they would see to it that he got a shot of penicillin...

As a result of the sterling fellow's information Marlene was picked up a day later back in Winnipeg.

The case against Tommy and Marlene eventually went to a preliminary hearing, with Greg Brodsky, QC, of Winnipeg, defending. Greg was one of several Winnipeg lawyers who were called to the Ontario bar, and as well he was a member of the Saskatchewan and Manitoba bars. For years he was involved in all the major cases in central Canada. Quite remarkably Greg could get by for days at a time on very little sleep, and this faculty stood him in good stead, because at trial Justice Haines forced the pace, and we were busy literally night and day. Now Greg is an old sparring partner of mine, and there was a lot of rough and tumble, but eventually Tommy was committed for trial, and Marlene was discharged. She underwent a miraculous metamorphosis and became a Crown witness at trial. After one of the most difficult trials of my career Tommy was convicted of manslaughter by a jury, before Justice Edson Haines, the same who had presided at the second trial of the first killing. This time Tommy drew life.

I shall never forget the sentencing. After Tommy was convicted and before sentencing he went through batteries of psychiatrists at the Oak Ridge division of the Ontario Hospital at Penetanguishene, Ontario's grim hospital for the criminally insane, as well as at the Clark Institute in Toronto. They all said the same thing: he was paranoid and dangerous. A keeper. During this period he had also spent time in the old Don Jail in Toronto, a relic of the nineteenth century. In his desperation he had peeled chunks of hard layered paint from the ancient walls and slashed his arms in an apparent attempt at suicide. The cuts had infected and created horrid red scars visible the length of the courtroom. Every soul in attendance wondered at the morality of what had to be done. In the end the judge did the only thing he could do, and sent Tommy back to Penetang. Everyone thought it would be forever.

Of course there was an appeal, and a new trial, with the same result, manslaughter again. Another appeal was heard later, but it was dismissed, and the conviction was affirmed. Leave to appeal to the Supreme Court of Canada was refused.

Oddly enough, Tommy functioned well in his permanent home in the psychiatric hospital, Penetanguishene. He was on a screening committee of inmates and brought his insight into his own paranoia to bear in assessing new arrivals. They say he was quite useful within the confines of Penetang and he led a relatively safe and sheltered life, except on occasion when an old adversary from Kingston Pen showed up and tried to bash him. Eventually, when they decided he was beyond curing, they transferred him back into the mainstream prison system.

In the remote event that Tommy is ever released from custody it is unlikely that he will again carry around books with pictures of tomahawks sketched on the covers.

And that was the way I originally wrote the story of Tommy Hawk, likely in the mid-1970s. I made a few penciled changes to the original from time to time, but it was not until after I retired in 1991 and started to pull these stories together that I actively pursued the destiny of Tommy Hawk.

In April of 1992, I made a few discreet inquiries about Tommy's progress, but ran into the confidentiality roadblock that so hampers effective communication in Ontario. I learned, however, that Tommy had been transferred from Penetang to Kingston Penitentiary many years ago, the reason being that Tommy was now a ward of the Federal Ministry of Corrections, and not of the Provincial Ministry of Health. One might see this as an unresponsive way of dealing with the problem of a young man facing life behind bars—how much better to be in a setting where one could make a useful contribution! But read on.

As of 1992, Tommy was on the street and self-supporting. He is married and productive in a real job in a town in southern Ontario. Of course he is closely supervised, but as of 1994 he apparently has it made, as with the passing of each month without incident it seems increasingly probable that a genuine cure and rehabilitation have been effected. Oh yes, and Greg Brodsky tells me Tommy will be going to law school, soon.

At Kingston they call him their success story.

The Bear and Grace Keesic

Why is it that some women take up with such low forms of life, bottom feeders, as I have heard them called? I don't intend to answer the question, but I observe that the phenomenon is puzzling.

Grace was about eighteen, and had a beautiful two-year-old baby girl. Grace was born and raised back in the bush, and what nasty trick of fate brought this shy, pretty girl into the orbit of Sam Johnston we will never know. I can't recollect Johnston very well, but when I think of him the word weasel comes to mind. The weasel had a shack just outside of Vermilion Bay, and he persuaded Grace to leave her home in the bush and move in with him, together with the little girl. Even with her background, she could have done better.

The weasel didn't have the guts to beat on Grace, so he took it out on the baby. Over the course of the two months Grace was with him he hit the child constantly. The postmortem photos showed a small body with literally dozens of bruises, so many that it was impossible to say which blow actually killed her or how it was delivered. That was one of the weaknesses of the case, although I later found out that the jury wasn't the least concerned with this deficiency.

The charge was murder, of course.

The real weakness was that Grace Keesic simply clammed up and wouldn't say anything. I got the case through a preliminary hearing by a fluke, and spent a lot of time trying to get the young woman to talk for the trial.

At the Grand Jury hearing I coaxed and cajoled, but to no effect. Grace wouldn't talk. As it happened, the grand jurors were all men, and great big friendly fellows, and they had a little more success than I did. The foreman was an oversized, pleasant gentleman, a friend of mine, named Zen Katz. He nodded at the door and flicked his eyes at me. "Why don't you take a little walk, Ted. You must have something you can do for a while."

As I left I could see the six big men leaning forward. Zen intoned in a friendly fashion, taking her little hand in his oversized paw, "It's all right, dear, he's gone. You can tell us what happened."

When I returned an hour later Zen had a complete statement for me, written in his own hand. It contained more information than even the police statements. Zen explained that my impatient manner, and that of the police officer who was assisting me, made Grace Keesic nervous and frightened, and she thought that "something bad" might happen to her if she spoke up. Zen advised me to get someone else, preferably a teddy bear, to take Grace through her story on the witness stand.

56

The actual trial was to begin two days later.

I put in an SOS to my boss, Bill Bowman, in Toronto: "Send me the biggest man you've got," I said. And that's how I met Don McKenzie, affectionately known to friend and adversary alike as "the Bear." You will notice that I did not say "friend and foe alike." That is because he had no foes worth mentioning. Don eventually was appointed to be a provincial judge, criminal division, in Kenora. He was brilliant, and his bust in bronze stands in the old section of the courthouse on Water Street.

The presiding judge at the weasel's trial allowed me to stall for some time, but eventually I had to call Grace to the stand. It was torture for both of us. All the threats and coaxing couldn't force anything intelligible out of poor Grace Keesic, who appeared to be on the verge of collapse. My questions went on for hours without answers. I was about to give up, and called for a recess.

In my office was Don McKenzie, the Bear, frantically gowning and reading Grace's statement. In a few words I told him what the grand jury had said. He barely had time to meet the girl, when court was reconvened.

I sat out of sight of Grace and watched Don McKenzie question her. He exuded good nature and calmness, carefully phrasing his questions, allowing the girl time to think. He looked big and safe and kindly standing there, waiting very patiently as if he had all the time in the world, and gradually you could see her starting to relax. Eventually, she told the whole sad story of how she and the child came to live with Sam Johnston, how he mistreated the child, and how she felt herself to be in his power, a rather frequent syndrome in women everywhere who are made to believe their only purpose is to serve men.

Johnston, as you may have perceived, was a detestable individual and had fired the local criminal lawyers one by one—either that or they quit. The presiding judge at the trial called Vern King in at the opening of the Assize and said simply, "Mr. Burton tells me you left the case at an early stage, but he also said you know more about the case than any of the other lawyers. I am appointing you to defend this man." In spite of his dislike for the weasel, Vern acted in the best tradition of lawyers, and did a really superb job of defending his client. He didn't have much to work with, but he emphasized evidence pointing to drunkenness and lack of specific intent to commit murder. His client was convicted of manslaughter and served several years in prison.

Vern was later appointed to the District Court bench in Fort Frances.

The Killing of Carl Rae

Carl was a disciple of the artist Norval Morrisseau, and in his time was almost as well known. Both of them painted stylized renderings of the ancient Indian legends, and became famous for it. They could have become wealthy, but neither was very interested in money. Carl, in addition to his stylized renderings, was an excellent wildlife painter.

I didn't know him well, but we had a mutual friend in Josias Fiddler of Sandy Lake, and Josias would often tell me about him. One evening when Carl and Josias were in Kenora we spent several hours together in intense conversation. We talked about a lot of things: the meaning of life, politics, native traditions, and so on. We also talked of Carl's alcoholism, and how he was trying to beat it.

Carl didn't really expect to master his problem. He thought he might reach an accommodation with it in due time, but master it—never. Carl thought it might even kill him eventually, but I am sure he didn't foresee how his death would actually come about.

It must have been in 1980 or thereabouts. Carl found himself at a house party in Sioux Lookout with Zacharias Netamageesic and Abel Keestablish and others. They all drank heavily, and one by one the others faded away. The last person to leave said that only Carl, Abel, and Zacharias remained behind, and Zach was spoiling for a fight.

Next in the sequence of events we have Carl crawling into the emergency room of the Zone Hospital in Sioux Lookout. This is a federally maintained hospital for the use of the native people in that vast hinterland area north of the Canadian National Railway (CNR) tracks.

On duty was a newly minted lady doctor on her first assignment. She took one look at Carl and called for reinforcements, and it was quickly discovered that Carl had broken ribs on both sides, and that some of his internals, most notably his liver, had been punctured by rib fragments. The medical team worked feverishly to save Carl, but he died later that night without being able to say what happened to him.

While the team was working on Carl someone else crawled into the waiting room. A nurse advised our good lady doctor that this new patient was in extremis, so she left Carl in the care of her colleagues and took a look at the new emergency patient. What she saw astounded her. The new patient, who turned out to be Abel Keestablish, had injuries which were the same as Carl Rae's. Warning lights began to flash in the doctor's head, as the similarity of the unusual injuries of the two men was too remarkable to dismiss as mere coincidence.

The doctor immediately put Abel in an ambulance and sent him to Dryden, where they had better facilities for dealing with emergencies, leaving the Zone Hospital people free to deal with Carl Rae. The doctor then called the police and told them what had transpired.

Abel Keestablish lived to tell what had happened to him, but he did not know what had happened to Carl Rae.

That was it, a pretty slender case.

Let me tell you about the lady doctor. She looked nineteen, but was really about twenty-five, and she was exceptionally attractive. She exuded competence, which is really what she should be judged on, but because of her striking good looks she got everyone's attention, and that was important because her evidence was what we had to build the case on; her evidence and that of Abel Keestablish.

Now I will tell you about similar facts evidence. This kind of evidence is not admitted if it is merely for the purpose of showing that the accused is a bad person. To be useful it must show that there is some sort of a connection between the similar act and the crime now being dealt with. Fans of famous murders will recall the Brides in the Bath case shortly after the turn of the century, in England. A man claimed insurance on the death of his new wife, who had "accidentally" drowned in a bathtub. In itself this was perhaps unusual, but not sinister. Not sinister, that is, until some clever detective turned up the fact that the villain had four previous wives with large policies on their lives in his favor, and they had all drowned in the bath.

At trial I convinced the judge, with the jury excluded, of course, that I was not offering evidence of the assault on Keestablish just for the purpose of blackening the character of Zacharias Netamageesic.

Abel said that the three principal people were at an afternoon party, which got rougher as the day wore on. Most of the people left, and

Zacharias postured his physical prowess. Abel said that Carl Rae was somewhere in the house when Zach put a choke hold on him, Abel, in the form of a half Nelson. Abel fell to the floor in a semiconscious condition, but was aware that Zach had jumped in the air and landed on his buttocks on Abel's chest. He passed out, and when he came to he realized that he was alone, and dreadfully injured with broken ribs on both sides. He faded in and out of consciousness, and managed somehow to get to the Zone Hospital. Abel did not know what had become of Carl Rae or Zacharias.

I asked the jury to reason like this:

Zach bum stomped Abel, and broke his ribs on both sides, a most unusual injury.

Carl was present at the time. Carl shows up at the hospital with injuries remarkably similar to Abel.

Therefore Carl's injuries must have occurred in the same way as Abel's.

Conclusion: Zacharias Netamageesic inflicted the assaults which caused Abel's injuries and Carl Rae's death.

The jury brought in a verdict of manslaughter, no doubt believing, and probably correctly, that Zacharias didn't have the *mens rea,* or the necessary guilty mind, to sustain a conviction for murder because he was so befuddled by booze that he could not develop the specific intention to kill. In a separate trial Zach was found guilty of a serious assault causing bodily harm on the person of Abel Keestablish.

I confess to a degree of satisfaction when Carl's killer was salted away.

Erica and I have an early painting by Carl Rae. It depicts a pair of moose about to bed down for a winter night in a burned over area. The cow is hunkered down in the snow among the blackened, snowcapped tree stumps. The bull, gentleman that he is, puffs ice crystal from his flaring nostrils, and takes a last look around for any danger that might be lurking nearby. Carl Rae had sold the painting to someone for four bottles of wine. Many years later I saw it hanging in a bar and bought it from the owner.

A Delayed Trial

Fourteen years is a long time to wait for your trial, but that's the way it used to be when you were found unfit to stand trial. In 1991 the system was improved by the building in of certain safeguards against unreasonable detention, but in 1957 the law was not so kind to the insane, or the mentally disordered, as we would call them in this gentler time.

Wilf MacIntosh was a Maritimer in his early forties, a miner by trade. Wilf had a bad alcohol problem and lost job after job because of it. Eventually he found his way to one of the gold mines in Red Lake, but before long he lost that job too. When he drank he hallucinated, and fantasized that those near him were somehow out to get him. He was considered dangerous, of course.

Wilf hit the bottom when he got out of mining and into bush work, or at least that's the way he saw it. He got a jobber to take him on, and moved into a bunkhouse a couple of miles from the highway, somewhere south of Red Lake. He was badly hung over the day he moved in to the camp, perhaps even with a case of the snakes.

There was very little conversation at the evening meal, as was traditional in bush camps, but it seemed rather sinister in MacIntosh's confused mind. He decided that his new mates didn't like him, and he would have to be careful.

Later in the evening MacIntosh was sitting alone when he observed several of the men with their heads together at the other end of the bunkhouse. He couldn't hear them over the hiss of the Coleman lamp, but they seemed to be talking about him, as they were looking his way. Were they plotting against him? He would certainly have to be on his guard. In fact, as it came out later, the men were matching shades of thread for one of them who was doing some mending, and for a brief moment they looked at Wilf and considered asking him if he had any thread, but decided not to when they saw the strange expression on his face. Everyone who saw him on this day and the next commented on the odd appearance of his eyes.

Wilf didn't sleep much that night, either because of fear or because of withdrawal symptoms. He thought about the day's events and concluded that there was some sort of a conspiracy to persecute him in Red Lake.

At breakfast there was again the customary silence and Wilf felt the silence to be directed at him.

Upon leaving the cookery Wilf was assigned a partner and handed a swede saw, chain saws not yet being common. As he plodded along with his new partner to the cutting area their horse (mechanical skidders were not yet common, either) quite suddenly lurched over and squeezed him against a tree. So even the horse was part of the conspiracy! In his altered state of mind Wilf felt he was a man marked for death.

When they arrived at the job site they got to work immediately, for it was a bitter cold day. Men who work in the bush are often not very articulate, and it is likely that Wilf's new partner gave him no instructions at all. In any event Wilf knew nothing about cutting green trees or handling a horse.

After a while Wilf's partner called him to help with a little task. Partner was on his knees in the snow trying to free a saw blade which had become pinched in a cut. Wilf understood that he was to stand directly behind partner in such a way that he could lean over and push on the tree to open up the cut, thus freeing the saw blade. When the tree moved partner jerked on the blade, and his elbow came back and hit Wilf in the pit of the stomach. Wilf was startled, and he saw this light blow as a declaration of war. He had to protect himself!

Wilf picked up an ax and swung it hard at the back of the other man's head, splitting it open and killing him instantly. He ran then, not to the camp of his enemies, but to the road, and hitchhiked in to Red Lake. The driver of the car made no comment on Wilf's ax, and probably didn't notice the blood on it.

Once in town Wilf felt he needed fortification, so he headed for a pub. The pub was not yet open, so he waited outside in the cold with the ax in his hand. Being Red Lake, no one took notice of the ax. When the door opened at noon he handed the ax to the waiter, who put it behind the bar. Wilf had a couple of fast beers, then collected his ax and walked on to the police detachment.

Constable Larry Moore had just finished his lunch and was manning the station alone when MacIntosh walked in and plunked the dirty ax down on the counter.

Without emotion and without any preliminary greeting Wilf said "I've just killed my partner."

Equally without emotion Larry replied, "That wasn't a nice thing to do, was it?"

"No, I really did." said Wilf, pushing the ax over the counter. This time Larry believed him, and took the ax. He was not sure whether Wilf was confessing to a crime or seeking protection.

Jack Doner, my principal, was assigned to defend MacIntosh, as the Kenora lawyers took these serious cases in their turn, without fee. Jack was not by inclination a criminal lawyer, but he was determined to do a good job, and he had me go out to the jail to visit his client almost every day. As an articling student the experience was good for me.

The defense was insanity, of course. A psychiatrist, Dr. Ruth Kajander, came from the Lakehead to interview MacIntosh and administer certain tests. Fortunately, she was quite knowledgeable with respect to the effects of prolonged alcohol consumption on the human brain. Dr. Kajander pronounced MacIntosh to be severely brain damaged from a lifetime of heavy drinking, and she diagnosed him further as being a paranoid schizophrenic, which is doctor talk for a mental disorder with psychotic delusions of persecution.

Insanity as a defense was not raised at the preliminary hearing, but was saved for the trial. The case was thought to contain a profound legal difficulty so Chief Justice McRuer assigned himself to the trial, which was to be held in two parts.

The first part of the trial was merely a hearing on MacIntosh's fitness to participate in the trial process. The jury agreed with the lawyers and the judge that Wilf MacIntosh was not fit, and so the presiding justice made the only order that he could in the circumstances, namely that Wilf be confined "at the pleasure of the Lieutenant Governor." This means that until the government officials have been satisfied by the psychiatrists that the accused is sufficiently rehabilitated, knows what is going on, and is able to communicate in a reasonable fashion with his lawyer he is to be confined. He was sent to the Ontario Hospital for the Criminally Insane at Penetanguishene.

The only thing notable about the insanity hearing, which was the first phase of the trial, was that Chief Justice McRuer and Dr. Kajander got into a poker game at the home of T.A. O'Flaherty, then the crown attorney, and she cleaned him out. The Chief Justice was widely respected but not well loved, and was so ill tempered that next day no one could tell if the poker game had affected his disposition or if he was just being himself.

Fourteen years later MacIntosh was finally pronounced fit to stand trial, and he had spent the whole time cooped up in Penetang. It is worthwhile noting that his ability to understand and communicate had improved considerably, but he was still considered dangerous. He was said to be the best home brew maker in the hospital, and in spite of Dr. Kajander's predictions was very much alive.

I had been the crown attorney for many years by the time the second phase of the trial rolled around, but I could not prosecute MacIntosh because of my previous relationship with him as Jack Doner's student. Bill Saranchuck had the dubious honor of heading up the prosecution, and because the objective of the hearing was now different the emphasis was now on the act of killing and the associated mental elements rather than on fitness to stand trial. Bill and the police had some trouble finding witnesses, but they had enough to go ahead with.

Mens rea, or the mental element of a guilty mind, must be present if a homicide is to be called a murder. This element was lacking in MacIntosh, as he apparently believed he was acting in self-defense when he split his partner's head open. But for this he no doubt would have been found guilty of murder.

The jury found MacIntosh "not guilty by reason of insanity" and he was again committed at the pleasure of the Lieutenant Governor, and returned to Penetang. This time he improved much more noticeably, so two years later he was released to return to the Maritimes, where he became an ordinary outpatient. Psychiatric drug therapy had made tremendous strides over the previous two decades, and as far as I know he has never had a relapse.

Wilf MacIntosh had been locked up for sixteen years before he finally gained his freedom, which is probably more time than he would have served had he been found guilty of manslaughter at the first hearing.

A small sidebar here. Crown attorney Bill Saranchuck put an Indian on the jury, I believe the first ever in Ontario, certainly in Northwest Ontario. There was some muttering by the traditionalists and the rednecks, but Bill's view was that an Indian had just as much right to be on a jury as anyone else. We heard later that the Indian was a bastion of common sense who was very knowledgeable in pulp cutting practices, and he turned out to be the only person on the jury who knew the difference between a single tree and a double tree, both of which were items of equipment used in the wood cutting industry in the 1950s, and which figured into the evidence.

It was partly a result of the MacIntosh case and partly as a result of another case in which a man was held for ten years and then found not guilty on the merits, as opposed to not guilty by reason of insanity, that the practice of long confinement without trial changed. The psychiatrists in hospitals for the criminally insane developed "fitness courses" and made a serious effort to get people to trial in much shorter time than was previously the case. I have had little secret doubts about the fitness of some of the people I have prosecuted over the years, but it was certainly not in the best interests of society or an accused person to hold these cases in limbo, and consequently my conscience didn't bother me if, on occasion, the Crown had to be a party to the semi-fiction that an accused was fit to stand trial, provided defense counsel was competent.

Frankly, I am content for some other official to make the decision on competence, and I was pleased when the law was recently amended to require closer scrutiny of matters pertaining to the locking up of mentally disordered people.

Two

Coroner's Cases

There is something about the work of coroners that is fascinating, witness the numerous TV thrillers and novels that have come onto the market in the last few years. The next group of incidents are mere vignettes that capture a moment in a coroner's investigation or an inquest. The Crown attorney's involvement may have been limited to the reading of a report, or it may have involved many days of preparation followed by an inquest. Each story exposes a difficulty, a small triumph, or a poignant instant. Death is no respecter of proprieties, and I have told the stories just the way I experienced them, or heard of them.

Caleb, the boy in the first story, is an example of several cases of children who were forced to grow up too fast, and whom "the system" had to find a way of protecting. Occasionally we in the system had to be very creative in how we did this. In a less sanitary time we did what we had to do, but we did not broadcast it publicly.

At the time, which was in the early 1960s, there were seven or eight coroners in the District of Kenora, and they could all be counted on to use common sense.

Justice for Caleb

The boy stood on the point of rock at the end of the island, looking over the water towards the mainland. The skin was drawn taut over his broad Ojibway face, and his belly protruded over his belt, as do the bellies of starving people everywhere.

Eventually he saw it. As the canoe came over the waves he could see the light flashing from the paddle, and he knew the motor was still. If there was no money for gas there certainly would be no money for groceries, and they would again be hungry till the next welfare day.

A dark emotion welled up inside the boy, momentarily pushing the hunger aside.

He turned and plodded slowly back to the one room shack that was the family home. He said simply to his mother, "The man comes." No more. His demeanor told her that he knew that once more there would be no food, and as was the custom of her people she asked no questions. There was no need.

The man lurched out of the homemade vee stern canoe, not bothering to pull it up on the little strip of beach, leaving it for the boy. He had a mean headache and a disposition to match. "A worm in his belly," as his people say of a man who carries too much hate around. Or guilt. He needed another drink. In an earlier time he would have burned with shame at having returned to his family without food, but he was past that now. Continuing poverty and lack of self-respect will do that to a person.

The man unscrewed the cap from one of his remaining bottles of Catawba and took a long sip. In his greediness, some of the amber wine spilled out of the corners of his mouth and made runnels down his neck. The liquid was much darker where it disappeared into his filthy shirt collar. He did not notice when the boy took his younger sister by the hand and led her into the shack.

The man stumbled over to where the woman was sitting on a stump, her head in her hands. He was conscious of hating her, but could not have said why, even to himself. When he held the bottle out to her she turned her head away and pretended not to see, as he knew she would. She had done the same thing last month when he came home without food and stinking of rot gut wine, and he had beat her unconscious then. It felt good when he beat her. She deserved to be hurt for trying to be better than he was, but he must be careful not to leave bruises where they would show.

His fist darted out suddenly, striking her on the breast, knocking her to the ground. She looked up at him through her pain filled eyes, but did not whimper. He lost what little remained of his reason—and began to kick her...in the legs, the hips, the ribs, the head...anywhere. He couldn't stop himself now, seeing nothing but the woman twitching on the ground, the woman who tried to make him feel bad.

Out of the corner of his eye the man saw the boy approaching. He reached out to cuff him, but his body did not respond properly, and he fell to his knees. The pain in his chest overshadowed the compulsion to do injury to the woman on the ground, and in the instant before he died he realized that the boy had shot him through the heart with a .22 rifle. He wondered vaguely if the boy had been saving the cartridge for a very long time.

Some days later, and many miles away, the coroner and the Old

Inspector and the Young Crown attorney conferred about what should happen to Caleb. After all, society expects officials to do something about such matters.

"The woman and the little girl will be well enough to leave the hospital in a few days," said the inspector.

"I hear the boy is in the residential school at Macintosh. They say he has already gained ten pounds," said the Crown attorney.

A fly buzzed in the window, taking the attention of the men. They looked from one to the other, each waiting for someone else to speak. The coroner thought for a minute, then spoke quietly. "Very well, gentlemen. It seems we are in agreement that I should write it up as an accidental death. No further action is called for here."

The men sipped their tea and went on to talk about other things.

Death in the O.R.

It was a bitter cold Saturday in February, the kind where exhaust smoke forms a layer next to the ground, and if you can see the sun at all it is silver, not gold. Erica and I were arranging the books in my new office in the courthouse, for I had taken the big leap from private practice, which had not been at all to my liking, to the service of Her Majesty. I was now the new Crown attorney for the District of Kenora.

A great huffing and puffing and stomping of frozen feet announced the arrival of Sam Burris, one of the two coroners in the Town of Kenora.

"We've got troubles, Ted. A lady just blew up on the operating table at the St. Joe's Hospital, and the staff are beside themselves. They don't know why it happened."

That was my introduction to my first inquest, the unfortunate death of a Mrs. Rivers. As it happens it was one of the most interesting inquests of my career. If I had known as much about my duties as I do now I would have been terrified, but in 1961 it was all a big game that a higher power had laid on for my particular benefit. Toronto and head office were 1,200 miles away and help would not have been made

70

available to me for anything short of a charge of an attempt on the life of the Queen.

Mrs. Rivers was a young middle-aged lady with five children. I have forgotten the nature of her operation, but it was routine, with no complications expected, and the local doctors were going to do it rather than send her to Winnipeg. The usual personnel were in the room: the doctor who was to be the surgeon; his assistant, the doctor who was to pass the gas; and two or three nurses and technicians. With the exception of the scrub nurse these people were not certified specialists, but were considered to be quite competent in the duties they undertook.

The precise technical details have faded over the years, but as I recall it the anesthetic machine was hooked up and the patient was induced by pentothal. The anesthetist turned on the fluothane and the breathing air was filtered through crystals to remove impurities. After a few minutes the crystals changed color, and one of the nurses reached over to change to a jar of fresh crystals. There was a hell of a bang with showers of flying glass, flailing tubes, and general consternation.

It was immediately obvious that the anesthetic machine had blown up, and with it Mrs. Rivers' esophagus and breathing passages. She became a human bomb, and died instantly.

Mass confusion prevailed. None of the medical personnel were injured beyond cuts from flying glass, but they were stunned and horrified, and it took a few minutes for them to collect their wits. They sealed the room and called the coroner.

My first order of business was to obtain some advice—an almost impossible task given the propensity of the medical profession to draw together in the face of perceived attack. I was firmly turned down by the other local doctors as well as Manitoba doctors, nearby Minnesota doctors, and Toronto doctors: "I'd really like to help you, but you know how it is..."

I telephoned Bill Wigle, who was the head of the Ontario Medical Association. I knew Bill casually, as he had practiced medicine in Dryden, a pleasant paper mill town eighty-seven miles east of Kenora. I figured he would do the right thing, and he did.

"Wait right by your telephone, and I guarantee that it will ring in fifteen minutes." said Bill.

When the phone rang it was Dr. Donalda Huggins of Winnipeg. She was a specialist in anesthetics, and a professor at the University of Winnipeg Medical School.

"I've just had a call from our mutual friend Bill Wigle. How can I help you?"

When I told her about the fatality she said she would pick up a friend who was also an anesthetist and be in Kenora three hours later. It was a refreshing change from the cool reception I had from the other members of the club.

Dr. Huggins looked over the operating room and talked to the people who were present at the time of the explosion. She gave the police and the coroner and myself advice about how we should handle the situation.

I attended at the postmortem, which was performed by Dr. John Potts of Dryden. John took the place of a certified pathologist in those days, as he had taken a six-week quickie course in forensic pathology. I recall that the temperature in the little morgue was stifling. John did his best to weed out the merely curious and restrict the spectators to people who had a serious interest in seeing the autopsy, but even so there were more than a dozen overheated, queasy people in the room.

The explosion had done an incredible amount of damage to Mrs. Rivers. In the autopsy the actual cause of death did not need to be pieced together, but the cause of the explosion was another matter.

Sam Burris and I were assisted in our investigation by Bob Etherington of the Kenora Town Police force. We did a tremendous amount of reading, and Dr. Huggins made it possible for us to visit several up-to-date operating rooms in Winnipeg in both old and new hospitals. Bob and I made several trips to Winnipeg to interview technicians and specialists, and by the time the inquest rolled around we were experts in our own right.

Early on it became clear that the height above the floor of the outlets was not critical. Explosions had been known to occur from outlets at all heights, and provided the outlets were not right at floor level it didn't seem to matter.

Conductive flooring came under scrutiny. Such flooring will bleed static electricity away from fixtures in the room, particularly the operating table, thereby (hopefully) insuring that a stray spark does not set off an explosion. There had been a lot of research into conductive floors and equipment, and opinions as to its efficiency were all over the map. In the course of our own research we discovered that a Winnipeg hospital had recently spent $10,000 on a new conductive floor, only to find a month later that it had lost its conductivity. Most small hospitals did not bother with it.

It eventually became plain that the St. Joseph's Hospital in Kenora was no model of safety, but it was about as good as most other small hospitals. It was also plain that the operating room people were aware of most of the hazards and took whatever steps they could to compensate for them.

As our research progressed and the issues were narrowed down, it appeared that the real culprit was underwear. There was very little in experience or literature on the subject, and we learned about it as we thought our way through.

Generally in a supposedly civilized society one does not enquire into the nature of people's underwear, particularly not ladies'. But where nylon, perhaps even cotton, uniforms swish against nylon underwear it is a recipe for the manufacture of static electricity, which may spell disaster in the operating room. This was not widely understood prior to the death of Mrs. Rivers. It therefore became necessary to enquire who was wearing what, and modesty be damned.

Various combinations of cotton and nylon were being worn by the O.R. personnel on the day Mrs. Rivers died. At least three people were near enough to the anesthetic machine to touch it, but they couldn't all remember what they had on when the machine sparked. Nevertheless, the betting was on a stray spark induced by the swishing of nylon when the swishing party was in close proximity to the machine.

As sometimes happens with a well prepared inquest, the hearing itself was only a formality. In many inquests we expect to learn something at the hearing itself, but in the Rivers case, by the time of the inquest we knew the answers before we got to the courtroom. We laid it all out for the jury, and they came back with predictable recommendations about conductive floors and equipment, and about wearing cotton as opposed to nylon in the operating room, but by the time we held our inquest the word had already circulated to the medical profession, and hospitals everywhere changed the way they did things.

The inquest was anticlimactic, but everyone involved in it nevertheless had the feeling that they had participated in a worthwhile exercise. Since that cold day in 1961, I have never heard of another anesthetic machine explosion exactly like this one.

Mr. Rivers sued the hospital and the medical personnel, but with-

73

drew his action in what was generally perceived to be a magnanimous gesture upon his remarriage, a year later.

Dead Trapper

One spring afternoon I was having tea (well, maybe it wasn't tea) with the Old Inspector when the phone rang. The caller was a young constable from Sioux Lookout, wanting permission to charter a plane into a remote lake where a spring bear hunter had discovered a body buried long ago, now partly exposed by the erosion of a creek bank. The inspector gave his permission, and turned to me.

"You know, lad, the body was an old trapper named Alfred Filipchuck. I buried him myself, and never got around to putting in a report about it, and eventually I just forgot about it.

"It was 1931 or 1932 as I recollect. I was on my annual canoe patrol of the area south of Lac Seul, and I knew the old man hadn't been heard of since the year before, so I made a point of finding his shack. The stink inside was something terrible, and when I forced myself to go in he was sitting at his little table, looking out the window. He was dead all right, and he'd shot himself right through the forehead with his 44-40 rifle. He must have been sitting there like that for more than a year. There was no food in the shack, and only a few skins. Nothing of value, and no papers to tell of any relatives. If he hadn't shot himself he would have starved before long.

"The old man wasn't much for reading and writing, but he'd left a penciled note telling what a rough time he was having, and saying he was going to finish himself off. I dragged him out and buried him beside a little creek.

"If I was to tell that to the boys in Sioux Lookout, like as not they wouldn't believe me. Anyway, there'd be all hell to pay because I buried him myself and never put in a report about it. Well, just let them dig him up. I'll tell coroner Hugh Allen about it myself and he'll make it all go away, nice and quiet."

And he did.

The Runaway, Charlie Wenjack

Charlie was an involuntary pupil at the Cecelia Jeffrey Indian School in Kenora in the sixties or early seventies. I mention that it was an involuntary situation because no kid in his right mind would ever of his own volition have gone to live in a church run residential school. Particularly not a kid like Charlie, a child of the lonesome places.

Not all residential schools were hotbeds of perversion and abuse, a phenomenon we hear so much of in the 1990s, and in fact, I know that Cecelia Jeffrey School was not. I know it because I conducted a confidential investigation into certain alleged wrongdoing not long before young Charlie died, and I am sure many people, including staff members, would have leaped at the chance to tell me about it if it had existed. This is not to say that this was a good place for children, for Charlie and most kids like him it was jail; but principal Colin Wasacase, an Indian himself, was doing his best to make it congenial when Charlie ran away.

Charlie and two other lads simply took off one day in the fall. The other two were headed for their grandfather's trapline camp near Redditt, a CNR village seventeen road miles north of Kenora, but Charlie set out for his home at Ogoki, or Marten Falls, about 300 miles further east down the tracks from Redditt, and 110 miles north.

He didn't have a chance.

The boys got to the trapline shack without difficulty, but it was a hungry reception. The grandfather and grandmother and the three boys shared two potatoes for their supper, and in the morning they sent Charlie on his way with their one remaining potato.

Charlie was in his summer clothes and the weather was getting colder. Perhaps he knew he was going to die as he walked down the trail to the railroad. The grandfather certainly must have known, but, as he said later at the inquest, what could he do about it when his own family was starving? In any event, it is a strongly ingrained ethic with Native Indians to avoid interfering in the lives of other people, and I believe it would have been perfectly natural for the old couple to simply allow young Charlie to go on his way, if he wished. Certainly it would never have occurred to them to contrive to have Charlie or his friends returned to the Indian Residential School.

Two days later an alert train crewman spotted Charlie's frozen body beside the tracks. He had made six miles before pitching on his face and dying of exposure.

Werner Lake

In the good old days, before they revised the Coroner's Act to require juries on all fatalities, and before government tried to create a saccharine empire by putting sensitivity and caring on such an impossibly high pedestal, we would often fly out to a mine site to get an inquest over within a day or two. Some said it wasn't considerate of the deceased's mates, but the results were not distorted by outside considerations and carried a degree of credibility that is often missing in the inquests of today.

One of these inquests took place at Werner Lake in the late 1960s. The miner suffered a fatal accident early on the day shift one freezing November day. By 10:00 A.M. Dick Murray, the District Engineer of Mines, had got the call. He alerted the police, the Coroner, and myself immediately. I found some way to shove my day's cases under the rug, and by 11:00 A.M. we were airborne. Erica came along to act as court reporter. Larry Gartner was the superintendent of the OPP, and in the absence of a junior officer he came along to assist the coroner. Fact is, if there had been forty men available he would have come along, as the trip smelled of adventure.

Thirty minutes after breaking ice on takeoff we landed at Werner Lake. The temperature was dropping fast.

Dick and I went underground to the accident site, briefly viewing the body in the head frame before taking the cage to the depths. I was no stranger to the underground, as I had worked at mining as a young man, during an absence from the dunghill of education, and I had been in several other mines in connection with other inquests. I always got a little thrill when the cage left the surface and plummeted down the dripping shaft. It seemed to be an unnatural thing to be doing. Like flying and scuba diving, both of which I have done, it caused me to wonder if man should really be making such bold attempts to triumph over nature.

Larry Gartner commenced to interview witnesses right in the head frame, as they came up from their work places in the mine. Lacking the policeman's little black notebook, he used a scribbler that someone gave him. Like the rest of the proceedings it wasn't regulation, but it worked just fine.

Sam Burris went to the office to assist the mine surveyor in selecting plans and blueprints for use at the hearing

Erica scouted out a suitable place for the hearing, settling on the dining hall.

Keith Parsons, our pilot, taxied the ancient Norseman back and forth to keep a path clear to open water.

At 2:00 P.M. the hearing opened, and I commenced to examine the witnesses under oath, using Larry Gartner's notes to guide me. As it happened we had ample time to take the evidence of the few witnesses, and Sam gave his verdict, or summing up, at 3:45. There was no jury, only the coroner sitting by himself.

By 4:15 we had poked out through tinkling ice to open water and were airborne, the body rolled in a piece of canvas and lying across the feet of the side seat passengers. Or perhaps it was tied to the top of the float; we did it either way when time was of the essence. We landed back in Kenora through skim ice just as darkness was settling, the last plane of the season to operate in or out of Kenora Bay.

If we had not gotten the inquest over with very quickly, within two or three days at most, it is likely that our key witnesses would have left for far parts, that being a custom of miners at the time. During the 1960s we handled most mining fatalities with what might be seen today as unseemly haste, but at the time it was the only way to do them, or we would have lost our witnesses.

Confederation Lake

I recall another fatality, this time at the mine at Confederation Lake, in the dead of winter. We convened the hearing in a brand new steel quonset hut which was destined to be the recreation hall but was not yet finished. We had power, but no heat, and a full inch of frost formed on the inside of the building from condensation of the people's breath. The reporter could not use her tape recorder because the bitter cold had seized it up. Fortunately she remembered her shorthand, and she was able to carry on with the aid of a 200-watt light bulb placed near her writing hand, and a mitten on her other hand. Everyone kept their parkas or skidoo suits on. In deference to the cold, hats were not removed. It was a mighty brief inquest, and we were pleased to pile into the unheated aircraft that was idling at high rpm waiting for us on the lake and to be on our way back to some place with a warm bar.

In the sixties and seventies, we had many such makeshift inquests into mining and aircraft fatalities, until changes in the Coroner's Act required a more structured approach. We don't have nearly as many inquests in the nineties, and they tend to turn into unnecessary productions that are often unsatisfactory in spite of the best efforts of the coroner and his advisor, the Crown attorney.

Drinking the Cargo

It was freezeup in the North and they were having the traditional pilot's wingding in Pickle Lake. George Harrison's Beaver was the only plane left in the water, and drunk or sober he intended to fly out to Big Trout the following morning. Two drums of gas plus the Christmas liquor were already aboard. Don't be shocked at the notion of booze being flown openly into Big Trout. Until sometime in the 1970s, white people in the North thought the liquor provisions of the Indian Act just didn't apply to them. Enlightenment did not come until the eighties.

Along about midnight George was bragging that he would leave before dawn. He was roaring drunk, and so were his buddies, but at least they had a little more sense than he did. When he finally passed out they put him to bed and hid his trousers and boots, just to be sure he didn't try to fly away.

The lack of trousers and boots was no problem to George. When he woke in the predawn he simply staggered out of the hotel in his long handled underwear and heavy socks, and down to the dock where his machine was tied. The hotel was built around a hollow square stairwell, and everyone left their doors open for heat, but even so, no one heard or saw George padding out.

George enlisted the aid of another early riser in getting away from the dock, but even so he was so drunk he fell in while trying to break the ice around the floats. He simply hauled himself out of the freezing water and into the cockpit, and was on his way, a fresh bottle of goof in his lap to keep him company.

The takeoff was uneventful, as the pilot managed to get out to open water before making his run. What happened next is not quite clear. Perhaps he selected cruise power and pointed the Beaver at Big Trout Lake, and then he fell asleep. Perhaps the wings picked up some ice. These are possibilities we simply can't know about. But we know that the flaps were down, and George Harrison still had the bottle in his lap when he was found a few days later.

Thirty miles out of Pickle Lake, the Beaver simply settled into a swamp. There was no great structural damage, but George was killed when the two drums of gas broke free and came ahead, squashing him into the instrument panel. If ever anyone could be said to be the author of his own misfortunes it was George Harrison.

Freezeup was too far advanced to get a plane to the crash site, so the RCAF sent a chopper over from Winnipeg. On the way they picked up a police officer and a coroner from Cochenour, that being simpler than detouring to Pickle Lake to pick up the local coroner and a constable.

They found the Beaver in the swamp easily enough, and dropped a man with a chain saw to clear a space for the chopper to land. Even with these precautions they managed to clip a rotor tip on a tree and put the big Sikorsky out of business. It was three days before the RCAF managed to fly a new rotor in and install it. The boys on the ground meanwhile had to content themselves with the little food they had with them, but there was the Christmas booze to pass the time and fend off the cold—there was even a generous supply left to welcome the crew of the rescue helicopter—before they were able to leave the swamp, hungry and hungover, to go back to their offices and write up their reports.

The part about the Christmas booze and its disappearance did not get into the inquest, nor did the story of how the plane was recovered. The details of the recovery would really make a story in itself, but basically what they did was to take skis to the downed Beaver, put them on backwards, and with the wings and tail feathers tied alongside, tow it out backwards with several snowmobiles. It was easily repaired and I was a passenger in it on several later occasions.

A Primitive Postmortem

In most jurisdictions a trained pathologist performs autopsies, or postmortem examinations, on people who have died in peculiar circumstances, just to ensure that the deceased expired from what he was supposed to have expired from—not from foul play. If a pathologist was not available we sometimes used an ordinary doctor. Sometimes we just used common sense.

Now, before the sanitation crews who purport to have a monopoly on decency and propriety in the 1990s advance on me with drawn sabres, I want to remind them that this particular incident happened in the early 1960s. The location was Pickle Lake, which the road from the south had not yet reached. At that time the Regional Pathologist program was not yet in operation in Kenora. It was still the good old days.

Some poor fellow had died in a rock fall at the Pickle Crow Gold Mine. They had a look at him, rolled him in a piece of canvas, and put him on ice in the curling rink, to await the arrival of a plane to take him down to civilization. Nurse Beloir informed Coroner Dr. Robbie Robinson that the boys at the mine wanted the rink for a bonspiel, and he would have to get the body out as soon as possible.

But the plane didn't come that day because of bad weather. Nor would there be any flying the next day or the next. In fact this story ended before transportation on ski planes opened up again.

Nurse Beloir phoned Doc Robbie again the following day. Robbie would have liked to authorize the local doctor to have a go at the body to see if it really did have crushed ribs as his mates had said; underground mines being such notoriously good locations for committing murder; but the local doctor was out on his annual holiday.

"How do you feel about taking a slice at him yourself?" asked the resourceful Dr. Robbie.

"Not all that great," replied Nurse Beloir, "but I'll do it if you will assure me I won't get in trouble over it."

"It'll be all right," said Dr. Robbie. "See if you can get the visiting cop to help you."

But the visiting cop was a milquetoast and wouldn't have any part of it. He was only in on a replacement basis while the regular officer was out in Kenora attending trials. Anyway, some people just never feel comfortable around corpses.

Nurse Beloir sat looking at the body all day, and every time she approached it with a scalpel she lost her nerve. By the end of the day she was in a bad state, and had not put so much as a nick in the skin of the deceased. And the bonspiel was to begin the next day.

Nurse Beloir's husband stepped into the breach. Early, early in the morning, before his wife was awake, he jumped into a mine truck and drove out to a nearby Mennonite mission where, he had heard, there was a male nurse temporarily in residence to dispense religion to the local Indians. Jackpot! The nurse had been a paramedic in the Korean War and had no scruples about carving up cadavers, and he willingly accompanied Nurse Beloir's husband back to the curling rink. With Nurse Beloir and the visiting policeman looking on he expertly zipped open the body's rib cage.

Voila! Four broken ribs! A massive crush injury! Just what the doctor ordered!

"Let the game begin!" shouted Mr. Beloir, as he threw out the first rock.

An Aircraft Fatality

It may come as a shock when I say that the best and most expensive private aircraft on the market has an inflight airframe breakup rate many times in excess of its closest competitor. The statistic was certainly a shock to me, and together with Regional Senior Coroner Bill Wigle of Dryden we determined to mount an inquest into a Beechcraft Bonanza fatality that would explore the limits of the aircraft's capabilities, exposing the dangers of the machine, if indeed it was dangerous. The Federal Department of Transport Aviation Safety Division was very supportive.

The enquiry arose out of a fatal acccident to a Beechcraft Model 35, better known as the Vee tail Beech, to distinguish it from its straight tail sister. This type of machine had been in production for more than twenty-five years, and was considered the Cadillac of small aircraft. Wealthy docotrs and lawyers tended to own them, as ownership was a status symbol. To fly one of these swallow-tailed beauties was proof that you had "arrived."

This particular Bonanza was flown by a pilot who had only nine hours of instrument time. He took off in an aft center of gravity condition with two friends and an overload of gear and fish, right into the teeth of a thunderstorm with severe associated turbulence, in spite of being advised that the storm posed a problem. He became airborne at 10:10 A.M. on June 19, 1977. Ten minutes later the pilot and his passengers were all dead, and the plane was scattered across a mile of bush just fourteen miles southwest of Red Lake.

Aviation fatalities were a subject of continuing interest to me, as I had been exposed to aviation all my life, and was in fact a pilot at that time. I may not have been a very experienced pilot, but I knew a great deal more about the culture surrounding aviation than many pilots much senior to me. This crash excited my interest, and I suggested to Bill Wigle that an inquest might bring out some valuable information.

The duty of the Crown Attorney at an inquest is quite different from his duty at a trial. An inquest is not supposed to call for an adversarial

82

approach by the attorney; rather, he is supposed to question the witnesses on the stand and act as the coroner's legal counsel, avoiding conflict with parties who are grinding an ax, as far as possible. In this case it was not possible to remain completely out of the arena.

The moment the inquest was called two competing interests became apparent.

Firstly, there were the families of the pilot and his passengers, who would have been pleased if the inquest found an airframe failure to be the cause of the fatalities.

Secondly, there was the Beech Aircraft Corporation, which had a number of product liability lawsuits pending against it at the time, arising out of in-flight airframe breakups. Beech was desperate to clear the good name of its products, and would like to have seen all the blame laid on the pilot. They didn't even want the issue of airframe breakup explored, which had the effect of spurring my interest all the more.

Other interests of lesser importance also surfaced. The meteorological people with the Department of Transport wanted assurance that no one would blame them for inadequate weather reporting. In fact, they were right on, but prior to establishing this fact there were a number of calls back and forth to arrive at an acceptable approach to the involvement of the met people.

Within the Air Regulations Division and the Air Safety Division of the Department of Transport there was some disagreement on the cause of the accident. One faction said there was an airframe weakness which caused the Beech Bonanza's unique tail to flutter and disintegrate and consequently to shed its wings at high speed. Backing them up was a well-known stress and materials engineer in the United States who had been hired by many of the people involved in suing Beechcraft.

The other faction was championed by a man who, while a pilot, was part of the engineering safety office of the department of Transport. He argued that the machine was unquestionably the finest aircraft in its class on the market, but the trouble lay in the kind of people who flew the particular type of aircraft. The Vee tail was powerful and fast and expensive. It was also a very demanding airplane, with a red-line airspeed just a very little faster than its normal cruising speed. It required to be flown attentively every single moment under turbulent conditions.

An example of the consequence of inattentive flying was told to me by a professional pilot. He was flying a Beech Bonanza over Lake Ontario when he fumbled a cigarette, and it landed on the floor. He leaned down to retrieve it and in the moment that it took, the nose dropped and the aircraft picked up speed and went through red line. Fortunately the air was dead calm, and the pilot was able to bring the aircraft back through red line without damage. Had he encountered turbulence the story might have had a different ending.

Now, to state the obvious, doctors and lawyers who work hard enough to afford a Bonanza have a lot on their minds, probably too much. They are apt to go months at a time without exercising their flying skills, and they tend to forget what they learned about the art, or science, of flying. Doctors in particular tend to develop a God complex, and believe they are immortal. They fly into turbulence, they let the machine go for a moment and it goes through red line and the pilot doesn't have the skill to retrieve the situation. Then, either the tail develops flutter and breaks off or a wing separates. The consequences are fatal either way. I don't believe the pilot in our particular case was either a doctor or a lawyer, but he nevertheless qualified fully in the God complex department.

The adversarial position was just beginning to be adopted by lawyers at inquests, and it became obvious that the inquest had the potential for turning into a circus. Dr. Wigle and I wanted to head off this possibility.

The bits and pieces of the aircraft had been taken to the National Research Council in Ottawa for testing. Bill Wigle and I went there to see the aircraft reconstruction ourselves. An astonishing amount of information had been turned up by the scientists, including the fact that a wing had torn off before the flutter and consequent destruction had been induced in the tail. This was confirmed when a wing was found farther back on the flight path than the components of the Vee tail. The significance of this is that the detractors of the Bonanza claimed that there was a fatal weakness in the tail which was causing all those crashes. We eventually concluded that the flutter in this particular case was a by-product of the breakup of the aircraft, and not the cause. The real cause was the excessive speed caused by loss of control induced by flight into a regime that was beyond the capabilities of the pilot.

All these preparations, including studies at the National Research Council, took two years. I had made the NRC findings known to the various lawyers representing competing interests, and when the inquest was convened in May of 1979 there was no opposition to the thesis of the Beech Aircraft Corporation to the effect that inept operation of the craft was the cause of the accident. The inquest jury found that a) the pilot was inexperienced, and b) he took off with an overload, c) in an aft center of gravity position, d) in unsuitable weather.

And so the reputation of the Vee tail Beech Bonanza was vindicated. But if you want to fly one safely, you had better not fly it into a thunderstorm at high speed.

Three

Behind the Scenes

A Crown attorney has to be able to improvise, and roll with the punches. Day by day he must face surprises and yet pretend he is not astonished by what he sees. He could not survive if he were not adaptable, and he would die of an internal ulcer if he could not cut loose and laugh once in a while.

Many of the next group of stories don't fit in to a specific category but some had a laugh in them for me, and I think they will cause you to laugh, too. Others caused me to think about something other than the never ending parade of misery to which I was exposed, and perhaps you, like I, will be moved to contemplate humanity's instinct for self-preservation, and the fine line that often separates the good guys from the bad guys.

Death of the King

They called him the King of McKenzie Island. He ran the post office and a private ferry service to the mainland, and what he wanted most in the world was for people to be happy. One evening in midsummer when I couldn't find accommodation in Red Lake I simply taxied over to the Gold Eagle Hotel and tied my rented Cessna 170B up to the nearest dock. Albert Kaye strolled down and took a line and invited me to leave the machine there for the night, hospitable man that he was.

"Will it be okay if I leave my stuff in the aircraft or should I cart it up to the hotel?" I asked as we snubbed the float up. I knew the doors didn't lock properly, but I just didn't want to bother toting a lot of junk up the hill.

Albert put on his best injured expression, letting on that the question had seriously wounded him.

"Why Mr. Burton, of course you ean leave your things in the airplane. You can't possibly think anyone from McKenzie Island would ever steal anything from a visiting airplane. Don't give it another thought."

Privately I could think of half a dozen residents of McKenzie Island who would have cheerfully stolen anything they could get their hands on, but I trusted Albert.

Albert must have remembered these same people some time in the night, for when I came down to the aircraft after breakfast there was Albert all twisted up in a blanket and fast asleep in the right hand seat.

"Oh, Mr. Burton," he said apologetically, "I meant to be out of here before you came down, but I figured the honor of McKenzie Island was at stake, and I'd better sleep in your machine in case some of those bad people from Red Lake or Cochenour decided to pay us a visit in the night."

Albert Kaye, the King of McKenzie Island, was truly one of the good guys, and he didn't deserve to die the way he did.

Some time after the incident with the plane, in the same year, I believe, Albert was standing on the grass adjacent to the post office and the ferry dock watching a young fellow playing silly bugger in his father's boat. It was a windy day, probably too windy for a little boat, and a number of other people were watching with interest from various vantage points. The shore where Albert was standing was composed of artificial fill hemmed in by a stone wall known as a breakwater, and Albert was more than a boat length from the edge.

As Albert watched, the boat skipped over a wave and a paddle flipped out. The driver circled around, came up on the paddle, and slowed down. The boat was operated from the front by remote control, so the boy pulled the throttle back and went to the stern to grab the paddle out of the water. He shoved the paddle forward between the driver's seat and the wall of the boat, and in so doing knocked the throttle up to full speed, with the predictable result that the boat shot forward and he somersaulted backwards into the water. He had no trouble swimming to shore on the mainland side, but the boat went on alone, straight as an arrow, heading for Albert Kaye's breakwater.

Albert had no idea he was in danger, no doubt thinking he was just going to see a dandy boat crash, until the boat spanked a high crest and bounced off the top of the breakwater and landed a full boat length inland. The propeller, turning at high speed, buried itself in Albert's thigh and destroyed his femoral artery. The injury was too high on the leg to permit a tourniquet.

Immediate first aid and a lightning trip across the channel to the Margaret Cochenour Hospital could not save Albert Kaye, and he was dead within five minutes.

The kid in the boat wasn't a bad sort, and he had really done nothing worse than play hooky from school and take an unauthorized joyride in his father's boat, something that many boys do from time to time. Nevertheless, he was very, very lonesome at the inquest.

The Redditt Train Wreck: Whiskey Galore

Some of the most interesting incidents pass into history without leaving bulging files for the archives. I couldn't find so much as a single piece of paper about the Redditt train wreck in the files of my Kenora office. There may be a few reports of the movements of the police in the OPP files. The newspapers had blurbs on it, with pictures of smashed boxcars and debris lying across the right-of-way. The CNR will have many pounds of paper hidden away in dark vaults, but it is unlikely that the officials could ever find it again, even if they wanted to, and the likelihood is they wouldn't want to. Not because of the wreck itself—train wrecks happen all the time—but because of the wholesale, un-checked carrying off of goods that went on during the salvage operation. After a while even the CNR gave up calling it stealing. It took many years to gather enough information from many sources to write this story as no one really wanted to talk to me about it, for reasons which will become obvious. Later, when people did open up and talk freely, it became difficult to sort fact from fiction. What I am setting down here is bizarre, but is basically all true, and either I had personal knowledge of it, or it was told to me in bits and pieces by the people whose names appear in the story. The names are real except for Harry Bluebird and John Hamilton.

It was a high-class merchandise train, you see. Clothing, jewelry, and manufactured goods of all kinds, but mostly liquor; whiskey galore. There were 59,781 cases of it, and 1,000 cases of beer, all lying on the right-of-way in an isolated area, and at the bottom of a lake adjacent to the tracks. All impossible to guard. The biggest problem the thirsty inhabitants of the area had was how to carry it away and how not to get so drunk that they couldn't manage another load the next day.

The strangest part about it was that some of the railroad officials got on the gravy train themselves, and so couldn't be heard to complain later about thievery among the rank and file. They tried, oh they tried. But I wouldn't listen.

It was 6:24 A.M. on July 28, 1971, and old No. 217, a high-speed express, was roaring westbound out of Farlane towards Redditt when it encountered a loose rail on a curve. The result was a monumental pile-up of twenty-seven cars, some in the bush, some on the tracks, and a number that careened into the lake alongside and sank. A few floated out as far as several hundred yards before sinking. Many of them burned on the right-of-way. All this was several miles east of Redditt, a CNR village some seventeen miles north of Kenora, right out in the bush and far away from the nearest road. It was typical Canadian Shield country of rocky terrain, lakes and swamps, and to add to the difficulty, the railroad was single track, and therefore, traffic was completely blocked from both directions.

The wreck presented a three pronged challenge to the salvage crew and the extra help hired for the occasion. The first priority was to clear the right-of-way and repair the tracks to permit traffic to pass. Then they had to save what equipment and cargo they could. After that they could get down to the serious business of backpacking or flying out what they considered to be their own fair share of the goodies. I was told that their share exceeded that of the CNR and its insurers.

The biggest bonanza was the cars that were at the bottom of the lake. Some were relatively intact in a few feet of water, but they nevertheless had to be unloaded by divers to prevent further breakage when the huge cranes pulled the cars out of the water. The unloading had to be accomplished a few bottles or a few sacks at a time until the little boats were full, and then dropped off at a dozen depot areas on the rocky tree lined shores. From there the goods had to be carried through the bush to some convenient spot by the track, kept there until a car could be spotted, and loaded by hand.

Of course, the cars had to be frequently moved to make way for trains once the right-of-way was cleared. All this activity required hundreds of men coming in on foot over the right-of-way or through the bush, or in small airplanes. And they all had to go somewhere each night, mostly back to boarding cars spotted at Redditt. There was no

91

way of accurately keeping track of them. As one of my raconteurs pointed out there is, after all, some honor among thieves, for at the request of the guards the salvage crews did not loot jewelry or firearms.

The degree of honor among thieves did not reach such unreasonable proportions as to prevent them from stealing booze from the wreck or from each other, however. Indeed, to swipe another man's booze became a higher mark of prestige than to swipe it from the company. The campfire talk was about the number of bottles hijacked from a pal, and how many gunnysacks had been retrieved and hidden. If a man found a bigger sack than he happened to be hiding, he simply put his own down and took the other. One exuberant fellow put down a sack of gin and picked up a bigger sack and slugged out seven miles through a mosquito infested swamp, only to find that he had acquired a sack full of jars of vaseline. When he returned the next day for his original sack of gin, it was gone, and a sack of cheaper whiskey was in its place.

Another bonanza was the merchandise cars that had rolled into the bush. Initially they were pushed back to clear the right-of-way, and those that weren't split open by the accident certainly were broken when the mammoth cranes and bulldozers started shoving them around. Their contents became easily accessible.

Harry Bluebird was lucky enough to discover a way into a car full of children's clothing. Harry was out of work until the CNR hired him shortly after the wreck. He was concerned about how he was going to support his growing family through the following winter at one of the reserves, many miles away. He was one of a group of extras detailed to unload several cars that had been shoved well off into the trees. Any intact boxes were to be carried on the backs of the men a distance of about a mile east, and deposited in a cleared area adjacent to the track, where they were later to be picked up. The men and goods were loosely supervised, at best. The supervisors were all company officials and most of them had far more to do than they could possibly manage. Many of them were busy caching their own hoards behind rocks and under the moss. All were aware that the others were doing it, and it became a game to find someone else's cache and then to hide it again. There was no one to watch the watchmen.

It was a game for everyone but Harry, and for him it was serious business.

Harry was an Indian of the old school, and was appalled by the senseless stealing of things that people couldn't use, and probably could never get away from the site. As a man of principle he determined to take only what he needed, and he planned to get every bit of it home to the chicks in the nest.

The first thing he did was to hunt around for a nearby lake, not the lake where the wreck was, but one where he could set up a cache that wouldn't be found. The lake had to be big enough to get a Beaver in and out of, and he knew of one a mile or so across some granite ridges and through a spruce swamp. It took two hours for the round trip on foot, but that was all right because it meant no one would be likely to follow him and find it.

The next thing he did was to send a message out to his friend, John Hamilton, the bush pilot. The note said to have his Beaver at Harry Bluebird's little lake at 5:00 A.M. on a day ten days hence, and a hand drawn map with the precise location of Harry's cache was enclosed. He knew that John would trust him for the charter fee.

For nine days Harry spent his spare time sorting clothing into boxes. This one for winter boots in various sizes, that one for running shoes, another for jeans, still another for sweaters, one for parkas, and so on. He even managed to find a fur coat for his wife. He made certain his family was going to be the best clothed family at the reserve that winter.

When the end of each work day approached, instead of making the last trip down the tracks to the depot, he simply disappeared into the bush towards his private lake, taking a different route each time so that he wouldn't leave a trail.

Every evening the pile of boxes at the cache grew larger. Then he would plod back down the tracks to the boarding cars at Redditt. The ninth day was pretty tense for him, as this evening was to be his final push. He quaked and quailed through the day, looking over his shoulder at every step imagining the penetrating eyes of CNR Constable Wolfe Thompson on his back. It was a relief to step out into the bush with the last box of clothing, and an even greater relief to hear the Beaver droning down through the dawn light the next morning.

Three hours later the Beaver dropped Harry back at the wreck. Not only had he swiped and stashed enough clothes to last his family for years, but he was the only man on the whole crew who had made love before going to work that morning. With his own wife, too!

Some of the best stories that came out of the wreck were about the booze that was flown out.

Kenny Race was an adventuresome young man with a J-3 Cub on

93

floats and he was an accomplished scuba diver to boot. As an experienced diver he was extremely useful to the CNR. Even better, he was able to use his little airplane to fetch full air tanks and run the thousand and one odd errands that needed doing.

Kenny's entrance to the scene happened this way. One day shortly after the train wreck he was flying over the lake when he spotted a shadow on the bottom in the slanting rays of the sun. Being a good samaritan, he landed and told one of the officials there was another car on the bottom. It turned out to be the mail car, and the company was desperate to locate it, so they rewarded Kenny with his odd jobs position and agreed to turn a blind eye to his comings and goings.

Kenny got away with forty-three loads of booze and was paid a goodly sum for his several weeks' work for the CNR. He has photographs of himself priming a sump pump with Chivas Regal, the very best Scotch whiskey.

Even though he virtually had a carte blanche to take anything from the wreck he wanted, Kenny wasn't dumb enough to flaunt it publicly. One evening he flew out with a large number of bottles of Drambuie which he had carefully amassed in a pile on the shore, well out of sight of the wreck. Given the untrustworthy nature of the people at the wreck it is a wonder that he was able to amass more than a few bottles at a time. His takeoff was thwarted by the fact that his rear spreader bar was under water, and he had to wait till the sun went down and the air cooled off before he could get airborne with the load. As he taxied his plane out to takeoff, one of the guards hollered, "You've got to share that load three ways!"

Now Kenny didn't want to fly straight home and unload the stuff right at his own dock; he didn't want to fly up to the English River to unload it at his favorite hiding spot near his camp, because he just didn't have enough daylight left, so he landed on a lake just north of Redditt, and taxied up to an alder swamp at the shore. He grounded the floats on the sand and waded in with his bags and boxes of Drambuie, simply setting them down in the swamp, out of sight of the water, each one out of sight of the other. Kenny then departed for his home in Redditt, feeling immensely satisfied with himself, as well he might, for that was the third load he had hidden that day.

All Kenny got out of that batch was three bottles. When he returned a few months later the alder swamp had been rooted up. There was dried blood everywhere. The swamp was covered with holes filled with broken glass. The only explanation, and one which I believe, is that a bear sniffed out a leaky bottle, broke it somehow and lapped up the ground under the bottle. Every time he sobered up he went looking for another bottle. The result was all the bloody holes Kenny found in the alder swamp.

"It was a cruel blow," said Kenny. "I've always loved animals, and never did them any harm except when I wanted to eat one. And now look what that black son-of-a-bitch has done to me. I hope all that glass and dirt constipate him for the rest of his life."

Barney Lamm was another bush pilot who had his booty hijacked, this time by a group of children. Barney owned a large tourist camp at Ball Lake on the English River, and the wreck was almost in a direct line between Kenora and Ball Lake. Barney was curious, and dropped down one day to see what was going on. As I have mentioned, the shoreline was difficult, and Barney pulled his Beaver in at a convenient place some distance from the wreck. As it happened there was a cache of Drambuie, just under the water where his float grounded on the bottom, no doubt hidden by Kenny Race or Slippery Walsten. Barney was an astute entrepreneur who was never known to miss an opportunity, and he didn't miss this one. Into the cabin went the Drambuie, all 104 bottles of it. Into the air went Barney, a song in his heart.

The problem of hiding the booze until it was cool presented itself. Ever the imaginative one, Barney solved it easily.

Out behind his main lodge was a big stack of fireplace wood. When no one was looking, Barney hauled his 104 bottles out to the woodpile, pulled chunks out of the woodpile at random and poked the bottles into the holes. Then he plugged the outer end of each hole containing a bottle with a short piece of wood, which he cut off with his chain saw, so that from the outside you couldn't tell there was anything else in the pile.

A job well done. He must have felt about the same as Kenny Race felt the day he left his booze in the swamp. He closed his camp in the fall, intending to retrieve the booze in the spring.

Unfortunately, Barney forgot about the children from the nearby reserve. When he returned in the spring the woodpile had been reduced to half its size, there was evidence of extended camping in the area, and 100 bottles of Drambuie were missing. He later found four full ones under a shed, no doubt hidden there by one of the campers and then forgotten about.

It appears that a couple of the kids from the reserve were out hunting, stopped to make a lunch fire with Barney's wood, and made the happy discovery. They went back and got their pals, and settled in for a few days of revelry.

Barney would rather someone had stolen one of his airplanes, however he didn't come out of it empty-handed. Several other expeditions netted him a large quantity of rye whiskey which he poured into three gasoline drums steamed out by his camp foreman, Stan Holmstrom. The drums were set back at random among the gas drums on the airplane dock, thereby becoming invisible to all but Stan and Barney. Reminiscing later, Barney said, "the stuff tasted terrible, but it sure traded well."

Throughout the six-week salvage period the police weren't idle. They knew, as did everyone between Edmonton and Ottawa, that a whole trainload of goods was disappearing, a little at a time. Trouble was, it was so extremely difficult to identify. The railroad officials eventually came to see me about prosecuting some little people, but went away to think about it when I opined that it might be a good idea to prosecute some company officials first, as that would be a better deterrent. Funny thing, I never heard from them again. Before the police ever came in I had heard that the booze for the wedding of a company man's daughter had come from a boxcar of salvage that was temporarily unattended on a storage track at Sioux Lookout. My informant told me that the whole town, railroad officials and all, stayed drunk for two weeks. It must have been a hell of a fine party.

The OPP had their hands full too. It would have taken 500 men to cordon off the area for six weeks, and that would mean every provincial and municipal policeman in northwestern and northeastern Ontario. It just couldn't be done. They did what spot-checking they could, but there were so many people coming and going that no one could tell whether any particular individual was hauling goods for the company or for himself. In the end, it was decided that there was insufficient evidence upon which to base any prosecutions.

Even the RCMP were active. At that time, all liquor was required to be sealed with an excise stamp and this particular trainload had not been stamped, as the excise tax had not been paid. Anyone in possession of liquor without a stamp was therefore theoretically in contravention of the excise laws. However, so much confusion was generated that no proof could be found of the origins of the various caches of liquor that were found and possession was difficult to prove. In any event, all the

Typical northwestern Ontario terrain.

Left: Ed Burton, *The Old Pilot*.

Below: Prospecting in 1950—black flies and mosquitoes in summer, and the bitter cold in winter. It was a very good period in my life, but I didn't realize it at the time. One day, ax or paddle in hand, I decided to go back to school.

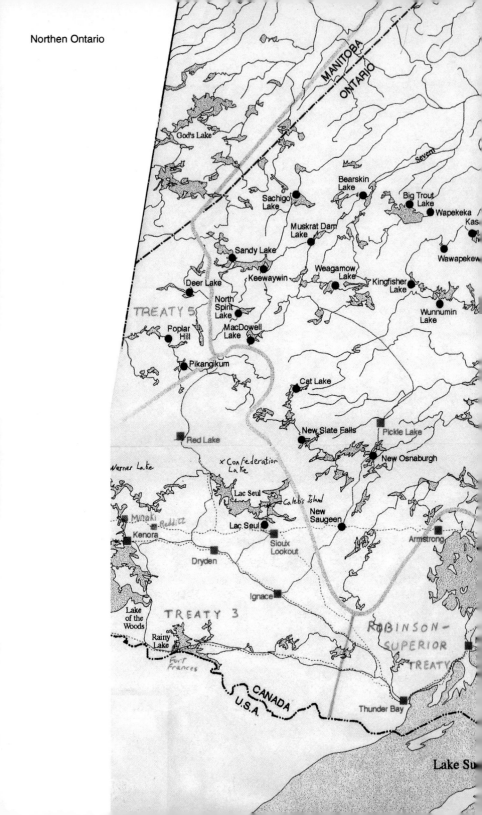

Northen Ontario

MANITOBA
ONTARIO

God's Lake

Sevent

Bearskin
Lake

Big Trout
Lake

Wapekeka

Kas

Sachigo
Lake

Muskrat Dam
Lake

Sandy Lake

Weagamow
Lake

Wawapekew

Keewaywin

Kingfisher
Lake

Deer Lake

North
Spirit
Lake

Wunnumin
Lake

TREATY 5

Poplar
Hill

MacDowell
Lake

Pikangikum

Cat Lake

New Slate Falls

Pickle Lake

Red Lake

× Confederation
Lake

New Osnaburgh

Werner Lake

Lac Seul

Caleb's Island

Minaki
Redditt

Lac Seul

New
Saugeen

Kenora

Armstrong

Dryden

Sioux
Lookout

Ignace

ROBINSON—
SUPERIOR

Lake
of the
Woods

TREATY 3

Rainy
Lake

TREATY

Fort
Frances

CANADA
U.S.A.

Thunder Bay

Lake Su

Bob MacGarva, who investigated many important cases in the 1950s and 1960s.

The old Inspector, T. G. Corsie, with his secretary, Grace.

Retired superintendent, Dick Bender, the former corporal at Red Lake.

100

Walking to court before the day of the skidoo.

Duty counsel (kneeling by overturned sled) at work in a northern village. The police had to collar the miscreants and hold them while the lawyer spoke to them, as they did not know what was happening to them. However, over the last twenty years the inhabitants of the north have learned all too well what the court process is about.

A typical group on the steps of a northern courtroom. Tikanagans, or back cradles, are still quite popular in the north.

Erica and friend Archie Stoney with wolf pup at Fort Severn.

In my bureaucratic mode.

The court house in Kenora as it was in the 1960s.

A home in summer, a smokehouse in winter.

Court in recess, Fort Hope in 1966.

An inland settlement in 1971. One of the few remaining tee-pee homes.

A stack of winter firewood.

A few seconds after the bomb went off.

A police artist's rendering of the "Mad Bomber."

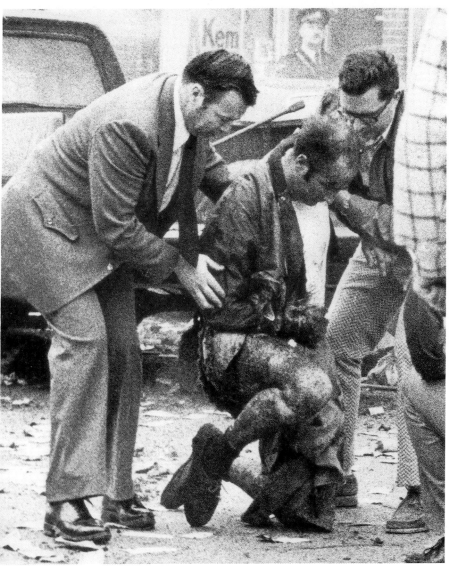

Just after the blast. Constable Don Milliard being helped to his feet by colleagues. Note the money on the ground.

Home to eight people on a northern reserve. Ample reason to leave home and join a protest or a march. Things have improved on most reserves since this photo was taken in the 1970s.

The only store within 30 miles, wrecked by bored children whose parents would not make a ball diamond for them.

One room of a four-room school and a three-unit teacherage wrecked by children with .22s and 30-30s with no intervention from their parents.

Louie Cameron of the Warrior's Society, the ringleader at Anicinabe Park.

Winisk village from the air, some time in the late 1960s, after the closing of the RCAF base across the river.

Winisk after the ice jam destroyed the village.

Anglican cemetery and spirit house at Big Trout. This view, from the back of the Natural Resources guest house, is known to everyone who traveled the north prior to the 1980s.

A church used for a court room. This could be any one of several dozen villages in Northwest Ontario.

With rented Cessna 180 at home in Kenora. Preparing to fly north.

Transferring to the Albany River's shore. Fort Hope, 1966.

labels had been soaked off in the lake, and the contents couldn't be readily identified without an analysis of each and every bottle. Any seized liquor was therefore given back or destroyed, and no charges laid.

People got involved in the train wreck in a variety of ways. Carl Hager was a sergeant on the Kenora Town Police, and he had his own plane and a tent camp on Botanist Lake about twenty miles from the wreck. Carl's camp was well known to the local pilots and sports fishermen and was a gathering place for men who wanted to escape from town for a day or a weekend. They were safe from their wives at Botanist Lake, as the only way in was by float or ski plane. Carl never swore and very seldom took a drink, and his credibility was of the highest order, although his friends were known to take a drink from time to time. Perhaps even quite a few drinks. It was while they were in their cups one night that they decided that Carl's camp would make an ideal hiding place for the liberated booze. Unknown to Carl, the bush area around his camp became the repository of dozens of cases of liquor, for what right-minded enforcement officer would ever have thought to search Sergeant Hager's property?

Generally speaking, I don't like stories of people beating the law. I have been conditioned to cluck my tongue and frown in disapproval because, after all, law and order are supposed to prevail. That's what I keep telling myself. In spite of it I had to chuckle when I heard about the booze cached at Carl Hager's camp. Ten years later, some of his buddies were still going back at the tail end of winter to look for stray caches. There are always a few days in late April when the ice is solid enough to take a small plane, the snow is gone, and the leaves are not yet out. Yes, the hunting is good at that time of year.

Another of Kenny Race's stories concerned a handyman he flew up to Tetu Lake to do some work on his camp, early in the spring following the wreck. Kenny dropped his man off on the dock with instructions to work at some camp chores until later in the afternoon when Kenny would return to pick him up. It was an efficient plan, except that Kenny didn't take into account that the water is always low in the early spring, and the sack of gin he had hidden in the lake at high water just before freeze up could now be seen. When Kenny returned his hired hand was still on the dock, passed out cold, and there was no sign of any work having been done that day.

Kenny Race and his friend Slippery Walsten were in close competition as to who could liberate the most booze. Slippery later gleefully reported that he had gotten away with forty loads. Kenny said he managed to make off with forty-three loads, but that was all right because he, Slippery, had found two of Kenny's caches and hidden them again.

Ever since the days of Aesop, stories are supposed to have a moral. If there is any moral to this story, it has to be that if you are going to steal something, steal lots of it, laugh a lot while you are doing it, and make sure that everyone else around you is doing the same thing, so there will be no one left to squeal on you.

Aesop was a light-hearted old gentleman, if we are to judge by his stories, and he might even have agreed with me.

The Art and Science of Highgrading Explained

The theft of gold ore is a special offense under the Criminal Code of Canada and is not lumped in with the general offense of theft. Section 394(c) of the Code provides that:

> Everyone is guilty of an indictable offense and liable to imprisonment for a term not exceeding five years who has in his possession or knowingly has on his premises (i) any rock or mineral of a value of fifty-five cents per kilogram or more, (ii) any mica of a value of fifteen cents per kilogram or more, or (iii) any precious metals that there are reasonable grounds to believe have been stolen or have been dealt with contrary to this section, unless he establishes that he is lawfully in possession thereof.

People in the mining industry and the administration of justice call it highgrading. At one time there was a lot of this sort of activity going on. A miner who was getting three dollars an hour could get ten dollars for a fist-sized rock showing visible gold (VG), and he might bring up such a rock every shift. If he beneficiated it by hammering some of the host rock away and stockpiling the gold he might clear an extra $300 or $400 dollars a month. Back in the fifties and sixties that would translate into an expensive new car every year.

The gravy train slowed down in the sixties when the price of gold was allowed to find its own level on the free market, and the citizens of the United States were permitted to own it legally. For much of the middle part of this century, gold was pegged by government decree at thirty-five dollars an ounce, and the black market in Paris would pay eighty-five dollars an ounce. It was said that in Bombay and Macao where it was much in demand as a symbol of family wealth, the black market would pay ninety dollars to ninety-five dollars an ounce. When gold was deregulated it bounced as high as $600 before settling down at $430, plus or minus. People could trade in it legally, and there was not the fantastic differential between stolen gold at the headframe, and legal gold landed in India, and the highgrading subindustry in Canada simply diminished like a low-grade vein in a stope. The game is still played, but it doesn't have the romantic overtones it once did, and the mines don't complain so bitterly about it.

While it was in its heyday, highgrading was a never-ending source of conversation and speculation in the gold camps of the North. Everyone knew someone who was doing it, and the practice of highgrading assumed an almost respectable status. The major figures, usually the buyers, all sported nicknames like the Russian Kid and Curley, and were well known in their communities. You just assumed that anyone who showed you a nicely speckled sample was in the business, or was a policeman trying to look like he was. This was a bad trip to lay on an innocent collector or legitimate prospector, but I must admit now, looking back on it, that there was a lot of justification for thinking like this in places like Red Lake and Timmins in the late 1950s. It was so prevalent that a small mine in the Goudreau area was put right out of business by its own employees. One of the mines at Red Lake that was just marginal at thirty-five dollars an ounce actually managed a return to profitability by buying back high grade ore from its own employees for fifteen dollars or twenty dollars an ounce. But the ethics of this were highly questionable.

The OPP spent a lot of money trying to keep highgrading within reasonable bounds. They used stool pigeons, undercover men, prostitutes, and regular officers, sometimes with surprising results. I became involved in several cases as a student, as a defense lawyer, and as a Crown attorney, and every case was interesting.

On one of my regular trips to Red Lake as defense counsel in 1960 I was approached by the chambermaid at the Red Lake Inn. I will call her Lisa. Her husband Tomas was employed by one of the mines, and he was in trouble over some highgrade the police had found in the basement of their home. She said no one in the family knew how it got there. I was barely able to suppress a snicker. Her English was not up to any further explanation, so I made an appointment to interview her husband at home.

As it turned out Tomas' English was somewhat better than his wife's, but he was strangely reluctant to talk. Lisa served us a delicious dinner of chicken paprikash and dumplings right off the wood range in her comfortable kitchen, washed down with quantities of sweet tea, but even those gastronomic inducements were not enough to persuade him to confide in me. It was plain that he simply had no faith in me, nor probably in anyone else. The oldest daughter, Maida, was thirteen and at the top of her grade eight class. She later explained to me that the reason Dad was in trouble was that someone had squealed on him, causing the police to search and find the gold, and they simply did not know whom to trust. Over a period of several weeks I managed to dig out the full story, not from my client, but from Maida, the very bright thirteen year old.

It seems that Tomas and two of his buddies were the Robin Hoods of the mine which employed them. All three of them worked in a stope where there was a lot of VG. They picked it off the vein like grapes from a vine, and beneficiated it before they ever got it to surface. They had some unique way of getting it up without being detected, probably in scrapped diamond drill rods or in discarded timbers. Once above ground they retrieved it and took it to some hiding place. Maida would collect it at intervals and bring it home on her bicycle or tucked in around her young brother on his sleigh. Further beneficiating would take place in the basement, then Maida would stash it again. When there was enough she would take it, now about fifty percent pure, to the buyer, Joe Fidlich. After that, she would take the money and distribute it to her dad and his friends, keeping some for herself. Fidlich would take the gold to a local service station operator who would then find some way to ship it out without detection. The police thought he might be melting it into bumpers which he affixed to automobiles heading south, but they were never able to prove it.

As it turned out Maida was not only the courier, but the group's strategist. At first I viewed this as highly unusual, but as I got to know the Hungarian refugee community better I came to understand that it was possible for a child who had lived by her wits all her life to be smarter than her parents. Maida was certainly a perceptive kid, and she had a cold feeling in her guts that Joseph Fidlich was the squealer who had set up the big bust. Tomas, who was an acquaintance of Fidlich, refused to believe it.

I knew there had to be a police informer and that the police would do anything to protect him. After I read the sections of the Criminal Code dealing with highgrading, I realized that the only way I could get Tomas off was to get so close to the informer that the police would abandon the case rather than have his identity revealed. George Groom of the Precious Metals Theft Branch kept mum and wouldn't give me a clue. "If you manage to figure it out I will ask the Crown attorney to withdraw the case," he said smugly as he consumed my whiskey, "but I don't think you're going to crack this one. And by the way, where the hell is the money for your fee coming from?" I could have been irritated at that, but I knew George didn't really expect an answer. Nevertheless, I prepared a cross-examination of the police which I hoped would force them to either admit the informer was Joseph Fidlich, or abandon the case.

It was getting on for trial day, and I still did not have a fee in hand, and I couldn't see any defense on the merits. I had told Maida and her daddy that I wanted $300 to do a quick trial at Red Lake before Magistrate Fregeau, that being a fair and reasonable fee at the time for such an undertaking.

Two or three days before the trial Maida called me and said she had come up with my fee, and it would be ready when I got to Red Lake. She added that she must have been wrong in distrusting Joe Fidlich, because it was he who had given the family the money to cover my fee, and he never would have done it if he was the stoolie who had fingered Tomas.

The part about the money was good news, but the down side of it was that my meager defense disappeared with the certainty that Fidlich was not the squealer. I decided to plead my man guilty and throw him on the mercy of the court. I bent my efforts towards convincing Magistrate Fregeau that my client was a hell of a swell fellow. I started by advising the court that his wife Lisa was our chambermaid at the Red Lake Inn. I banked on the fact that he would recognize her in the front row of the courtroom. It must have worked, because Tomas only got six months in jail.

Several months later I became the Crown attorney and I learned all the secrets of the Precious Metals Theft Squad. For example, I learned that Joe Fidlich was playing both ends against the middle, and Maida was right to be suspicious of him. When Joe sensed her suspicions he went to George Groom and told him his cover was about to be blown. They decided that if Joe were to give Maida the money for my fee it would throw Maida (and me) off the scent. George then went to the manager of the mine that employed the three Robin Hoods and asked him to come up with my fee. He agreed, stipulating a cap of $900 on what he would put in the pot. Of course, I had only asked for $300, thereby leaving $600 on the table. Fidlich's code name with the OPP was Kokomo Joe, and they eventually discovered he was in the buying business for real, keeping about half of everything for himself. It was outrageous of him to cheat his employers, the police, and it was even more outrageous for him to blow the whistle on Maida's little ring of enterprisers. It was my pleasure to learn that some former colleagues of his own stripe invited him to leave town, which he wisely did.

I prosecuted or defended several other cases during the early 1960s, most of them being souvenir cases. The only one that resulted in an acquittal was a case in which the accused testified in his own defense to the effect that he was not in possession of the gold. He theorized that a former resident of the mine bunkhouse must have left it behind the wall next to his bed. It was unusual in highgrading cases for a lawyer to put his client on the stand, thereby subjecting him to cross-examination, but the accused stood up well enough to establish a reasonable doubt in the mind of the presiding judge, who promptly acquitted. A secret fink had told the police he saw the accused place the gold in the wall; however, the Crown could not call him to testify without exposing his identity.

Well, it could have been true. Secret finks are not well thought of by the underworld or by the police, and the reward for information of this nature might have been as little as fifty dollars. The whole story might have been a frame-up by some enemy of the accused. I don't mean to be inventing fanciful defenses, but when you are dealing with people of this strata, possibilities of this nature are something you have to keep in mind, whether you are prosecuting or defending. It is just possible the accused was really telling the truth and deserved to be acquitted.

I had a qualified admiration for the undercover police who pursued the highgraders. They had to look scruffy and keep bad company in order to be seen playing the part, and often they went months at a time without any success to show for their efforts. It was just as discouraging to be a regular officer pursuing a faceless, shapeless quarry, and seldom catching him.

On the other hand, when the police made a pinch, the news reverberated through the highgrade community with the speed of light, and even a so-called "souvenir pinch" caused quivers down the spines of wrongdoers in mines many miles away, for such is the nature of the human conscience.

The Girl in the Boat

She was only a kid, not more than twelve or thirteen years old. She was dressed in pants and a thin jacket, even though there was snow in the air. Her bed was the center seat of a sixteen foot outboard skiff.

Her pretty, youthful features had a determined cast and you only had to look into her face to know that her life was not easy.

Mary ran the night ferry from McKenzie Island in Red Lake to the mainland at Cochenour, a distance of a half mile or so. In between passenger trips she curled up on the seat wrapped in a blanket and a length of canvas. She got all the sleep she needed that way, or so she said.

I locked the car and walked down to the dock on a cold November night, avoiding the half frozen puddles. The far shore was not visible through the spitting snow, so I pushed the button, causing a buzzer to sound at the post office dock on the other side. In a moment a light flashed, and I knew the boat was on its way. A few minutes later several miners on their way home joined me on the dock, stomping their feet to ward off the cold. One of them said, "It's a hell of a night to be out on the water." The rest of us just grunted.

By the time the boat was actually visible it was almost at the dock. The wind was from an awkward angle, but Mary landed in an expert fashion. She left the motor running.

"Get in quick," was all she said. There were four of us, and we stumbled in awkwardly. Mary handed a length of canvas to the two men on the windward side, without explanation. They knew the drill, and held the canvas up to deflect the spray. The girl hunched down at the stern, hanging on to the tiller through the cuff of her sleeve, and opened the throttle, appearing to be totally unconcerned. If there were life jackets, I didn't see them. There were no navigation lights on the boat.

In less than five minutes we were at the dock on the other side. Mary put her hand out and said, "twenty-five cents each," and she popped it into a pocket without counting it.

As I walked towards the Gold Eagle Hotel, I could barely make the kid out in the gloom. The snow was coming down hard now. She had wrapped herself in the blanket and was in the act of pulling the canvas spray deflector over her head when I lost sight of her.

I felt sorry for the kid, but the thought dissipated when I walked into the warmth and laughing companionship of the Gold Eagle, and was able to forget for a while that I was the Crown Attorney.

Many years later I met Mary again. This time she was a grown woman with a family of her own, married to an assayer friend of mine. Her life was still hard, as she had an autistic child. Her still pretty face had premature lines in it. When I reminded her of that snowy night a lifetime ago she merely shrugged her shoulders and said, "You do what you have to do."

Sinbad The Police Dog

For many years Minaki was a one-man detachment, and the only way to get to court or to OPP headquarters was to take the train to Redditt and be met by cruiser from Kenora. If you were real adventuresome you

120

could make the trip by boat, negotiating two sets of rapids on the way. The point is, Minaki was very isolated, and a cop had to be resourceful to survive. There was a succession of big, mean dogs named Sinbad to guard the policeman's family when he was away. Even after they punched a bush road in from the Trans-Canada Highway, thirty miles south, a Sinbad was kept at the detachment house.

During a winter cold snap Constable Eric Miller had to go away on a course, and left his wife Lois and two children at the detachment with Sinbad. A relief officer was sent in to board with Lois. He and Sinbad didn't get along at all, and Sinbad would have loved to eat him alive.

As it happened, the relief was not too fond of work, and Lois could see it piling up. She knew Eric would have a busy time of it when he returned, and she and Sinbad just didn't think it was fair. Lois and a friend hatched a plot to get rid of the relief cop.

Lois' friend faked a call to draw the relief out of the house. He groaned as he walked up the trail to where the police car was kept, and went off to investigate the phony complaint.

Meanwhile, back at the police house, Lois put Sinbad on a long chain and told him not to let anyone near the house. Sinbad understood. Lois then threw the relief cop's stuff in a bag and put it on the trail just beyond Sinbad's reach. When the relief returned it didn't take him long to get the message, and he fairly flew down the new bush road, arriving in Kenora within the hour.

The Old Inspector was snoozing with his back to the radiator when the phone rang. "Sir, this is Lois Miller in Minaki. I just want you to know that I have sent that lazy son-of-a-bitch on his way, and if you send him back I'll have Sinbad chew his ass off."

The inspector knew he was no match for a fiery, determined woman. "All right, lass, just be calm. I'll send the man back to his own detachment and you take the dog in before he eats one of the neighbors up. I'll see that your husband comes home as soon as possible."

A few minutes later when the relief cop stormed in the inspector said, "Well, lad, I hear the detachment commander at Minaki has fired you. You'd better get on back to your own bailiwick and forget about Minaki."

Sinbad wasn't such a hero one day the following spring. He got off his chain and followed Eric to where he was bagging the bits and pieces of someone who had been hit by a train. Eric tried to make the dog go home, to no avail.

Eventually Sinbad disappeared, much to Eric's relief. But when Eric got back home there was Sinbad on the step chewing on what appeared to be a large human bone. Eric jumped to the conclusion that the bone was from the tracks and was nearly sick to his stomach. Sinbad wouldn't give it up and continued to gnaw on it with great relish.

Later that day when Eric was having a cuppa with the cook on the track gang train, he learned that the cook had given Sinbad a huge ham bone earlier on. He took Sinbad back into his good graces, but until the day they moved Lois was the only one who could control the dog.

The Rifleman

The Old Inspector and the Old Pilot planned very carefully for their encounter with the Old Prospector. They didn't want holes shot in either their airplane or themselves, knowing full well that the prospector was a deadly shot with a rifle. A hole had recently appeared in an airplane which flew too close to the remote mine site at which the prospector was a watchman.

They landed on the other side of the lake from the mine site, well out of accurate rifle range, and chatted as they untied the canoe from the rack on the starboard float, knowing that the prospector would be watching through his binoculars. They made sure the prospector could see they had a bottle of whiskey with them. Neither of them thought it necessary to take a gun.

The two men paddled back and forth on the lake very slowly, trolling for pickerel as they went. They laughed uproariously at each other's jokes and whenever one of them pulled in a fish. With each pass they came closer to the prospector. Eventually they were close enough to yell at him.

"Do you want a fish, Harvey?" the inspector called.

"Sure do!" replied the prospector. He had set aside his rifle, and was watching them intently. He was no longer suspicious of them, and he hoped the two men from the airplane would offer him a drink. It had been almost a year since he had a drink, and even longer since he had been with a woman. He was developing a powerful thirst.

After a while the whiskey was almost gone, and the three men had become firm friends. The pilot had taken very little, merely putting the bottle to his lips and moving his adam's apple, but the inspector had actually taken a few genuine snorts. The prospector was out of practice and the whiskey had the effect on him the other two had planned.

"It's getting late, Harvey, and we've got to be going," said the inspector. "Why don't you come along with us and spend a week in town?"

Old Harvey the prospector did just that. They saw to it that he checked into a hotel where they weren't too particular about female guests in the room, and started him off with a new bottle of whiskey.

A week later the prospector's outlook on life had improved considerably and he chartered back to his mine site in behind Sioux Narrows with the same outfit in whose wing he had put a hole, several weeks previously.

The Old Pilot was philosophical about it. "He's got a piece of paper from the Lakehead Psychiatric Hospital saying he's sane, which is more than most of us have. All the same, I'm going to be damn careful about flying over the mine site from now on."

Deadman's Run

In 1950 the CNR branch line between Thunder Bay and Sioux Lookout was quite active. Today weeds grow between the tracks, but in those days it was a main route for grain trains into the Lakehead. In the summer these trains ran in convoys with a twenty minute space between trains, that being the minimum interval allowed by the rules. The trains were shorter, too, as they were powered by cantankerous old steam engines, which meant more of them were required to pull a given amount of grain. In order to get over the tracks faster, the crews of trains everywhere often cooked their times, thereby shortening their intervals by a few minutes. By a few minutes I mean two or three, usually not more.

Alfie Sommers was a young constable at the time. He was a big, good-natured farm boy who fit right in to police work because of his common sense approach to his duties. At the time I first heard this story I was working as a brakeman on the CPR and I later got to know Sommers well. I watched with satisfaction as he progressed through the ranks to superintendent. One of his outstanding characteristics as a senior police officer was that he had a lot of empathy for young cops in a jam, as he no doubt remembered some of the shenanigans he had been involved in.

On a hot summer day in about 1955, Constable Sommers received orders to attend at a remote section house several miles from the nearest station to pick up the body of a railroad worker who had died of unexplained causes. Alfie proceeded to the nearest village with a helper from the funeral home, and they borrowed a push car from the station master, taking with them a metal coffin with a screw down lid, thinking the body might be pretty ripe. It was.

It was mostly downhill to the section house where the body lay, so they were able to coast without expending much effort. It would be different on the way back. They left at a time when there were no trains running and reached their destination without incident. For the return trip they were firmly instructed to get behind a passing train, glue themselves to its tail, go like hell for twenty minutes, then get off the tracks until the next train went by.

All went well at the section house, and they quickly stuffed the body into the coffin and battened down the lid. As it was a hot day, the boys lolled in the shade waiting for the next train to go by. They were mildly perturbed to find the trains were running at intervals of seventeen minutes or so. One of the deceased's buddies from the section gang was to accompany them back to the station, at the village down the tracks, and he assured them the trains often shaved their times, but it would be all right.

As soon as the next train went by they heaved the push car onto the rails, but being amateurs they used up a few precious extra minutes. They noted the time and began to run down the track with as much speed as they could, pushing their grisly load ahead of them.

Twelve minutes later, as the boys were riding the car on a slight downgrade, they thought they heard the baleful sound of a whistle behind them. There is very little in the world more terrifying than the sound of a train whistle behind you when you are on a narrow track and that is as true today as it was forty years ago. If you don't believe it, try crossing a single track railroad trestle on foot some day when a train is due. "Sacre collise," exclaimed the railroader, "It is not yet time. It is only twelve minutes."

The whistle sounded again, and this time there was no mistake about it, as the engine suddenly appeared around the bend behind them, coming fast. Now the boys were really panicked.

"Mother of God," yelled the section man, "She will nevair be hable to stop, an' we won't eider!"

"Holy shit," screamed the funeral director's assistant, "Hit the bush! Hit the bush!"

By this time the ancient steamer was snorting at their backs, the whistle blowing, the bell ringing, and the brakes squealing crazily and throwing sparks. Alfie ran alongside attempting to wrestle the push car off to the side, body and all, but he only succeeded in tearing the heels off both his boots. The boys leaped into an alder swamp just as the engine flashed by, the white faces of the head end brakeman and the fireman peering openmouthed from the side window.

There was a terrible crash and the push car was smashed to splinters by 120 tons of steel locomotive. The coffin took off like a ballistic missile. It landed in the swamp, one end buried in the mud. The lid had sprung open and the body was hanging half out with broken bones it had not possessed before the crash. The push car crew was not badly hurt, but they were bruised and winded.

The freight train stopped with the caboose opposite the bedraggled men in the swamp. "Is anyone hurt bad?" called the conductor, implying that he would only be concerned with serious injury.

"No, but you bastards who can't tell time are going to be hurt bad when I catch up to you," replied Alfie.

The conductor looked confused, and he called down, "You might as well know it now as later, but we are running at fifteen minute intervals. There's someone right on our tail and we've got to haul ass out of here. We'll wait for you at the station and notify someone to pick you up in about an hour." As he spoke he gave a hand signal to the engine man to get moving.

The boys had a terrible time cramming the dear departed back into his twisted box, and they just managed to get him back to the tracks

125

when the fifth train in the string stopped and took the party aboard the caboose. The coffin rode in style, crosswise on the rear deck.

The offending train crew had taken the siding at the village, and were waiting sheepishly, fully expecting to be transported immediately to the gallows. However, Alf sensibly reasoned that if he took action he would never again get cooperation from any railroader on the subdivision. The section hand volunteered to steal a push car from the next section gang in order to make the station master's inventory come out right, and the funeral director's man undertook to charge the damaged coffin off to the next wealthy customer. Alf figured he could explain the extra injuries to the deceased to the satisfaction of the coroner, and besides, he might be in serious trouble himself if headquarters ever found out about it. Everyone was happy with the new arrangements.

And that is how the illegal practice of cooking the station passing times came to an end on the Alcona Subdivision.

Hiding the Nitro

"No, Mr. Isaacs is not in. If you wish to see him you might try the Marlborough coffee shop. It's where he usually sees his clients in the morning."

There was no problem, as I happened to be staying in the Marlborough, a comfortable, old hotel of fading decor that had once been the pride of Winnipeg. I took the elevator to the lobby and Max Isaacs was the first person I spotted when I walked into the coffee shop. He was elegant in cream colored trousers and white shoes. Max was surrounded by several guys who looked like they were trying to pass for hoods, but being prairie farm boys they didn't quite make it. There is a certain innate decency about prairie farm boys that cannot be completely obscured even by a life of crime.

"Boys, this is Mr. Burton from Kenora, he's the Crown attorney there you know. Say hello to him nicely and then leave us please," intoned Max in his cultured English voice. The boys who passed for hoods in Winnipeg glared daggers at me and shuffled off to another table.

"Sit down, Mr. Burton. I believe you prefer tea, don't you? And to what do I owe the pleasure of this visit?"

Max was one of the most affable adversaries I ever had. He was an effective lawyer, with a persuasive manner that charmed judges and juries into acquitting his clients. At law school they used to tell us there were two kinds of lawyers—fact men and law men. But they forgot to reckon with Max Isaacs. Max didn't know an iota of law and never cared about the facts, but he fell into a third category, that of persuasive men. The breed has all but disappeared as of 1995, and the profession is poorer for it.

"Max," I said, "when you got those fellows discharged on that robbery prelim last week I meant to make a deal with you to tell me where your boys hid the nitro-glycerine they were going to use on the safe. The police never found it, and there are children in the neighborhood. I told Chief Pike I would inquire."

"Those oafs!" roared Max. "I told them never to leave that stuff around. Just sit tight and I'll be back in a moment." Max ambled over to a pay phone, and I saw him dial without looking the number up. He talked briefly, listened even more briefly and returned to the table.

"It's all right, Mr. Burton. My clients are not totally without a sense of responsibility. They went back over the weekend and found the stuff and poured it off the Keewatin bridge. It was a very unstable batch and they didn't want to bring it all the way back to the city. And now, will you have some sugar in your tea?"

Night of Terror

It was a very interesting situation, with the people expressing total indifference, the dogs expressing outright hostility, and the rain blowing horizontally against the sides of the quaking cabin. And dark. My goodness, it was as dark as the inside of a dog with its tail tied down! The single-engined Otter, affectionately known as the stoneboat, was tied to the shore of the mighty river that ran past the village and poured noisily into James Bay. Even though it was snubbed down by every inch of rope we could lay our hands on, it grumbled and thrummed like a live thing. It was more than interesting, it was bloody unnerving, like a scene out of an old Vincent Price horror movie, just before the villain comes on.

We were snug enough in the forestry shack, with a wood fire hissing in the stove and an oil lamp glowing on the table, but we were afraid to set foot out the door because of the damned dogs. They were all around in the dark, and when you stepped out the door on to the porch to relieve yourself you could sense the dogs moving up. When you heard a low growl in front of you, you just knew they were close enough to attack, and you imagined one of them snapping the end of your whatchamacallit off. You stood with your back to the wind and did what you had to do, then scuttled quickly back inside where it was warm and dry.

You probably want to know what I was doing on the coast of James Bay on that dreadful night. I was traveling with Chief Coroner Beatty Cotnam and his executive officer, Jack Hills. Our pilot was Al Stuart, one of the senior pilots with the Ministry of Natural Resources, a man greatly respected in the flying fraternity. He had spent years traveling in the North, and knew the customs of the country well. The purpose of the trip was to pick up on unreported deaths in the North and we were flitting from village to village to talk to the chiefs and the nursing stations.

There was nothing in the regulations to say we couldn't enjoy ourselves, but so far the trip had brought us nothing but hardship, with rain, high winds, ice on the wings, and unfriendly people. No fun at all. No fun, that is, until all that after dinner tea began to find its way to Jack's bladder. Then the fun started.

I don't remember the year, but it was before there were any airstrips in the boonies, and it was before Papa State got all uptight about people carrying revolvers. I used to lug my favorite piece around when I was in the North. It was a big, old .455 that was RCMP issue at one time. I left it by the door to the porch along with the only two flashlights the party had.

By and by, all that tea began to cause Jack unspeakable agony. He put off doing anything about it as long as he could, but when he could bear it no longer he opened the door, took a flashlight in one hand and the .455 in the other, and stepped resolutely to the edge of the porch. Now I don't go around peeking at men who are peeing, but I would give a lot to know how Jack managed to effect his purpose with both hands full of revolver and flashlight.

There was no growling from the dogs, but all of a sudden there was a lot of delighted squealing and giggling from just beyond the circle of light, accompanied by unintelligible strangling noises from Jack Hills, who backed into the room, still wee-weeing and still clutching the flashlight and the gun. He looked decidedly ill at ease. A bevy of seven local belles followed him in, laughing and pointing at Jack as they came, apparently totally unimpressed by the revolver, but amused at a certain physical attribute of Jack's.

It didn't take Al Stuart and me long to size up what was happening, and before the ladies' eyes could adjust to the light we dove for our bunks and pulled a blanket over our heads, leaving the two city slickers to cope with the guests while we pretended to sleep. I could just make out Al's eye peering at me through the gloom. The eye gave me a big wink. Beatty Cotnam and Jack Hills later accused us of cowardice. They were right, of course.

One of the visiting ladies spoke a bit of English, having been to convent school as a youth, but what she told us she didn't learn from the nuns. They must have been watching us through the window for they had us all picked out, and they made it plain to Beatty and Jack that they expected certain services which we were totally unwilling to deliver. The leader of the delegation was a large—shall we say 250 pound?—lady who had dibs on Beatty Cotnam and she wouldn't take no for an answer. She sat on my feet and resolutely refused to budge while the rest of the ladies made free with our grub and tea.

Eventually the other six ladies tired of the sport and left in a group, kicking at the dogs as they went. But not Two Ton Tessie, who became downright angry. Beatty's voice rose by half an octave as he pleaded with her to go. She finally got the message, but refused to get off my feet. She didn't want to go out alone among the dogs. Al hissed from under his blanket, "For God sakes, Doc, give her a flashlight and make her get the hell out. If her old man finds her in here he'll lynch us."

By this time Jack and Beatty really were in a state, and they reacted in a most ungentlemanly fashion. Each took an arm and they hauled her, protesting all the way, to the door. As she passed the door she grabbed both flashlights and ran into the night. As she left the porch we heard

"Mutchun animoose," a rough translation of which would be "Get the hell out of the way you mangy mutts," followed by a grunt and a howl, and we knew she would be all right.

Fortunately one of the boys found a large, empty Javex bottle, and a small kitchen funnel, making it unnecessary for anyone to go out the door again that night.

In the morning we went on our way under the clouds, congratulating ourselves for our diplomacy of the night before, and feeling smug at having escaped that fate which is worse than death.

A Survivor

Alice Sigurdson first swam into my field of vision back in the early 1960s, when she was a girl of about fifteen years. She lived with her family on the shores of Red Lake, a few miles out of the village. Her dad was a sometime laborer who was never able to provide adequately for his large family, and didn't try very hard. Her mother was a long-suffering Native woman who eventually had to just give up trying. It was not one of the better families in the area.

One summer afternoon the police received a hurry-up call to attend at the Sigurdson shack. It appeared Alice had gone berserk and was smashing up the house with an ax. My friend Corporal Bender suggested I should go along "to better my education."

The police approached very carefully, thinking they had another nut on their hands. To our immense surprise, Alice ran out of the house and jumped into the police car, flinging an ax aside as she came.

When the police finally got the full story it seems that Alice's father had sold her to a man from one of the northern villages for a boat and motor. This was quite without Alice's knowledge or approval, and when her husband-to-be showed up to claim her she would have none of it, and to show her displeasure she started swinging the ax.

I don't believe any charges were laid, but I do know that she was a big, strong girl who could look after herself, and eventually she returned home and became the protector of the younger children. I recall that on several occasions the police or the Children's Aid would find the parents drunk and disabled, and when they checked the house Alice would be there, serenely in charge and rationing out what grub there was.

This sort of thing continued even when the family moved down to a shack just outside Kenora.

Eventually the father was convicted of incest, but not with Alice. Later, he was again convicted of a sexual offense against one of his family, and it was said the family did better without him when he was in jail than with him when he was free.

As you might expect, Alice grew up to be a cantankerous, dangerous woman, very good with a knife. I prosecuted her for cutting up a little weasel of a boyfriend, in the 1980s, and was not sorry when she was acquitted. And recently, in 1991, I saw where she went down for carving up her landlord when he objected to her making too many long-distance telephone calls to her boyfriend in Winnipeg.

Alice Sigurdson makes a hell of a lot better friend than enemy. She now lives in Winnipeg. I wonder what she tells her grandchildren when they ask her about what sort of a life she has had.

Crazies I Have Known

I have always sensed that I don't have anything to fear from ordinary people who get in trouble with the law, but crazy people are a different matter. Ordinary people who break the law expect to be prosecuted, and so long as the Crown attorney is fair about it there will be no serious grudges. Time and time again I have encountered people whom I was responsible for sending to durance vile, finding to my surprise they wanted to tell me I had done a good job or given them a fair trial, which is not to say that I won any popularity contests with that element of the population. Even people I exerted myself considerably to salt away have told me I was fair with them. But none of them were crazy. Most judges and lawyers don't worry about their safety for the same reason—they simply aren't in any danger. I think people instinctively understand that judges, lawyers, and police are just doing their jobs.

There is an exception with officials who deal with family matters. Sour domestic relations and resulting court action can cause otherwise sane people such terrible stress and hatred that they become temporarily disordered, and are capable of attacks on the perceived causes of their misery. But I am not discussing these exceptional people, rather I have in mind people, usually men, who darkly nurse a hatred, perhaps for years, and then spring out of nowhere to attack. The target may not even remember the incident that was the root cause of the trouble. Other people may know all along of the danger, but not the victim. Prison authorities, family, the boys at the Legion—may all be aware of it, but the target may carry on in blissful ignorance for years before the attack comes. It is even possible the unnatural burden of hate has nothing to do with the fact that the subject of the hatred is a person in authority. And sometimes the subject of the hatred is not even a person in authority. Whatever the circumstances, the victim often can't see it coming.

Before we get down to cases I want to explain the use of the word crazy. It is quite legitimate in this context, and I have heard respected psychiatrists use it often. It refers to people who are not insane in the sense that they have no understanding that what they are doing is wrong, but they have bizarre and sometimes unpredictable behavior problems of an antisocial nature. The practitioners of the discipline of psychiatry do not always agree among themselves about who might fall into this category, or what to do about them, but they know the real ones when they see 'em, and so do most of the rest of us who deal with this type of person.

Consider the case of Jonathan McIvor. I knew him for more than twenty years before discovering that he bore me a serious grudge, and could be dangerous when drinking. I had always sensed that he didn't quite like me, but what the hell, I don't like a lot of people either, but I don't let it churn in my guts. In the interests of civilized living I try to be somewhat cordial to them. I certainly don't want to kill them. I avoided Jonathan and we coexisted peacefully for many years without incident.

I was acquainted with Jonathan's son Robbie, an up-and-coming young policeman. We had confidence in, and respect for, each other. We worked on a few cases together, and we may even have shared a glass from time to time.

One day Robbie came to me in great distress. "Ted, I don't know how to tell you this. I feel like a fink because it concerns my own father,

132

but it is so serious I just have to do something about it." I waited for him to get to the nub of the matter.

"Years ago you had an argument with Dad's boss, at a social function which he attended as Dad's guest. It was a serious argument about a matter which affected the whole town. You bested him at it and he looked foolish to the onlookers. Dad took it as a personal insult, and he has brooded about it all this time."

I thought back over the years and remembered the incident vaguely. Being just out of university at the time I was full of piss and vinegar and eager to take on the world. I was also very stupid, as no young man with ambitions to change the world should ever demolish an older man gratuitously without an exceptionally good reason. But I had done exactly that, and in the presence of people who mattered. He may have been a pompous old jackass, but he didn't have it coming, certainly not from me. As a matter of fact, I didn't know until Robbie told me two decades later that the gentleman had been the guest of Jonathan McIvor, Robbie's dad. Robbie fidgeted, and went on. "Every time Dad gets a snootful, which is every Saturday night, he thinks back to that incident. After that he never received further promotion, and he feels your run in with his boss was responsible for it. He hates you like poison, and means to do you dirt. It wells up in direct proportion to his alcohol consumption. On Saturday nights he sits in his car on Main Street and broods and watches people go by. I am afraid that you are going to walk in front of his car and bingo! There is going to be an accident. Ted, I just want to tell you to be careful."

I was stunned by this revelation. For the next little while I watched myself carefully when I thought Jonathan might be about. Jonathan died a short while later after my conversation with his son Robbie, and I was spared the fate of being run down. The episode confirms my belief that you never know who has it in for you.

Another case in point is Sam Frescoe. Sam and his wife Jessie were longtime acquaintances of mine in Dryden, through mutual friends. I had even been a guest in their home on occasion. For some reason we drifted apart, although we were still friends. Sam was a moody sort of a guy in contrast to Jessie, who was bubbly and outgoing. They longed to be thought of as movers and shakers in the community, and as far as anyone knew they were good citizens.

Jessie was the executive director of a publicly funded charitable organization, and her assistant was another well-thought-of lady. It was a terrible shock to the community when they were charged with extensive thefts from the charity that employed them. "Not Jessie and Helen!" people exclaimed. "They would never do anything like that." But they had, and they were both convicted of it. They were disgraced, of course, and they lost their jobs. The disgrace was particularly hard for their husbands to bear, but to give them their due they were loyal to their wives.

The local newspaper did not pick the story up, but the widely read Thunder Bay paper splashed it across the pages in big letters.

The two husbands, Sam Frescoe and Willis Abrahamson, were outraged at the publicity. Tracking down how the story was made public became an obsession with them. They had been in court when Jessie and Helen were processed, and they knew the public and reporters were absent. They soon discovered that my mother, who was at the time the editor of the Dryden paper, had once been a stringer for the Thunder Bay paper that had printed the news, and they jumped to the conclusion that she had tipped the city paper off to the events in Dryden. They thought a dirty trick had been played on their wives, as such matters are often not reported in small towns.

I pointed out that sneak attacks were not my mother's specialty, and that in any event she was on the outs with the Thunder Bay paper at the time, but they persisted in believing the worst about her, and me too. There was nothing I could do to change their minds, so I just went on living my life. After twenty years as a Crown attorney I was used to cool relationships, but it was unfair to my mother.

At the time of which I speak I had another friend in Dryden in the person of Donald Plessis. You wouldn't call him a close friend, but he was a trustworthy sort of a guy who was known as a leader, and people listened when he had something to say. He hung out at the local legion, as did Sam Frescoe. One day, on one of my regular visits to Dryden, I got a message that Donald wanted to see me after court. I had a feeling it would be something out of the ordinary.

Donald told me he and a group of older men, including Sam, often drank and played cards of an evening. This had been going on for months, and the group was increasingly concerned with Sam's attitude. He was brooding with resentment towards my mother over the imagined newspaper scoop, and it got worse when he drank and lost money at cards. The group had elected Donald Plessis to speak to me about it, their advice being that she should not deliberately have any direct dealings with Sam on an eyeball-to-eyeball basis, particularly not on weekends.

My mother moved away from Dryden, and the necessity of avoiding Sam Frescoe disappeared.

The point is, to outward appearances, Sam was a rational man. Without the good will of his drinking buddies, we would not have known of the dark thoughts he harbored.

Another crazy was Tony Horseman, who brooded over a presumed injustice by a local policeman in a small village for years, without coming out of the woodwork. One dark night he tried to burn the policeman's house down, not knowing that the policeman and his family had moved out and were living elsewhere. Horseman was given four years in the pen for that job.

A lot of people don't like the local cop in a small town, but Tom Varga was a real gentleman, and had done nothing he could remember to merit such a degree of hatred.

Assistant Crown attorney Richard Cummine was Horseman's prosecutor on the arson case, and word filtered out from Stoney Mountain Penitentiary that Tony was going to get him. We kept in touch with the prison authorities to know when he would be released, and we waited. One day the prison psychiatrist called. He was chuckling. "You won't have any trouble with Horseman," he said. "Tony's got religion. He's all caught up with Jesus now. All he wants to do is go back to his village to pick up a few clothes and his tools and be on the way back to his fundamentalist brethren in Winnipeg."

Tony Horseman had fizzled out, but not before causing us a few bad moments. The prize of all the jerks was an evil little fellow named Alphonse Perrault. Given his background he never had a chance to be anything but a psychologist's nightmare. He came from a dubious subculture scattered over the Lake of the Woods, becoming mean and devious in order to survive. He was forced to fend for himself for long periods when both his parents were locked up in town. Bitterness and distrust were his portion. His mother's name was Archangel, "call me Arckie," who, when crossed, was known to remove her colostomy bag and swing it around her head, causing the contents to fly away, but never far enough. I mention these things not merely to horrify you, but to cause you to understand that Alphonse had a truly hopeless upbringing, and with his background it is no wonder he became a problem. As a kid he never really had a chance to be a normal person. All his life he drifted back and forth between the state we call psychopathy or sociopathy, and a state of true insanity. Every one who knew him said he was crazy.

As a boy of fourteen or fifteen, Alphonse had numerous brushes with the law, but fortunately I was never involved with him. My first real contact with him was when I accompanied the police to pick him up on a warrant one peaceful day in the late winter of 1961 or 1962.

Alphonse was fifteen and was hiding out in a shack at French Portage Narrows, an island village about twenty-five miles south of Kenora. His neighbors were developing a siege mentality with him so close by, so we were going over the lake to check the situation out and see what could be done.

George Orosy, and another constable, two young commercial fishermen who owned a puddle jumper, and myself, all set out to do our bounden duty. Fact is, it was a spectacularly beautiful winter day just a few degrees below freezing, and the expedition smacked of adventure.

As we neared the place our guides became visibly nervous, suggesting to the two police officers that they should position themselves on the front deck of the puddle jumper, and hit the ground running, otherwise Alphonse would leap out the back window and disappear into the bush. They pointed the contraption at the shore and ran it right into a snowbank, having the effect of catapulting the officers head first into a snowdrift. It was very difficult not to laugh, but I learned in my youth never to laugh at an angry police officer, and the lesson stuck.

Alphonse lit out through the back window in his socks, but with directions being shouted by the two guides and myself the officers soon nabbed him. The interest of our two young guides was, of course, that they were under suspicion for some of Alphonse's break-ins. They had problems of their own without being blamed for Alphonse's crimes, and were glad to see him under wraps.

The arrest of Alphonse was not a pretty sight. With his little animal face screwed up and contorted by hate, he punched, kicked, scratched, and bit, but the police could not use these tactics. Finally they were able to cuff his hands behind his back and drag him to the puddle jumper, still cursing and fighting. In order to keep him subdued they tied him just ahead of the propeller arc, in such a manner that if he moved more than a few inches, he risked getting his fanny nicked by the whirling propeller blade. The situation was both funny and pathetic. We all admitted to a premonition that Alphonse would be a problem for years to come.

But let me tell you about the puddle jumper. This conveyance was invented by denizens of Lake of the Woods during prohibition in the United States, and was originally used to ferry loads of booze into northern Minnesota in the wintertime. Basically it was a lightly built barge with the bottom sheathed in tin. Power was by wooden propeller, often hand whittled, hung on engines ranging from Ford Model A to Rolls Royce aircraft engines. The machine we used to pick up Alphonse had a 150-h.p. engine taken out of a wrecked Super Cub, and in addition it sported hard oak strakes on the bottom, causing it to go like hell in places where the ice was showing through the snow. The excess power and the oak strakes caused the machine to lurch about in a most unpredictable manner, and therein lay the secret of Alphonse's tranquility on the ride back to Kenora. As I said above, he was tied just ahead of the arc the propeller made in the back of the puddle jumper, requiring him to hold himself still to avoid the nasty blade tips.

Alphonse Perrault swore that day he was going to get George Orosy. Years later, after another chase he said he had once had George in his sights, but his gun misfired....

Early in his career Alphonse committed mostly property crimes, and maybe a few assaults. One of his first offenses was the wanton and gratuitous destruction of a beautiful boat he had swiped. After running it on a reef he sawed a hole in the bottom to ensure it would sink. This could have gotten him serious time, but the wise Magistrate Fregeau opined that he was still pretty young, and inasmuch as the law was certain to have him in its clutches off and on for the next forty years or so (psychopaths sort of fizzle out in their middle years) there would be lots of opportunity to give him heavy-duty time. Alphonse was still a juvenile, and capable of attracting sympathy because of his background.

Shortly after this Alphonse was arrested for throwing a pail of kitchen slop and fecal matter over his mother and her lover of the moment, and beating them up. *Fragrante delicto,* his lawyer T.A. O'Flaherty called it. He didn't get much time for this, either, as even in the criminal law there is a certain *quid pro quo.*

I have forgotten the precise nature of all Alphonse's offenses, but they became more serious as time went on. In 1975, he found himself charged with the rape of a middle-aged lady in a village east of Dryden. When her husband found her, she was disabled and unable to speak, because her mouth had been jammed full of stones. Alphonse locked himself in an outhouse and waited for the police with a .22 rifle, but was subdued without a fight when an officer broke in and found him asleep. His defense to the charge was that the woman consented to the act.

John McIsaac, who was defending Alphonse Perrault, watched him deteriorate during the trial. First there was the incredible fact that he claimed the victim consented to the vicious rape. Then he threw fecal matter around in his cell. Then he claimed he was having sex with the Queen by remote control.

Alphonse iced the cake when he attacked one of the few people who had ever been kind to him. During the trial, Constable Don Hakli was assigned to pick him up at the jail and return him in the evenings. He bought cigarettes for Alphonse out of his own pocket. They became friendly, to whatever extent a friendship can develop in such circumstances, but not so friendly that the constable allowed him to go without handcuffs on. Alphonses right hand was cuffed to Don's left hand, and the prisoner preceded him through doorways.

One afternoon when Don was taking Alphonse out of the courthouse and reaching ahead for the door, Alphonse swung his free left hand in a wide arc, catching the police officer unaware, and knocking him to the floor. Hakli's nose was broken badly and he was dazed. As Alphonse reached for Hakli's gun, a bystander, Bob Popadynitz, intervened and knocked him out with one punch.

Assaulting an officer was the charge, and this time Richard Cummine drew the short straw, Alphonse having worn out the good will of the other lawyers. He refused to plead guilty, so they imported a new judge unaware of his past. When Alphonse clanked into the courtroom in irons and shackles, the judge rumbled objections until Richard pointed out that even he, as his lawyer, wouldn't come in the courtroom unless Alphonse was thoroughly fettered. The judge finally agreed.

Alphonse drew two more years for that episode, on top of the ten he got for raping the lady and stuffing her mouth with stones.

And so went the life of Alphonse Perrault. I haven't even told you about the time he raped the magazine salesgirl, or how he caused the earthquake in Nicaragua, or about many other episodes that have faded from my memory. He was one of the most grossly offensive people I ever came across as a lawyer, and I often reflect sadly on the possibility that the system I worked for may have had some measure of responsibility for his being that way. But my conscience clears when I consider that no system, not even one with a multitude of social workers like ours, could ever have coped with Alphonse.

Four

Sex and the Thinking Crown Attorney

If we are to judge by television, newspapers and supermarket tabloids, sex is the number one preoccupation of the English speaking world. O.J. Simpson's trial, which is really about sex among the rich and famous, merits national coverage by U.S. television. The sexual proclivities of the Royal Family are blazoned from every newsstand, and the size of every movie starlet's bra is known to all the fans. It seems that we are forced to contemplate sex wherever we turn, whether we like it or not. Most of us like it. There's the rub.

As society pursues the Holy Grail of sex, and at the same time continues to wallow in the fashionable pit of victimism, it becomes the duty of the courts to bring a certain balance, or sense of perspective, to the prosecution of sexual crimes. But the overwhelming number of such crimes that come to the attention of the Crown Attorney make it virtually impossible to pre-try every case in the office, so the temptation today is to proceed with everything.

The following chapters illustrate the sometimes sad, sometimes humorous foibles of humans in their determined and bumbling pursuit of crime, sin, or damn good fun.

Abuses of the Clergy

There was a young rector of Kings
Who thought about heavenly things
His loins were on fire
For a lad in the choir
Whose ass was like jelly on springs

Why is it that the sections of limerick books dealing with this subject are entitled "Abuses of the Clergy?" They should be entitled "Abuses by the Clergy." But being a total conformist I have followed precedent in the title of this chapter.

I have mentioned Inspector Tom Corsie elsewhere in this book, although sometimes not by name. He was a powerful man both physically and in terms of the influence he wielded, and he had a lot to do with my development as a Crown attorney. I had known him since I was a kid, and had reason to be in awe of his right arm, as he had used it to propel me out of the office once when I had the temerity to apply for a job on the OPP.

In the early 1960s the Crown attorney and the police worked much more closely together, perhaps because both were under the jurisdiction of the Attorney General. And so it was that the Inspector called me first thing one morning.

"Lad," he said in his Orkney accent. He always called me lad, I took it as a sign of kindly friendship and not of patronization. "Lad, that young constable from Hudson is here, you know, the one with the good lookin' wife. He's got a remarkable story. I'm sending him up to you. We'll talk about it later."

Constable Adler did indeed have a remarkable tale. It was funny, too, but he was so furious that I didn't dare laugh.

The constable and his family lived in the detachment house close to the CNR crossing in Hudson, a sawmill village eleven miles west of Sioux Lookout. It was a hot summer night, so he and his wife moved down to the ground floor, and pulled the couch over by the open window where they could get some air. They slept fitfully. By and by the 4:15 blew for the crossing and they wakened. It was much too early for the Adlers to get up, and it was too late to go back to sleep, and so they did the only other reasonable thing.

In the dim light of dawn (it gets light early in Hudson in midsummer) Mrs. Adler saw a pair of eyes peering in through the screen at her elbow. With an outraged yell she threw off her vigorous young husband, who looked out and saw a figure disappearing into the gloom. He thought, but wasn't quite sure, that the figure belonged to Red O'Brien, the local Anglican parson. It was quite a stretch, but the constable managed to get his underwear shorts on, and he legged it out into the dawn, taking up a position behind some bushes adjacent to the reverend O'Brien's home. Sure enough, in a few minutes the reverend came skulking in from around the corner.

Constable Adler thought better of confronting the reverend, the more so because he was wearing only his boxers, and the mosquitoes were driving him mad, and not the least because real dawn was about to break and he might be seen. He returned home and typed up a brief report and set out for the three hour drive to Kenora, and the redoubtable Inspector Corsie. That's where I came into the picture.

I made an appointment for Inspector Corsie and myself to see the bishop later in the day, promising Constable Adler I would do nothing to embarrass his wife. The constable drove back to Hudson, still steaming.

It was a dull, rainy day as a young officer drove us over to Bishop Hives' residence. His Grace helped us off with our slickers, and we sat around drinking tea and eating biscuits. We talked about trivialities until at last His Grace invited us to state the real purpose of the visit. With some trepidation we told him about Constable Adler and the Reverend O'Brien.

His Grace was not amused. He ushered us out in perfunctory fashion, not being as much help in getting us into our slickers as he was in helping us out of them when we arrived.

"Gentlemen, you are slandering O'Brien. I know him personally, and he is totally dedicated to his parish, and he most certainly wouldn't do anything like that. Men in your position should be careful about your allegations. You will hear from me, and soon."

On the way back to the friendly old courthouse on Water Street Inspector Corsie would only say, "I knew I did right not to hire you that time. You can't trust a university man to do anything right, particularly not a goddamned lawyer."

Two weeks went by during which I avoided looking Tom Corsie in the eye, wishing that Constable Adler's infernal report would go away.

It was again a dull rainy day when Bishop Hives called and invited the inspector and me over for tea. The ride over was again cool, as Inspector Corsie thought we were going to catch whatfor from the Bishop. The cruiser felt more like a tumbrel than an automobile. I dragged my shoes through the puddles on the way up the walk, like a little boy being taken before the principal for a licking.

Bishop and Mrs. Hives were the epitome of grace and courtesy, and we made small talk as before, but avoided any discussion of Red O'Brien and the Adlers. Gradually we relaxed.

Eventually it was time to go, and we were not anxious to prolong the visit in spite of the storm that raged. Neither of us had the courage to raise the obvious question, and I pretended not to notice on several occasions when the inspector nodded at me and flicked his eyes towards his grace, even though I knew I would hear about it later.

As Bishop and Mrs. Hives helped us shrug into our rubber slickers I heard him clear his throat and I knew that something momentous was coming.

"Gentlemen," he intoned. It sounded like the voice of doom. I think bishops practice that sort of thing. "Gentlemen," now building up a head of steam, "I want to tell you again how shameful it was of you to make those allegations about poor O'Brien. I went to the village myself to look into the situation, and I assure you that there is nothing wrong with him."

As he herded us out the door he added, almost as an afterthought, "And besides, just to make sure nothing like that happens again I have invited him to leave the church. Case closed.

There was nothing funny about the case of the Good Father of Reedy Narrows, that being a reserve name that doesn't actually exist, as far as I know. In this case Reedy Narrows wasn't even in my bailiwick, but I handled the case at the request of a neighboring Crown attorney.

The good father was a young man with his fair share of natural instincts, and he let his biological urges get the better of him. There was nothing particularly startling about this until he started openly keeping company with a very young girl. Even so, he might have got away with it if he hadn't got her pregnant. To make matters worse he bought a layette by mail order, and had it delivered to himself at the reserve.

Enter the offended ladies of the village.

There are two ways you can handle a case like that, at least there were before the depredations of the Christian Brothers in Newfoundland became public knowledge and rightfully caused the Crown everywhere to take a much more rigid stance. The easy way is to lay charges and let the chips fall where they may. This route may blight lives and is a black eye to the church. I have never had any strong religious convictions, but I have always thought the churches did more good than harm, and endeavored to support them.

The other way is to open negotiations with the church involved and hope it will take a responsible position in the matter. You can only do this when you are absolutely certain of your grounds, for it would never do to put a person in a position in which he might make certain admissions, either by word or deed, thereby prejudicing himself if the matter were subsequently put before the courts.

In the case of the good father, I chose to enlist the aid of the church, having been advised that the ladies of the local church and the girl's family supported this action.

The older, established churches were pretty good about this sort of thing. The Catholic Church, in particular, understands about human

143

frailty, although today I would be more hesitant to put my faith in efforts the church might purport to make at rehabilitation, my ideals having been rubbed raw by many encounters in the last thirty years.

The result was that the young priest was transferred out and sent off to be rehabilitated. The girl and her baby had a trust fund set up for them by the church. Perhaps they all lived happily ever after. At any rate they lived less unhappily than if the young priest had gone to jail and the church had been forced to disown him.

The last of the three offending clerics was a minister in a United Church in a small town in the District of Kenora. I will call him the Reverend Schmidt. Schmidt yearned to be considered a part of the local establishment in his little town, but he didn't quite make it. Perhaps it was because he was an immense, unattractive slob with a stern, plain wife. Or perhaps it was because he was said to have an improper interest in young girls. Whatever it was, he certainly was not invited to belong to any of the local clubs, and generally was frozen out of every organization but his own church. Very sad, it was.

Eventually a representative of the Board of Deacons came to ask for my help. He said that "everyone knew" that Schmidt was messing around with girl children, and what could I do about it? Of course, I was well aware of the perils of simply accepting something as a fact just because "everyone knew" it to be so. Besides, we had not yet arrived at the day when the Crown attorney had to knee-jerk react by having a charge laid whenever someone hollered "Rape!" As it turned out something else happened which caused Schmidt to rapidly leave town before I was forced to act on the deacon's complaint. By the time I had reliable evidence of the deacon's facts (it ultimately turned out to be true about the young girls) Schmidt was long gone.

One evening I got a call from some people I didn't know, requesting me to come around to their country home. They asked me to bring Erica along, because they knew she spoke German. They were aware that it was an unusual request, but they said they had a refugee in their home, and she was afraid to leave it.

We were introduced to a rather strange young woman who spoke not a word of English in spite of being a world traveler. If the story hadn't been about the Reverend Schmidt, concerning whom I had already heard a lot of bizarre things, I wouldn't have believed it.

She said she had answered Schmidt's ad in a Hamburg student newspaper, asking for a German nanny to come and live in Canada.

Right from the beginning it was made clear to her that she was to have nothing to do with anyone who was not family. They all but sequestered her, and she never heard a word spoken in English. The only time she got out of the house was when the reverend took her out to a little farm he had purchased a few miles from town.

Before long the reverend started coming to her bedroom on pretexts. He always wore an old-fashioned nightshirt, and made suggestive remarks which she thought were inappropriate, particularly since his big belly would have made sex repugnant to her. Up to this point she was more annoyed than frightened. She was greatly put out by the fact that not only did Mrs. Schmidt know about her husband's behavior, she seemed to approve of it. It is important to the story to know that the girl believed the reverend to have tremendous power and influence locally, because he hung around the local militia unit and pretended to her that he was an officer. I suppose in her Teutonic mind she thought he would be impervious to the local police.

The whole thing came to a head the night before Erica and I interviewed the girl.

Schmidt took her out to the farm house, and told her they would be spending the night alone there, a prospect not much to her liking, the more so because she could not lock the bedroom door. Shortly after lights out Schmidt appeared in her bedroom door, resplendent in a fresh white cotton nightshirt. He stood for a few moments looking towards her in the dark, then flipped the light on. Lo and behold, the nightshirt was up around his neck, and a rat was hanging out!

It would have been funny if it weren't such a serious predicament. It's no joke for a girl to be stranded in a strange place, alone with a jerk who has sex on his mind and is intent on having his way.

What happened next is not clear, but there must have been a hell of a scuffle, ending with the girl running out with her clothes in her arms, fighting mosquitoes, dressing in the dark, ducking into the trees every time a car came along, and making her way down the bush road toward the highway. One can just imagine her terror. Every twig that snapped would be a wolf about to eat her alive; every owl that hooted would be an Indian about to scalp her. And yet I remember being of the impression that her anger quotient exceeded her terror quotient. Eventually she found herself at the door of the people who called and asked me to come out and interview her.

Fortunately the girl's hosts were kind people. They could speak a little German, and had some understanding of what the girl had been through. They gave her a bed, and when she had slept herself out they called me.

The girl did not want to get involved in court proceedings, for which I could not blame her. I assured her that Schmidt could not touch her or influence proceedings, but all she wanted was to collect her few belongings from the Schmidt residence and get to the nearest Lufthansa office. She would not complain to the police.

I didn't think I should leave the matter like that. I telephoned the reverend and in my most authoritative voice I told him who I was (not merely Ted Burton, but the Crown attorney, no less; I might even have said I was the Clerk of the Peace) and commanded him to have the girl's possessions neatly packed and in my office first thing in the morning. He complied, of course, and I told him that the authorities were in the course of translating a rather interesting statement from the girl, and he would hear from me "in a few days." I may have mentioned something about the immigration authorities being interested in his real reasons for bringing the girl over to Canada.

The end of the story is that Reverend Schmidt immediately left town, and his family followed when his wife had cleaned up their business affairs.

Two years later a returning traveler from a former British colony in the Caribbean told me he had met the reverend in a military setting. He was doing well, had a fashionable church of a protestant denomination, and was the official chaplain for the island militia. There was no mention of his wife.

Times change and attitudes change. These were clear-cut cases, and I would handle them this way again if I had to do them over, but the fact is that Crown attorneys in the 1990s feel they have very little discretion in cases of sexual abuse. They are made to feel they must prosecute even the most dubious cases. This is an unfortunate state of affairs, as one of the nobler functions of the Crown attorney is to weed out those cases which are bound to fail, and to discourage cases mounted out of pure vindictiveness. However, the pendulum always swings, and I am sure that one day the situation will return to a position somewhere between the two extremes.

A Perspective on Rape

I have never been very successful at rape prosecutions. There were a few trials which resulted in convictions for lesser offenses such as indecent assault and attempted rape, and a number of saw offs (that is the rather inelegant term for a plea bargain in which the Crown accepts a plea of guilty to a less serious offense), but my overall batting average was low.

I don't know why this is so. Women are frequently raped, but I have had a lot of trouble getting juries to buy the proposition. My record on murders and manslaughters and crimes of violence generally was good. Perhaps Kenora juries are just cynical.

It has been said that rape is one of the easiest charges to allege and one of the hardest to prove. The law is hedged about with checks and balances to protect the persecuted male from being unjustly convicted by a vindictive woman, but if a woman makes up her mind to pursue a man through the courts she thereby subjects herself to being put through the hoops. Often she doesn't realize what an ordeal this will be for her.

Many women would never make the complaint if they could foresee the prolonged distress that may result. First a complaint must be made to the police, often to a man who is just as embarrassed to hear the story as the woman is to tell it. Or he may be jocular, or skeptical, or just plain bored. Next there is a very personal physical examination by a doctor, highly distasteful to most women, accompanied by a retelling of the story. Then the woman must face her family, perhaps even a husband who is not supportive, and if the rape happened partly as a result of her own stupidity, facing the family can be as bad as the original ordeal. Then there will probably be further interviews with the police and the Crown. In due course there is a preliminary hearing, usually public, at which the whole story must be told again, and at which a skillful and occasionally unethical lawyer might challenge both her credibility and her virtue. If she has the fortitude to face it, and many don't, there is still a trial and its attendant publicity. The courtroom procedure is particularly hard on young women and on cultural minorities. They find the sordid revelations highly stressful. It is no wonder that many women freak out before the case ever gets to trial. Rapists often go free simply because a woman cannot bear the ordeal and refuses to proceed with it. The Crown has ways to force an unwilling witness to testify, but as a matter of common humanitarianism, it usually doesn't.

Amendments to the Criminal Code which abolished the use of the term rape in favor of the all-embracing charge of sexual assault have done nothing to make it easier to obtain convictions, although the amendments were well intended. The courts have not wholeheartedly accepted changes in the substantive law or the rules of evidence, but have often struck them down as infringements on the right of an accused person to make full answer and defense.

Some of the losers stick in my crop. I may have said elsewhere that I like the jury system, and if I haven't I say it now. Most juries are perceptive and are able to pick up on a good case. I have often gotten convictions on weak cases where a coldly logical and objective judge might have acquitted. Unfortunately, most of those few cases in which the opposite was true seemed to me to be good rape cases.

Let me tell you about some of the women who stood up through the whole process, only to be denied their vindication.

Elizabeth Wildflower was an eighteen-year-old girl who had lived on Rice Bay Reserve all her life. She had the distinction of being the only girl on the reserve over the age of sixteen who had not had a baby. She lived in relative poverty in a standard Indian Affairs house with her mother, an old uncle, and an assortment of children and young teenagers. I say relative poverty, because by the standards of the rest of the country at that time cooking on a wood stove, carrying water by the pail, and using kerosene lamps made for a rather low standard of living. On the other hand, the Wildflower family lived pretty well by the standard of their neighbors because they didn't spend much of their money on scutay wabo, which translates literally to firewater, the scourge of the once proud Indian race. At least they had food to eat, clothing, and oil for the space heater, and this somehow set them apart as being better than their neighbors, to many of whom drinking, fighting, and misery were a way of life. To be "better" than, or "higher" than one's neighbors is offensive on many reserves, and consequently Elizabeth was not a favorite.

One winter night in 1964, young Eddie Keesic appeared at the locked door and demanded entrance. Eddie was a mean and ornery drunk, and he walked around the house yelling at the windows. The people inside became uneasy, and left their beds to gravitate towards the kitchen; no doubt they were driven to band together in mutual protection of one of their member, like a herd of caribou bunching up to ward off a predatory wolf. Eddie eventually smashed a window and crawled into the darkened house, demanding access to Elizabeth. The family retreated into a bedroom and locked the door. Elizabeth was petrified. Eddie, scenting the quarry, yelled, and threatened and kicked at the door.

Now at this stage you may ask, as the jury most certainly asked itself, why didn't the family gang up on the intruder and beat his head in? It was one of the two weak points in the case, but I hoped the jury would be intelligent enough to bridge the cultural gap. Certainly any reasonable WASP or WASC family would have fired Keesic out into the snow without further ado. But not the Wildflower family. They shamefacedly admitted that in fear for their own safety, they opened the door and pushed the unhappy Elizabeth into his arms.

Keesic marched Elizabeth Wildflower out of the house at the sharp point of a broken broomstick, on past several neighbors' homes, down a trail through the dark bush, and to a small shack beyond the houses. Elizabeth forced herself to overcome nausea, and steeled herself to face the act that was to come. She did not call out to the darkened houses, both through fear of the broken broomstick and because she knew there would be no response. At the abandoned shack Eddie threatened to insert the broomstick into her private parts if she resisted. She shut her eyes tightly and did what was required of her. And that was the other weak point in the case. Why didn't she yell and scream, or run to a neighbor's home and ask for help?

Why not indeed? It was a legitimate question, and counsel Len Compton would have been remiss if he hadn't asked it. He led the witness on past the various houses, drawing from her the names of the occupants and what her relationship to them was. He then asked her, in a mildly outraged voice, why she hadn't run to one of these neighbors for help. I had a sinking feeling, as I could see the case flitting out the window.

There was a long pause before Elizabeth answered. I had ample time to wonder why in hell I had ever become a Crown attorney, and to hope that there might be some greater reward in later life.

After an eternity Elizabeth spoke slowly and deliberately in a strong, clear voice. Her answer was eloquent in its simplicity. "You have to understand that Rice Bay is not a community like Kenora, or Dryden, or other places where people will help you. In Rice Bay the people are afraid of each other, and if there is trouble they lock their doors. They will not give a helping hand." There was an audible sigh from the jury, who nodded and smiled in understanding. I had it made after all.

Or so I thought. For some unfathomable reason the jury brought in a verdict of not guilty!

Keesic went back to the reserve a hero, and Elizabeth went back feeling like a tramp. Somehow the system failed Elizabeth Wildflower, and after the fashion of all mankind I don't want the blame for it on my shoulders—it must have been a perverse jury.

Lawyers used to talk to juries to find out just what facets of a case impressed them. Frequently a defense lawyer and myself would split the cost of a jug and invite some jurors in for a few snorts after a trial was over. Sometimes the judge would join us. Invariably we got criticisms which improved our subsequent performance. An amendment to the Criminal Code later prevented this constructive exercise.

After Eddie Keesic's trial (or was it Elizabeth Wildflower's trial?), Len and I quizzed several of the jurors about their verdict. The jury's reasoning surprised me. They believed her story, all right, but they had made up their minds to acquit long before we got to the end of the case. Their reasons were quite discreditable. They boiled down to two. Either they thought they "shouldn't mix in" with what they thought to be an Indian lifestyle, or they figured that any girl whose trashy family wouldn't protect her probably just wasn't worth protecting.

By the time the bottle was empty I wished I hadn't been so generous with the whiskey.

Mary Nogeeshik was another case in point. She was raised on the Pike Lake Reserve, and had a pretty tough time of it in her formative years—no father, no guidance, sporadic schooling, and police troubles. Mary was bright and resilient and managed to survive it without too many scars. By the time she was fifteen the Children's Aid or the correctional authorities or Indian Affairs placed her in a good home in Thunder Bay, and for the first time in her life she knew love and security. She did well in school and began to develop a sense of self-worth.

Life was looking good for Mary Nogeeshik in her sixteenth summer, and her white foster parents encouraged her to take an interest in her Indian heritage. Mary's irresponsible past as a juvenile was well behind her, so they let her go back to the reserve to visit her mother. It seems that Mary behaved herself with proper decorum in spite of the example set for her by some of her relatives. Now maybe she wasn't as sophisticated as a white girl raised in an ordinary way would be, perhaps not as cautious as the ordinary Canadian girl would be, but the point is she wasn't a bad girl and she wasn't looking for trouble or thrills.

I have always thought the law should protect the unsophisticated and careless girls of this country just as much as the women who are in better control of their own destiny. In fact I don't think the women in my life need the same degree of protection that the Mary Nogeeshiks of this world do, because by training they simply avoid situations which are apt to cause them problems.

One might say that Mary Nogeeshik was partly the author of her own misfortunes when she got in the car with Big Bill Norbert, a local tough on the reserve. But then, as I have pointed out, Mary did not have the training and instincts of the average North American girl. To put it bluntly, she was just plain stupid to get in that car, but it didn't mean she was asking to be raped.

Instead of driving Mary to her auntie's place, or wherever it was to be, Big Bill drove her to the proverbial gravel pit. She wanted to jump out, but the car was going too fast. When it finally stopped she hit the ground running, but Big Bill was too fast for her. He threw himself on her and overpowered her in an instant. Mary screamed and struggled but was powerless. She ultimately relaxed and accepted her fate. Big Bill told her that Indian women shouldn't resist their men, and he apparently didn't think she would complain, but complain she did, and with vehemence. No one would have had to know about it if she hadn't raised the hue and cry herself, so the complaint was not for the purpose of protecting her reputation. The police were convinced that the girl was genuinely outraged by what happened. Time has dimmed my memory of details, but one way or another there was ample corroboration of what the girl said.

T.A. O'Flaherty, by now a QC, defended Big Bill Norbert at the first trial. I thought it went off rather well, but the jury couldn't agree, so a new trial was ordered. In due course we went through all the motions again, with my old sparring partner T.A. defending again. Once

151

more, I thought I had put in a pretty good case, but it was not to be. This time the jury returned with an acquittal—Big Bill Norbert returned to the reserve in triumph, and Mary returned to her new life wondering if white man's justice was very effective, and if being a "good girl" was a worthwhile effort. I wondered too, and I have wondered many times since.

Not all bad cases are the result of insensitive or unperceptive juries. Sometimes a female complainant will distort and exaggerate in a misguided attempt to make the case stick, or perhaps to paint an inaccurate picture of herself. For whatever reason, the woman may contrive to tell something less than the truth. Sooner or later she gets tripped up, and when her credibility crumbles, so does the whole case. What the police may know, and what the Crown can prove in court, may be two different things.

Such was the position the Crown found itself in when prosecuting Dick Hill for the rape of Cindy Mechanski near Sioux Lookout, in 1964. Hill was a big, rawboned young man, a stranger to the area, and was by all accounts most attractive to the ladies.

Cindy, on the other hand, was a sixteen-year-old virgin, a high school girl. This was one of the rare cases in which a doctor could positively say that the girl was *virgo intacta* until she suffered the very recent insertion of some object in her private parts. Very unusual in an era in which little girls climb picket fences and ride bicycles just like little boys. However the fact that Cindy was in close possession of all her private physical property until she was dragged off to the bush by Dick Hill was not disputed.

The story is a brief one. Dick inveigled Cindy into his car with the aid of some beer, drove her out to a bush road behind an abandoned mine, dragged her into the underbrush and had her. Twice. Dick drove her back to town and dumped her off in the wee hours. Perhaps the incident would never have come to light if Cindy's mother hadn't decided to sleep on the couch that night, and wakened up and noted Cindy's disheveled condition as she passed by. Cindy burst into tears and wailed about the theft of her virtue and the hunt was on.

At first it looked like a pretty good case. We had violence on a young virgin, and ample corroboration, all of which should have locked the case up tight. The trouble was with Cindy herself.

The peculiar thing about Cindy was that she wanted people to think she was the town tart. I don't suppose I'll ever understand teenaged girls, but in fact Cindy worked at giving that rather ridiculous impression. There wasn't a boy in the local high school who didn't think that Cindy was putting out. She talked rough and tough and dressed like twenty, not sixteen. She knew all the hip expressions of the day.

Somehow I got the case through a preliminary hearing and obtained a committal for trial, although it was plain that the wise old magistrate, Joe Fregeau, wasn't terribly impressed. If he had been a trial judge he probably would not have convicted. Dick Hill languished in durance vile for six months before a High Court Jury and Judge were assembled for the trial. In those days a Grand Jury had to be satisfied that the evidence was such that it warranted putting the accused on trial. This was an added protection to an accused person which no longer exists, and I was likely one of the few people in Canada who was sorry to see the demise of the Grand Jury, because it gave me a dress rehearsal just before trial.

Now, Cindy was an intelligent girl, and she knew that the Grand Jury proceedings were secret and not open to public view. She was at her Mae West best—a slinky dress cut too low at the top and too high at the bottom, jewelry, pancake makeup, and horror of horrors, eye shadow! The Grand Jury consisted mostly of middle-aged men who immediately took a dislike to the girl. In the first five minutes she told about how she "got pissed up on beer" (she had one bottle), and how the rapist "put the brute to me a second time because he didn't get his rocks off good enough the first time." Six minutes after she walked in the door she was shown out by the foreman, and the unanimous decision of the Grand Jury was that they wouldn't give me a true bill if I kept them there a hundred years.

No bill. That meant no trial.

Cindy went back to Sioux Lookout more than ever confirmed as the local pincushion in the eyes of the townspeople. She did it to herself.

Years later I met Cindy again. She was a receptionist in a real estate office in Fort Frances, dressed to kill, and looking for all the world like a streetwalker. Her employer told me later that she was happily married and a model of propriety in her domestic life. "Damnedest thing," said her boss, "she comes on like a big city harlot and brings in more business than I do myself."

High Court trials are supposed to be attended with great solemnity, but once in a while some merriment creeps in. Justice Lerner and a jury were trying three young ne'er-do-wells in the Town of Kenora for

153

raping and committing gross indecencies on a girl. Those were the days when everyone knew what was grossly indecent and what was permissible. John Bowles, QC, of Winnipeg and Toronto, was cross-examining a witness when Justice Lerner said in front of the jury, "Surely, counsel, you aren't suggesting that three men and a woman all linked together on a bed isn't an indecent act?"

John Bowles put on his most offended air and huffed, "Surely, My Lord, such a comment should not be made before the jury, and in any event that is precisely what the jury is going to have to decide, and you shouldn't decide it for them."

Justice Lerner was jolted by this unexpected objection, which was well taken. He sat back in his chair, and John stood swaying at the end of the table, waiting for the ax to fall. We all watched the judge. Evidently he felt that offense was better than defense, for he leaned forward, eyes glinting in mirth, jiggling on the edge of his chair, and waved his finger alternately at John and the jurors. He fairly squealed in self-righteousness. "Of course it was an indecent act. When I charge the jury I am going to tell them it was an indecent act. In fact I'm going to tell them right now. Jurors, that is an indecent act, I tell you. In fact it was grossly indecent! So there, Mr. Bowles."

Justice Lerner thought about the matter overnight and concluded that the Court of Appeal would get him for what he had done, even if God didn't. The next day when John Bowles moved for a mistrial for some piddling reason, he granted the motion, dismissed the jury, and ordered a new trial. I have never been sure that John wasn't put up to making the motion by the judge himself, but John won't admit to it. The next trial, before another judge, resulted in a conviction of the three male miscreants on charges of gross indecency. That was a partial vindication—I had really hoped for a rape conviction.

Not all Crowns have dismal records in sexual assault charges. Many Crowns are as successful at rape as at any other prosecution, and my speculations as to my lack of success have brought no answers. Vern Frolic, for example, was a lighthearted, young Crown attorney who persuaded juries to convict on impossible cases.

I cannot leave the subject of rape without indulging myself in my favorite fantasy of playing psychiatrist.

Everyone understands the ordeal a woman must go through in preparation for and during a trial. Many women choose not to do so, and that is their business. However, after talking to many rape victims who did not go through trials as well as many who did I feel strongly that in most cases women should complain and carry it through. The reason is simple. If they say nothing, then the specter will return to haunt them again and again. Most people who quietly suffer unredressed violence to their dignity do so only at great cost in bitterness, guilt, and confusion. They cannot passively shrug the incident off and forget it. Such unrevenged trauma can eat at the soul of a sensitive person and blotch their ordinary human relationships forever.

On the other hand complaining about it has a therapeutic effect. The woman thereby protests her virtue and causes her tormentor a hell of a lot of trouble and embarrassment. Rapists are not favorites in the prison system, and if the villain gets time, so much the better. Win or lose the matter is laid to rest, and the evil is exorcised. If the woman has done her best to obtain redress she can then pick up the pieces of her life, and start living again. This process can be called closure.

Whores

Whores. Never had much to do with them. I discouraged prosecution and ignored people who refused or were unable by natural disinclination to make a distinction between crime and sin and fun. At least I did until some damn fool invented the concept of political correctness. Nevertheless, my limited contact in the courtroom leads me to observe that madams are not all fading beauties with a heart of gold who are putting their nieces through an education at the Sorbonne, nor do they make chicken soup for visiting policemen, nor do they hand out ten dollar bills to old prospectors who are down on their luck. They are tacky women who wear too much perfume to cover up the body odor. Their families disowned them long ago. They pour whiskey for crooked cops and honest cops too, and their only thought for the poor old prospector is how to get his next pension cheque from him. Even so, something positive that can be said for them all is that they are genuine characters.

Some of the girls who work for the madams are pathetic creatures who were mistreated early in life to the extent that they are warped and have come to believe they are good for not much else. Others seem to be above the more base aspects of the profession and are more agreeable than their twisted sisters.

As for the pimps, they do nothing for the tone of the enterprise, being sleazy, often smelly, and worst of all some of them are just plain uninteresting.

All the same, if men want to have recourse to whores to get their jollies my view is that the law should butt out. After all, the Creator endowed us with the ability to achieve just so many orgasms, and if you don't take 'em you lose 'em. Just fancy waking up on your sixty-fifth birthday and thinking " My God, I'm entitled to 2,500 orgasms and I've only managed 500 with members of the opposite sex and just a thousand that I have achieved by myself—a mere handful, really. I've missed the boat. It's too late to recoup. A wasted life."

Panicksville. Get it where you can, I says.

Anyway, at the risk of contradicting my high road moralizing on prostitutes, I offer the following gems:

My Dad was a bush pilot and flew many people about in the quest to open the North. Over the years it had been his dubious privilege to know Boxcar Annie, Patsy Cameron and many other ladies of the frontier. Back in the late 1940s he flew a court party from Kenora to Pickle Lake to try a lady known as Muskeg Myrtle for keeping a common bawdy house. Old Magistrate Wolfe was not exactly filled with the milk of human kindness, and he relished the job of giving Muskeg Myrtle her comeuppance. He solemnly intoned the charge in his best funereal voice. "You are charged with keeping a common bawdy house. Do you know what that means? Do you understand the charge? How do you plead?" Myrtle drew herself up to her full height and shot back in an injured tone, "Well, perhaps some people would call my establishment by such a name!" with emphasis on "some people." Score one for Muskeg Myrtle.

By and by the trial got started, and a witness was called to the front of the beer parlor to be sworn. Yes, that's right, the trial was taking place in the beer parlor in the local hotel, that being the only place other than the school that would accommodate such a large number of people, and of course it wasn't fitting and proper to hold a whorehouse trial in a school. Fifteen years later, in 1961 or so, I got to know that same beer parlor well, as we did many inquests in there. The wild and woolly days were over, however, and we didn't do trials in the beer parlor anymore.

156

As it happened no one had thought to bring a bible along, and the Gideons had not penetrated as far as the Pickle Lake Hotel. The learned magistrate was mulling over this unexpected lapse when Myrtle piped up and said, "Well if it's a bible you're wanting I have one you can use, and it's probably the only one in town. " The perceptive reader will no doubt have gathered that Pickle Lake in the 1950s was not exactly a great center of religious practice.

Myrtle turned to the spectators and in her best stage voice said, "Fred, will you slide over to the house and fetch the bible from the parlor. You know the one, it's under the magazines at the end of the couch." Fred had more sense than to acknowledge that he knew anything about the place, because as the local taxi driver he wanted to stay on the good side of the police. But as the local taxi driver it was in his best interest to stay on the good side of Muskeg Myrtle, too, so he was off like a shot.

Ten minutes later Fred was back with a huge bible and he triumphantly plopped it down before Magistrate Wolfe, who was not amused. But the spectators were, and they gave Fred a round of applause. Score again for Myrtle!

Ultimate vindication was to belong to Magistrate Wolfe, and he convicted her and fined her $400. Sorry, but that's exactly how my father told the story until the day he died and it's not up to me to doctor the facts.

Being inspired by such stories I eventually decided to go into law myself. When I was under articles to my mentor, Jack Doner, he would send me out of the office to interview people in their homes, people who were in need of legal services but were too frail to come to the office in person. Actually, I think Jack just wanted to get rid of me for the afternoon when there was nothing for me to do around the office, but it usually suited me fine. One of the old-timers I visited was Joe Derry, who had come to Kenora as a babe in his mother's arms in the same freight canoe as his lifelong pal Agar Fitzgerald, well before the turn of the century.

Joe and Agar grew up together and were properly raised by their good Christian parents, which meant they got a switching if their mothers found out they had peeked over the jail wall at one of the rather frequent hangings that were a feature of the times. But if their fathers heard they were running errands for the madams of one of the numerous whorehouses that graced the town in, say, 1890, it was an occasion for a really serious licking, the kind that hurt for a week.

Do I hear a gasp at the mention of whorehouses in pristine pure Kenora, where they still don't have condoms in the high school washroom? Well now, you should know the awful truth. The place was positively crawling with bawdy houses at the time of the building of the railroads, when there were twenty randy men in the area for every honest woman. Apparently the railroads, both Canadian Pacific Railway (CPR) and the Canadian National Railway, tolerated them, and if it was okay by the railroads, it was okay by the two rudimentary but competing police forces that kept order after a fashion when they weren't chucking each other in jail. Truth! They actually did that. There is research on file in the Kenora museum recording the antics of the Keystone Cops and documenting the locations of the many houses of ill repute.

There were two houses catering to the Chinese coolie laborers in nearby Keewatin. Over by the CPR roundhouse on the east side of Kenora was an elegant Edwardian edifice with red plush wall hangings, and a circular driveway with a boy to hold the horses. Upstairs there was even a gentleman's gentleman to see that the clients had their flies buttoned up right. In between these two extremes were at least half a dozen others catering to all tastes and levels of affluence.

But the one I want to tell you about was built atop a large log crib in sixteen feet of water just off what is now the Second Street dock, where the float aircraft now tie up. Goodness knows what was going on in the vicinity at the time. Perhaps sawmills, boat building, freighting to the many mines, and the coming railroad by long boat and primitive steamboats...whatever it was, it involved a lot of lusty men. Oh yes, and women too, several of whom were living in the house on the crib.

There was only one door into the house on the crib, and no dock or landing stage, making it exceedingly hard to take by surprise. Gentleman visitors had to hire a boy with a rowboat or a canoe to scrabble around the door until someone on the inside opened it and let them in, whereupon the boy with the boat would collect a nickel from the madam. If the visitors had anything left over after their trip upstairs the boys might collect another nickel. Sometimes the madam, whom I will call Melba, would give the boys an apple pie. Inevitably the small boy's father would hear about it and whale the daylights out of him, whereupon he would have to turn his ferry business over to some other small boy whose father was not wise to him.

However, getting back to Madame Melba, who ran the establishment on the crib, Joe Derry told me she stayed sober most of the time, and insisted that her young ladies be models of decorum who must not swear too much and who were forbidden to fight when drinking. One day the mistress of the establishment, she of the nickels and apple pies, developed a powerful thirst, one which could only be slaked by a trip to the mainland. She left her number one girl in charge of the house with instructions to be kind to policemen, and hailed the nearest wharf rat for a ride to town, which took no more than five minutes.

There is a break in the yarn here. In truth I do not know what troubles assailed Madame Melba in town, but whatever it was it must have involved a lot of cheap booze and a fight and a night in the digger. Not the jail at which the boys watched the hangings, but the one that belonged to the other police force, downtown. At any rate that is where Melba woke up on Sunday morning, a dry day even in Kenora. The turnkey wouldn't give her a sip of his whiskey, her head ached, her blouse was torn by some lowlife who didn't know a lady when he saw one, her corset was pinching, and her money was gone. One can imagine that Melba felt mighty low.

Every cloud has a silver lining, and help was at hand in the form of our two young Tom Sawyers, Joe and Agar, who were spotted by Melba strolling along looking for mischief on a fine summer Sunday morning. They found it all right.

Melba whistled through her steel mesh window, thus luring the boys into whispering range. She induced one of the boys to row out to the shack on the crib and wake up her head girl. He was to ask for a bottle of rum and a fresh blouse. The other lad occupied himself by whittling a groove down the middle of a long, thin cedar stick which could be poked through a wide spot in the screen mesh, and down which an enterprising boy could dribble rum into a thirsty gullet on the other side. Madame Melba didn't have any money with which to pay the lads, but being sportin' gentlemen of the full age of ten years they were drawn into the play by the promise of blueberry pies to come.

The turnkey, or someone, reported the episode to the boys' fathers, who promptly tanned their hides and put an end to a budding economic consortium.

And that's exactly the way Joe Derry told it to me in his upstairs bedroom in the winter of 1957, and Agar Fitzgerald's relatives reluctantly confirmed it.

You would think that in thirty-five years of going to court in what was comparatively recently frontier country I would have encountered many of the dubious ladies of which I now write, but such was not the case. Most of what I know is hearsay.

The only whorehouse episode in which I came close to making a cameo appearance was actually pretty tame. It happened in 1959, shortly after I was called to the bar. I went right into private practice in Kenora, and kept in close touch with Jim Barclay, a pal who was just starting out in Thunder Bay. He in turn was a friend of Wally Dubinsky, a young lawyer who was a year ahead of us, and who, like Jim and I, aspired to do criminal law.

Enter the lady who kept the legal establishment of Thunder Bay agog for several weeks. Her name was Martha Adams.

Madame Martha ran the poshest house of ill fame in all Thunder Bay, and there were a lot of them at the time. The bush camps were full of single men who had to be serviced like so many rampant bulls, and the harbor was full of ships and sailors all of whom believed that a visit to Martha's was the equivalent of dying and going to Nirvana, or a sailor's notion of Valhalla, or at least it was fashionable to talk as if they thought so.

There had been occasions when Martha's friends on the police force had not been quick enough to warn her of an impending raid. These were dark moments in Martha's life, almost enough to destroy her faith in human nature, and over time she paid a number of fines. She didn't mind paying the money, for she looked upon it as a license fee but she knew that license fees would not go on forever, and sooner or later she would have to go to jail. She knew it because the Fort William magistrate had told her so. Magistrate Davies was afflicted with a certain moral fervor, a dreadful liability in a member of the bench, no doubt urged on by Vic Ibbetson, QC, the Crown attorney, who was a bit of a blue-stocking himself. A few weeks before the episode of which I write His Worship had fined Martha $400 for keeping a common bawdy house, and publicly stated that the next time he saw her in his courtroom he was going to lock her up and melt the key. For some reason Martha dreaded jail.

Like a good madam, whose customers always come first, Martha kept a little black book with the names of her clientele, and beside each

160

name was a notation about what it was they expected from the girls upstairs. In the book, of course, were the names of many prominent Lakehead citizens, not merely the names of the Mustache Louis and the jack-tars. Municipal politicians, business people, and the cream of Lakehead society were all there. Included in the little black book, which was kept behind that proverbial loose brick in the chimney, were the names of some prominent Conservatives, and, I blush to say it, Liberals. Be reminded that the Conservatives formed the provincial government at the time.

Of course, Martha was picked off again. She wasn't in the place at the time, but her number one girl was running it in her absence. Someone squealed about the little black book, and the police took that, too. When Martha appeared before the court she was ordered to post bail or be locked up pending trial. As I have mentioned Martha was petrified of jail, so she posted bail, which, if I recall, was in a fairly high amount.

In that antediluvian time, high bail was a signal to an accused to hotfoot it out of the country. Bail would be forfeited, the province would be spared the expense of a trial, and the accused could wait till the heat was off, then sneak quietly back to town and resume his or her normal occupation until the next time. Occasionally the procedure would be varied by having a lawyer appear at court and plead the accused guilty in absentia.

The accused would then have the offense on his record, and the Crown attorney would not have to be troubled making an application to forfeit the bail money as it would all be taken as fine.

This procedure was all very neat, in theory, but it didn't work out in practice. Magistrate Davies did the unthinkable and issued a warrant for Martha, who by this time was comfortably ensconced in Montreal. For some reason the policeman and the matron didn't take the train, but drove to Montreal to pick her up. This gave Martha plenty of time to visit a big city lawyer and cook up a defense, and she took full advantage of it. In order to stall off the day of reckoning, and incidentally, to give Wally Dubinsky back in Thunder Bay ample time to work out the details of her defense, Martha paid the expenses for the trip back with the police officers. They trusted Martha, and drove back through the States, eating and drinking very well along the way.

In the meantime the big city lawyer told Wally what to do. He was to go to the Crown attorney and tell him that he was prepared to call as witnesses all the respectable people, particularly those who were affiliated with the Conservative party, whose names appeared in the dreadful little black book. He was to tell the Crown attorney with a straight face that these good people were expected to say something like, "What, a bawdy house? Goodness me, I don't remember seeing anything like that going on in there. No, all I did was sit and discuss literature and the arts with a cultured young lady. Drink? Nothing but a cup of tea, with lemon, I believe. No, I don't know why anyone would put my name in a little black book. I have no idea why anyone would write 'round the world' after my name." But Wally couldn't keep a straight face, and Crown attorney Vic Ibbetson wouldn't have any part of it, and Wally was told to take a hike.

Wally went to Jim Barclay and asked him to try to make some mileage with the Crown, but he wisely forbore. Jim called me in Kenora, and I drove to meet him in Ignace, where he filled me in on what had been happening. Jim and Wally wanted me to take the defense, as they knew that any lawyer who would bring such a defense would never be able to practice in the courts of Thunder Bay again. I, of course, would have nothing to do with it, and a good decision it was, because twenty-five years later I became the Crown attorney for Thunder Bay.

Fortunately Magistrate Davies had a change of heart (what motivated this will be forever unknown) and he came to the assistance of the defense by letting it be known that if Martha pleaded guilty he would take $400 from her and not put her in jail, but she would have to leave town permanently. She did and he did and she did. Many a citizen mourned her passing.

One could hear of her at election time well into the 1980s. She ran in a Montreal riding for election to parliament on several occasions, her platform being the legalization of prostitution. I don't imagine Martha got many Conservative votes.

I suppose I should really cut this chapter short before someone accuses me of being preoccupied with round-heeled ladies, but first I have to tell you about Anastasia Treblink.

This lady variously ran a poolroom, a taxi business, a not-too-respectable boarding house, and it was rumored that for a fee she would dispense intimate personal favors. I had prosecuted her for bootlegging on several occasions, but oddly enough she had a sort of resentful respect for me.

One day Anastasia appeared on the docket of the provincial court in one of the outlying towns of the district, charged with impaired

162

driving. This is before being convicted of impaired driving carried any stigma; in fact it was almost fashionable. I was therefore surprised when she entered a plea of not guilty, and even more surprised when she asked my help in retaining a lawyer, not a local lawyer. When I pointed out that we had her cold turkey she would only say, "I got to try, I got to try."

When trial day rolled around, Cliff Brock, QC, appeared for Anastasia. He was an old war horse from Winnipeg and was not on good terms with Magistrate Cox, who was presiding. Magistrate Cox usually found against Manitoba lawyers. As it happened, the trial was to be held in a brand new courtroom, and all the lawyers present had to make little speeches before the trials got under way. A lot of monotonous oratory took place before Cliff finally rose to his feet.

Perhaps Cliff knew he was going to lose his case on the merits and just didn't care about the effect of what he said. He looked Magistrate Cox in the eye. "Your Worship, I will be brief. I anticipate that in this beautiful new courtroom you will dispense with justice just the way you did in the old one." And he sat down. There was a chorus of suppressed snorts and giggles, but no one dared to applaud.

It was all tough sledding from there. A young constable gave impeccable evidence which resulted in a conviction. Magistrate Cox sentenced Anastasia to a fine of $100 plus seven dollars costs, or fifteen days in jail. He gave her a month to pay.

Anastasia was crushed. She had bags of money, but refused to pay her fine.

One day after the time to pay had elapsed I met Anastasia on a street corner in Kenora. "Did you pay your fine yet?" I asked in all innocence.

"No, I not payink it nohow!" she wailed.

"What's the matter?" I asked. "What's the big deal about this fine? You've always paid your fines with a smile, like it was a patriotic duty. You can pay it right at the OPP office back home."

"That is the trobble. It's that Goddamned corporal at the poliss office. I don't vant to see him. He's been screwink me for fourteen years, and now he's let his polissman put a charge on me, and I do not wish to pay him."

It was soon after this that the practice of taking fines at the police office was changed, and people were required to pay at a court office.

Collecting the Evidence

Sometimes dreadful things happen, or funny things, and they are so embarrassing that you really don't want to take them to court. The wise Crown attorney will find a way to wriggle out without infuriating the victim. Unhappy victims have a way of writing to the Attorney General....

Such was the case of four hormone-driven young lads from the reserve at...whoops, I almost said it, but that would never do as will be seen as the story develops! My purpose in writing is to entertain and instruct, and not to trash peoples' lives.

The four boys were all inflamed by passions that inflict teenagers everywhere, and after the custom of boys the world over they were not too particular about how they satisfied themselves.

Enter the victim in the case. We'll call her Susie. Susie, at the age of thirteen, was not as innocent as she may have appeared to be, and somehow she fell in with the four young studs, and the inevitable happened. With all four boys. Susie told her boyfriend about it later in the evening. Fool that he was, he imagined that his property had been trespassed upon, and he either complained, or made Susie complain, to Peter, as I will call him, a First Nations constable.

Now you must understand two things. The first is that First Nations constables deal well with the nuisance crimes we hear about so frequently in northern villages, but they seldom, if ever, have to do serious investigations, and their latent skills as detectives are rarely developed. Secondly, the law says you must not mess around with young girls. However, in Canada, the law also says it is a defense, in cases where there is no suggestion of force, if the boy is not more than two years older than the girl. Questions like this always take time to sort out, and to the constable his present duty was clear. He must commence an investigation into the facts.

The first thing Peter did was to take the girl over to the nursing station for an examination. I will digress and say that all across northern

Canada a truly fine network of health services prevails. The federal government has well trained and well motivated nurses assigned to strategic villages, and they are given a much higher degree of responsibility than nurses are expected to have in the populated areas. In Northwestern Ontario the nursing stations are anchored to the Zone Hospital in Sioux Lookout, and they can be in immediate communication by phone or radio, if advice and instructions are needed. In this case one of the nurses began an intimate examination of Susie for the purpose of gathering evidence of the dastardly crime of which the poor girl was the victim, a procedure that elsewhere would have been carried out by a doctor.

The next thing the constable did was to go out and collar the four boys. This really presented no problem, as the boys didn't realize they had done anything wrong, and when the officer told them to meet him back at the police shack they simply wandered over to see what the problem was.

As it happened, Don Hewitt, a coach officer from the Northwest Patrol of the OPP, was staying in the living quarters at the back of the office, together with Rupert Ross, the assistant Crown attorney from Kenora. They went to bed early, and knew nothing of the problems the First Nations constable was having until he walked into the bunk room and woke them up to tell them about it. Don forced himself awake and groaned, thinking he had to give some guidance. "You know what to do Peter, take samples. Take lots of samples from all of them."

Rupert later said he had a sort of an uneasy feeling that perhaps the two officers had not communicated very well.

Along towards dawn a commotion in the cell block pulled Don and Rupert out of their sleep. Don put on slippers and shuffled to the outer office to check the situation out.

To his horror, surprise, chagrin, and whatever, he saw the four boys sitting side by side on the plywood sleeping platform in the cell, all naked as jaybirds, and all pulling their wires with grim determination. Each one had a sterile jar in his other hand. A centerfold of Flush magazine was pinned to the wall to aid them in their endeavors. Constable Peter, in line with his duty, was collecting samples. Of everything.

"Jesus, Peter, I ain't got any left," said one.

"My pajagwin's gonna break off," said another.

"Fill the jars, you assholes," said Peter.

When the smoke cleared it was found that Susie had dallied with

165

another boy that night and was on her way to look for her boyfriend when she hit the jackpot with the four studs. Consent was not even an issue. The four boys were all within two years of Susie's age, give or take a year or so, and Susie didn't want to testify anyway.

Case closed.

The Transvestite

I got a peek into Leon Conlon's strange mind when I was on a visiting assignment in a little town over in the northeast part of the province. I won't name the town, for that in itself would be an identification of Leon Conlon, and would result in acute embarrassment to his family, still resident in the community twenty-five years later. As often happens when a local official is out of town, there was a sudden flurry of activity and in the absence of the local Crown attorney, I found myself drawn into a coroner's investigation that lasted more than a year.

Conlon was the welfare administrator for a large but sparsely populated municipality that included several villages. He knew every unfortunate person and lame duck for miles around, but never exhibited cynicism about his charges. Though not highly educated, he was widely respected and served on several public boards around the area.

The details of Conlon's private life were not nearly as well known as his public life. His wife was an attractive young woman who was very much church oriented, and they had three lovely children. Mrs. Conlon was a nurse employed full time.

It was well known that Leon was not allowed to have much fun, as in Mrs. Conlon's eyes, fun somehow equated with sin. For example, he was never seen to take a drink in his own community, but he enjoyed a beer or two with friends when he was overnighting elsewhere. He tended to make his friends among policemen and businessmen rather than in his church.

The picture that was painted for me was of a youngish man who was somewhat repressed by a highly developed sense of duty in several areas of his life. He liked to laugh and drink in appropriate company, but in moderation. Always in moderation.

The day Leon Conlon died was not a routine day. Early in the morning Mrs. Conlon caught the bus to Sudbury, for a medical appointment. Leon got the children off to school, and was to get lunch and dinner for them, and to meet Mrs. Conlon when she returned on the evening bus.

Leon sent the children off to school, then went to work himself. He didn't stay there long, but left his very competent secretary in charge of the office. He returned home and entered the secret world that only he knew about.

From its hiding place under the eaves he retrieved a box full of women's clothing and his precious manuscript.

Leon removed his own clothing and laid it neatly on the bed. Item by item he put on the ladies' outfit from the secret box, and admired himself in the mirror. First the sanitary pad and belt to compress his genitals, then the frilly half-panties with no crotch. Over that, the garter belt to hold up the black mesh stockings. He looked again in the mirror. Sexy!

The brassiere presented a problem. He was lean and firm and had no excess flesh on his chest. He solved it by stuffing Kleenex artfully down into the cups. Under a patterned blouse, it looked quite realistic. Erotic, he thought.

And so went the dressing. Pausing at intervals he would pirouette in front of the mirror. He took particular pains to get the makeup just right. The lipstick...just so. A little powder on the freshly shaven face. A wig. A real honest-to-goodness woman looked back at him from the mirror. Her name was Leona Conlon.

Leona gathered her scrap book with the pictures and clippings from porno mags showing straps on the bare bum, spankings, and the like, and went down to the kitchen table. She took along her cherished and very private manuscript to read over again.

Leona poured herself a mug of coffee, admiring the lipstick marks she left around the rim. She idly traced the pattern of her hand on a piece of paper and painted the finger nails with the red polish she intended to use on her own fingers. She would have to hurry, as the children would be coming for lunch.

The manuscript claimed her attention. She had worked on it for years, and hoped to publish it some day. It was about a man who was bored with his job and dissatisfied with the way his life was going, and he sought illicit thrills. For his annual vacation, he went to a certain hotel in Montreal which catered to people of his persuasion. They gave him an injection in the throat to raise his voice, and hormones to make his breasts grow. For three weeks, the man in the book became a woman, enjoying spanks on the bum and other pseudo-sexual pleasures. Everywhere the words "spank" or "strap" or "beat" appeared, they were written in red.

Leona didn't finish reading her manuscript. She looked at the clock and realized there wasn't much time left. There was still something she had to do. She flew to the doors, locking them from the inside. Then she ran down to the basement.

The children were perplexed to find the doors locked. They were never locked when the family was home, and they knew their dad was home because his car was in the drive. They walked around the house peering into the windows, and were horrified to see the body of a strange woman hanging by the neck from a rope tied to a basement beam, eyes bulging and tongue lolling, swinging back and forth, back and forth...

Five

Unfinished Business

Neither the police nor the Crown attorney like to leave loose ends dangling, in the form of cases unsolved or files not closed. It is human nature to want to finish something off, or lay a mystery to rest. I put far more effort into the two cases next described than I did on many cases on which the files were eventually closed. However, we still don't know who the principal players were. In the case of the girl found in the coal bin there never was an accused person, and we were unable to identify her. In the Mad Bomber's case, he was blown up and scattered beyond recognition.

Both stories are engrossing, and in both there is still a possibility that someone will come forward with information that will help the Crown close its files.

For the purposes of this book I have continued to use the phrase "Maggoty Maisie," instead of the more proper "Unknown Female." If any young Crown were to do so today, I would skin him alive for being insensitive, not that I pretend to be a living monument to the notion or the practise of sensitivity, but a generation ago such monikers were more common. A small injection of levity once in a while does more to make an unhappy situation bearable than does strict adherence to formality. It is a sort of a psychological mechanism to offset the effects of the gloomy fact situations we encounter.

Bomber, Mad

Who knows this man?

He was short in stature, middle aged, had brown hair and a red beard. He was undoubtedly a psychopath.

He is dead now, blown to bits by a bomb he made himself. His name is unknown. What little is known about him was largely reconstructed after his death. He is officially known under the file name of "Bomber, Mad" in the office of the Crown attorney in Kenora, for there is no question in the minds of the authorities that he had a serious mental disorder.

To the people of Kenora, a tourist town of 11,000 in northwest

Ontario, his story began and ended in seventy-eight dramatic, tension filled minutes on a spring afternoon.

The day was Thursday, May 10, 1973. It was sunny and warm, with a gentle breeze blowing off Lake of the Woods. In the business section of town, Trans-Canada Highway 17 became Kenora's main street for a distance of three blocks with stores, offices, restaurants, and banks. As on any day the streets were busy with automobile and pedestrian traffic. Along with local residents there was an early influx of American tourists and campers from Winnipeg, the nearest city to the west.

The business of law enforcement in the town was carried out by a municipal police force under Chief Webb Engstrom, and on any average day consisted of traffic patrols, the pick up of drunks, investigating car and boat thefts, break-ins, attending court, and office duties. On this day the routine was to be shattered by a telephone call. At 2:55 P.M., Chief Engstrom answered the phone and in disbelief heard the voice of Al Reid, the manager of the Canadian Imperial Bank of Commerce. Reid announced that there was a man with a bomb in his office holding up the bank. Simultaneously the bank alarm rang in the police station and the chief realized that Reid was in earnest.

At the Scene

As 3:00 P.M. closing time drew near the Bank of Commerce was still busy with a few customers. Al Reid was at the desk in his private office talking on the telephone when he noticed a man had entered and was sitting facing him. He was dressed in bush clothing and wore a checkered hat. Around his neck hung a satchel, and on his back he wore a packsack. Reid's first impression was that he might be a hitchhiker who wanted to call home for money. Reid finished his telephone conversation, left the office to talk to someone in the main lobby of the bank, then returned to his desk, sat down, and asked the stranger what he wanted.

Indicating the satchel slung around his neck, the man said he had a bomb.

"Phone the police," he ordered. "Tell them I am here and I want the money from the bank." At the same time he pulled a .32 automatic from his pocket.

Reid says, "He didn't actually threaten me with it, but I got the distinct impression he wanted me to know he meant business." Reid was stunned, but he remained calm.

171

As Reid was putting the call through to the police and tripping the alarm switch under the desk, the stranger produced a device resembling a large clothespin, connected to wires leading from the satchel.

"Do you know what a deadman switch is?" he asked Reid, explaining that it was connected to a bomb in the satchel, and if the ends of the clothespin were allowed to make contact it would detonate the bomb.

The potential bomber then proceeded to don gloves and a black balaclava which completely covered his head except for his eyes and an opening for his mouth, and put his hat back on. "Clear the bank," he said. "Everybody out," and inserted the deadman switch between his teeth.

Reid and the robber now entered the main lobby where some customers were still transacting business. Corporal John Lechkun entered, along with Inspector Walter Mychalyshyn and Constable Bill Grynol. They were told to stay inside while the robber and the bank manager proceeded to clear the bank of all persons. A few minutes later a citizen strayed in from the street and the robber fired a shot at the floor near his feet. Al Reid says laconically, "That moved him; he got the message and left."

On the floor near the office door the robber had left a large kit bag, and he now went over to it and pulled out a Parker Hale 30-06 rifle with a shortened forestock, and another smaller bag. With the aid of his rifle he pried open the tellers' drawers, emptying the cash into the kit bag. As he levered at one drawer, the rifle discharged accidentally. Having emptied the tellers' drawers he now turned his attention to the main vault. "I want the cash out of the main vault, or I'll blow the place up!" he said. Reid told him he did not have the full combination but would have to phone for his accountant, and was directed to do so.

While waiting for the accountant to call back the stranger ransacked the manager's desk and found a loaded .38 revolver which he examined and fumbled with in an effort to unload it. Reid calmly showed him how to open it and dumped the shells out on the desk. The robber stashed gun and shells in his pack.

The awaited phone call came and Mr. Reid was given the combination. He opened the vault and the robber proceeded to stuff his bag with bills. He must have underestimated the bulk of his haul, for when his packs were filled, he asked Reid to help him find some plastic bags for the remainder of the loot. After a brief search this idea was abandoned.

At some stage the robber demanded Corporal Lechkun's gun. The corporal told him to go to hell and walked out on the street. The robber made no effort to stop him.

The robber now ordered Reid to phone the police station again and to have them send over a policeman with a pickup truck. Reid complied.

Reid had received several telephone calls, and now the telephone rang again. It was an Oakville, Ontario radio station asking for details of the robbery. Reid told the robber who was calling and asked if he would like to speak to them. The robber thought for a minute and declined. The telephone conversation continued for a few minutes until the robber nodded to Reid to cut it off.

The robber remained visibly calm and unperturbed during the whole episode. His voice was quiet and controlled. Reid made a deliberate effort at small talk.

"Why did you pick Kenora for a job like this?" he asked.

"I wanted to give them something to talk about," was the unhurried reply.

At one point the stranger volunteered to Reid, "I don't like the smell of dynamite. Do you know anything about it?" Reid said that he did not.

When the subject of drinking came up, the robber commented, "I can't afford to drink on a job like this." The bank manager was convinced that the man was deadly serious and that there was every reason to believe the bomb was real.

Over an hour had passed since the stranger entered the bank. He held the deadman switch in his teeth except when talking to Reid, when he would hold the ends apart with his gloved fingers. He was showing his first signs of nervousness, or impatience. Reid struggled to remain calm, to do nothing that would alarm the human bomb.

At the Police Station and on the Street

Immediately upon receiving the call from Reid, Chief Webb Engstrom put his organization into high gear. He dispatched men to the scene, had off duty men called in, and telephoned the local detachments of the OPP and the RCMP for assistance. Officers were sent to keep people off the streets, to guard the rear of the bank and to keep a lookout from rooftops across the street from the bank. People were warned to keep clear of plate glass windows.

Walter Mychalyshyn, soon to be deputy chief, boarded a helicopter in order to get a bird's eye view of the scene and to follow any possible getaway vehicle.

Very little concrete planning could be done as no one knew what to expect; all that was known was that there was a man in the bank who was armed, and claimed to have a bomb. He was obviously not in a hurry and did not conform to anyone's conception of how a bank robber should behave. The police did not know whether the bomb was real or a fake, and they wisely decided to act on the premise that it was real.

On the street the word spread quickly. People who found themselves in the downtown area were warned by the police to stay away. Some beat a hasty retreat and listened to the progress of events over their radios, but many others were attracted to the scene. Soon a crowd of several hundred people formed, making it imperative for the police to exert efforts to keep the area clear in the vicinity of the bank. Across the street and down several doors the announcers of radio station CJRL had a grandstand view and were reporting events as they developed. In spite of their broadcast warnings the curious, the foolhardy, and the bloodthirsty were continuing to make their way to the downtown area. Complaints were heard from a number of young thrill seekers that the police were violating their civil rights by interfering with their right to move about at will.

Across the street in Johnson's Pharmacy the employees and customers moved nervously towards the rear of the store away from the windows. Some of the adjacent storekeepers locked their doors. In Findlay and Hook's law offices above Johnson's pharmacy, all work stopped as lawyers, students, and staff took hurried peeks out the window. Someone thoughtfully closed the venetian blinds to guard against the possibility of flying glass. An OPP sniper made a brief appearance and one of the law students followed him up to the third floor to a better vantage point.

Police with rifles and shotguns stationed themselves on rooftops and at both ends of the block. They kept their guns ready, snapping at kibbitzers. A loudspeaker periodically barked out orders to keep back. All eyes were on the front of the bank.

The Chief was having trouble keeping in touch with his scattered forces and took a tour to the danger area. Faced with the threat of the bomb and the difficulty of communicating with over thirty men there was little planning he could do. Satisfied for the moment that every precaution had been taken, he stationed himself in Newman's Jewelry

Store across the street where he could keep his eye on the situation and be available to the phone.

Sergeant Bob Letain took up position at the north end of the block, at the intersection. He had an open sight .308 rifle that someone had brought him from the station, but he would vastly have preferred his own .308 with the telescopic sight. A staff writer and photographer from *The Toronto Star*, Don Dutton, moved up beside him with his camera. Letain, thinking him another idle spectator, told him to move on, however Dutton convinced him he was aware of the risk and was prepared to take it, so he stayed.

At the other end of the block, local photographer Bob Ponton took up a position by the police. He was armed with a movie camera. The event therefore had excellent photographic coverage.

Constable Don Milliard was due to report on duty for the 4:00 P.M. shift. Hearing that trouble was afoot, he walked in early, just as Chief Engstrom at Newman's Jewelry had received the request for a pickup truck and driver and phoned the station. Milliard was the man on the spot.

"Don, someone has to take a truck and drive that bastard out of town."

In retrospect neither the Chief nor Milliard could say whether it was an order or a request for a volunteer, but Milliard knew what he had to do. He raced home, changed into plainclothes, and was back in fifteen minutes. In the meantime a municipal employee found his truck commandeered for Milliard's use.

Milliard drove the commandeered half ton to the bank, double-parked and walked in at about 4:05 P.M. As specified by the robber, he was unarmed. The robber asked him if he knew what dynamite looked like, and he looked inside the satchel and saw six round objects with wires from the deadman switch disappearing into them. At the same time the robber twisted what sounded like a windup ratchet on his belt. Milliard was certain it was a real bomb, not a bluff.

Reid had an open line to the police station, but he abandoned it as the robber and his hostage moved out of the bank. At a signal from Milliard, Reid slipped over to the far end of the lobby, away from the large plateglass doors and windows.

Bloody Hell, the Bomb's Gone Off

A few minutes later Milliard and the robber came out into the open,

Milliard carrying the duffel bag, the robber a step behind, awkwardly carrying a bag, a backpack, and the dynamite satchel. One hand was up by his shoulder, the automatic dangling cumbersomely from his fingers. The deadman protruded from his mouth like an open duck's bill. At a distance his black mask would make him appear to be a black man. Milliard could see perhaps a dozen of his colleagues with their guns trained in the direction of the robber. As they stepped out onto the sidewalk the helicopter carrying Inspector Mycalyshyn flew overhead, and the two men wheeled and went back into the bank. As it turned out, the robber had forgotten his rifle leaning against a counter inside.

A few seconds later they emerged again, Milliard in the lead, the robber a few paces behind, the rifle now added to his clumsy load. As Milliard stepped forward, part of the truck box screened him from the robber for an instant.

As the moment of truth drew closer, Sergeant Letain's hands began to sweat. Like the other officers with their guns trained and ready he had no positive instructions as to what to do. Contingencies of this nature are not planned for by the Kenoras of this world. Circumstances dictated that the men must use their own discretion. Unlike many of them, Letain was a skilled hunter and bushman. He was used to acting decisively, almost by instinct, and was a superb marksman. He had an excellent view of the truck parked 150 feet away.

Later he told it this way.

"As Milliard came around the corner of the truck he looked at me. I felt I was damned if I did and damned if I didn't. With my own rifle I would have tried for the deadman switch in an attempt to blow it apart before the points could make contact. As it was I saw my moment and aimed for the heart."

The time was 4:13 P.M., an hour and eighteen minutes after Al Reid had first looked up to see the stranger in his office.

Here is how radio announcers Chris Paulson and John Berry told it in words which were rebroadcast hundreds of times by radio and television across the English speaking world:

"The man is coming out. He has got a black stocking on his head. He is carrying a clothes-peg in his mouth. He is moving back to the bank now. He has dropped three duffel bags...three duffel bags apparently filled with money. Ah...he has moved back in with his...ah...with the man, and we are waiting now to see what happens. The helicopter did a flypast as the man just walked out. Whether he was frightened off or not, he moved back in.... Now they're coming out again. He is a colored man...it's a clothes-peg in his mouth. He is carrying a flight bag, a..." (A shot is heard in the background followed by a louder explosion.)

Chris Paulson: "Bloody hell, the bomb's gone off!"

John Berry: "The bomb has gone off, the bomb has gone off. He has been shot...it's gone...." (Words obscured by background noise.)

Chris Paulson: "Everything is just rancid. Stay back. A bomb has gone off!"

Loudspeaker in background: "Everybody stay back...."

John Berry: "Ladies and Gentlemen...."

Loudspeaker: "It's gone off!"

John Berry and Chris Paulson together: "The bomb has gone off! Ladies and Gentlemen...get off the street...a policeman has been shot...a man...men are running...two cars are completely heavily damaged. The entire front of the Canadian Imperial Bank of Commerce has just exploded. A helicopter is flying over top now...(obscured by background noise)...people right off the street. Windows have been blown out literally all over the place. There is debris...(obscured)...the policeman who was with, the policeman who was with the man, appears to be not that badly injured. At least he is able to stand up. He has stomach wounds. He has been driven to, he is being helped to the police car. This is the policeman. Now the bank robber is lying, we would well and truly suppose that he is dead...."

Loudspeaker: "Clear the roadway up there...further up Main Street...."

Richard Cummine, an observer in the law office across the street, put it this way: "We could see plainly into the front windows of the bank. Al Reid and the bomber were talking and Al kept putting matches to his pipe as if it were business as usual. Eventually Milliard walked in, and after a few minutes came out again with the bomber. They ducked back in, and almost immediately came out, Milliard in the lead. Milliard nodded towards Letain. There was a shot, followed by a terrific bang, and clouds of smoke. The building shook, and several of our windows were broken. As the smoke lifted there was a terrific scramble on the street."

The Aftermath

Don Dutton, from his position beside Sergeant Letain, took a series of excellent photos showing Milliard and the robber coming out of the bank; a few seconds later a huge cloud of smoke hanging over the debris strewn scene; Milliard on his knees in the street, the raw flesh of his hip and thigh showing through his shredded trousers. Other photos showed a street littered with money and broken glass, the frantic activity of officers clearing the scene, bystanders helping the police gather up money, and everywhere broken windows.

Bob Ponton's movie camera, from the other end of the block, had recorded the total scene as it unfolded. His films were rushed to Winnipeg and a scant few hours later were shown in TV news broadcasts in North America and Europe.

Don Milliard was immediately rushed to the hospital, along with a colleague, Constable Don Munro, who suffered ear damage from the blast. Nine persons on the street were treated for minor cuts, and one for shrapnel. Milliard was in the hospital for ten days and returned to his duties on a sporadic basis several weeks after his ordeal. He received commendations from several sources over his part in the event. Later he transferred to the Kenora Fire Department, where the hazards are at least of a definite nature.

Al Reid never did reveal the exact amount of money taken, but it ran into many tens of thousands of dollars. Only an insignificant amount, less than one percent, was not recovered. It will probably never be known what was stolen by bystanders and what was totally demolished in the blast. Rumors circulating around the town to the effect that large sums of money were grabbed up by greedy people at the scene proved grossly exaggerated.

Opinions varied widely as people assessed the situation in retrospect, and some strong feelings were vociferously expressed condemning the police forces and in particular Sergeant Letain's actions. However, the vast bulk of public comment was favorable, even laudatory. Milliard himself credited Letain with saving his life.

At an inquest several weeks later, a coroner's jury commended the local police force, the OPP, the RCMP, and in particular, Constable

Milliard and Sergeant Letain. In its recommendations they urged the police to continue their efforts to determine the identity of the bomber.

Gathering the Evidence

The difficult task of seeking information fell largely to Inspector Mychalyshyn, who was the chief's deputy and also the man in charge of the Kenora Police Criminal Investigation Branch. As a highly experienced investigator he knew that only painstakingly detailed effort would bring results. His efforts were totally professional and perhaps outside the full appreciation of the layman.

The bomber and his clothing were spread over a radius of 500 feet, yet the information Inspector Mychalyshyn was able to accumulate was remarkable in quantity and detail. The clothing was purchased in many different places in both the United States and Canada.

One arm and hand was found in Johnson's Pharmacy directly across the street, having been blown through the front window and by a macabre coincidence into a manicure showcase. Fingerprints were taken and revealed no criminal record with the RCMP, the FBI, nor service in military forces.

The bomber was of short to medium height, according to witnesses and as indicated by his shinbones. He may have been overly conscious of his short stature, as the insoles in his boots were built up to three thicknesses at the heels, or he may have had foot trouble. Some witnesses said that his posture was peculiar; others said it was normal. Several pairs of neatly rolled socks left behind in his hotel room were worn through in round holes at the heels.

The hair of Bomber, Mad was brownish; his beard was reddish. He habitually wore dark glasses, either as a means of disguise or because of eye trouble, and he had been observed at all previous times wearing a sporty checkered fedora hat.

On the day before the robbery, he had been in the Kenora Sport Shop and purchased a hunting knife. Clerk Dot Dunford had passed a pleasantry, "Nice day, isn't it?" to which the man had replied, "No, this isn't a nice day" and had walked out. Dot and many other witnesses remembered numerous seemingly insignificant encounters with the man who turned out to be the bomber, and told about them at the inquest.

Mychalyshyn's attention turned to the bomber's effects, including his clothing, the gear in his duffel, and numerous articles left in his hotel

179

room. He gathered these and catalogued them carefully, laying them out on the floor of the police garage.

The robber had been registered in the Kenricia Hotel on Main Street under the false name of Paul Higgins, of 435 Glen Drive, Toronto, a nonexistent address. He had stayed for two days, checked out for ten days, then returned for five days before the robbery. During the days when he was in town he was seen by a number of people, always alone, always wearing a hat and dark glasses. During the period he was away he left a large yellow steamer trunk in the hotel storage room. This type of trunk was sold only by Eaton's Department Store, a major Canadian chain. There were only a few of them in existence and Eaton's had no record of their individual sales.

In the bathroom of the robber's hotel room were numerous sinister looking fluids in bottles, together with Atlas detonating devices. These detonators are sold only in the United States and not in Canada. Does this clue indicate he might have been a construction worker, or perhaps a miner? There was paraffin wax which might have been used to seal off the ends of the dynamite (large diameter sticks of unknown length) which he was carrying. He undoubtedly knew how to handle dynamite, but it is believed he did not acquire his skill in the bush or in military service. Perhaps in the construction industry? But where do the bottles of fluid fit in?

In the bomber's room was also found an eight-inch Emerson TV set, fairly new, of a type sold only in the United States.

How did he get it into Canada? How did he bring the rifle and explosives into Canada, if in fact he came from the United States? Public transportation would be very risky, and even crossing the border by car would present difficulties in concealing items such as these. Perhaps he came in by way of a lake, by boat or canoe, through Quetico Park, a large wilderness area in northern Minnesota and Ontario. Perhaps he came across Lake of the Woods.

The only other significant thing about the hotel room is that a lot of clothing was left behind, all neatly folded away. The neatness of his effects would suggest a military background, although the lack of a fingerprint record would negate this, if indeed it can be relied on. Perhaps he had spent some time in an institution. A mental hospital?

Paul Higgins, to use the name under which he registered at the Kenricia Hotel, may have been an outdoorsman, or perhaps he had merely read a great deal about the outdoors. It is not unlikely that he had previously visited Kenora, but it is probable that he was not familiar with life in the north. That is the conclusion that can be drawn from the type of gear he was carrying. It would take several pages to list the duffel contents in detail. He had most of the items one would expect him to carry for survival, such as a sleeping bag, twine, tent, concentrated foods, warm clothing, tools and ammunition. Some of the items, however, seem to be superfluous or unsuitable.

The following articles which were among the many in the bag he was carrying and were strewn about in the explosion, or which were in the duffle placed in the back of the truck, seem especially significant:

A book about flying with floats.

Surely an odd type of manual to have at a time like this. If he knew how to fly on floats he wouldn't need it. If he was a pilot he would have known you can't learn to fly on floats by reading a book, and equally so if he was not a pilot.

The bomber had many aerial maps and a book on air navigation aids covering Northern Ontario eastward from Kenora as far as Georgian Bay. Most bush planes on floats do not carry equipment capable of using such facilities. Did the Mad Bomber know this?

A map of Quetico Park, a vast wilderness area covering part of both northern Minnesota and northwestern Ontario. Inspector Mychalyshyn checked certain spots marked on the map, but found nothing of interest there, not even good camping spots.

Then there was his Parker Hale Safari caliber 30-06 rifle (serial B39743M) with clip and ammunition. This is an excellent rifle, not the type of gun a gun lover would use to pry open cash drawers. A real expert would not fire it by accident. Nor, for that matter, would a professional criminal momentarily forget it upon leaving the bank. Did he know what a fine weapon he had? Why had he cut down the forestock?

One .32 caliber Galesi-Brescia automatic pistol (serial 207570) and a supply of ammunition. He fanned it while scaring the citizen out of the bank, which could indicate a familiarity with guns. On the other hand no one fans an automatic, not even in old movies. His total lack of familiarity with the rifle and with Reid's revolver seems to rule out any great familiarity with guns, which in turn tends to rule out a military background, and probably a professional criminal background as well.

A number of keys and a Slaymaker lock.

One pair of Pic handcuffs (serial 16845). Has a policeman somewhere in North America received brownies for allowing them to be stolen from him?

Wallet with handcuff keys, $175 in Canadian money and $5 in American money.

Two small transistor radios.

Cigars.

Small Rupen two lens magnifying glass; eye trouble? prospector?

Scissors and hair clippers; to shave off his beard? What did he look like before he grew his beard?

Canvas repair kit: "The Awl for All." For canoe repairs?

Two cans of spraypaint for touch-ups; to disguise a vehicle or boat which he intended to use?

Supply of concentrated foods, including a package of natural and health foods, barley groats, and hulled millet.

One Nordlund ax and case. This hatchet is too small to be of any real use in the bush, as any self-respecting bushman would know.

One small length of fish net; the mesh size is too small to be of use in Northern Ontario, although it might conceivably be of minimal use as a small seine.

A variety of tools, including a sixteen-ounce hammer, three screw drivers, two metal punches, tin snips, and wire cutters, a chisel, and a hand brace. The weight of these tools was considerable, and one would not expect a camper or one familiar with tools to so encumber himself, unless, of course, he had some specific use in mind for them.

Bush clothing and street clothing; if he was carrying his street clothing with him he very possibly did not have a cache.

It should be noted that no compass or fly dope were found in the effects of the robber. Both are absolute necessities in northwestern Ontario bush survival.   •

Many articles of clothing, wire cutters, American and Canadian beer bottles, scraps of paper, and miscellaneous items were left behind in the hotel room. A few of the more significant are listed:

Several pocket books including *Burn After Reading, OSS in World War II,* a Spanish-English dictionary, *Student* (a Nazi pictorial book) and *Canoe Trails Through Ontario.*

A pink comb and a blue comb; a Beau Brummell?

A variety of bullets, some thought to have been manufactured in Germany; any connection with the Nazi literature? A German immigrant, perhaps?

An Emerson eight-inch portable TV, (model 9FP02, serial E2026842) with ear plug and antenna; what sort of a traveling man carries his own TV set around? A loner? A man who broods in rooming houses? A psychopath?

The task of sifting this evidence and following it up is never ending. For example, several letters and a trip to Winnipeg were required to determine that the Parker Hale was a dead-end clue. Parker Hale keeps no records that can be traced. The rifle was not purchased at the major outlet in Winnipeg which might have sold it, had it indeed been purchased in Winnipeg. It could have been obtained anywhere in North America. Did the bomber win it from someone in a poker game in a logging camp? Did a disgruntled brother-in-law miss it the last time he passed through town?

And what of the speculation that the robber was a psychopath, or a sociopath, as they are sometimes called? Some of the more common symptoms of psychopathy have been catalogued, and there is general agreement by psychiatrists with whom I have discussed this case that the bomber possessed at least fourteen to sixteen possible characteristics of psychopathy.

Infinite possibilities assail the mind. Was there an accomplice? There is no evidence to so indicate. Certainly there was no accomplice on the scene.

Did someone know of the bomber's plans? It is a possibility, but one would not expect it, as the observable indications are that the bomber was a loner. On the other hand, at about this time a half-ton camper with B.C. plates was abandoned at a service station in Winnipeg, and the man and woman who left it never returned to pick it up. Further, it is said that at the time of the detonation, a woman standing beside her car stalled in the traffic tie-up west of town jumped into her car, shouted "My God, he's dead!," and turned around heading back west. These reports, whether or not they are true, can lead one down endless rabbit warrens of speculation. Does someone know that woman? Are you that woman? Have you been bottling something up, choking on it over the years? Now is the time to get it off your chest.

Somewhere in Canada or the United States, the bomber will have been seen by a psychiatrist. Are you that psychiatrist? Are you a social worker who tried to gain the man's confidence or insight into his problems—and probably failed? If so, come forward with what you know. A case study of this man, properly documented and written up, will be of value in assisting responsible authorities to recognize a future Mad Bomber, and to straighten him out before he kills people.

Somewhere the Mad Bomber has a relative who will remember. A mother, wondering what happened to her rolling stone son, the one who never had any friends, but had a lot of problems. Or a sister who hasn't seen him for years and doesn't really regret it. Or an older brother who got sick and tired of bailing him out of trouble and who has washed his hands of the problem. If you are this relative come forward and tell us about the identity of the man we seek.

Somewhere there is a landlady who remembers the habits of her one-time roomer who disappeared without a trace. Or an ex-bunkhouse mate or a shipmate who remembers the way the Mad Bomber built up his insole in steps, higher at the heels. Or a flying instructor who washed out a kook who resembled the man I am describing. Or a construction foreman who employed him as a powder man, but never quite trusted him. Or you may be a policeman who had a nasty brush with him and has a lot of sympathy for a fellow officer who was told, "Someone has to take a truck and drive that bastard out of town."

If you are one of these people drop a line to me. You could be the key to solving this case. I do not undertake to reply to all letters, but if you are in any way responsible for identifying the Mad Bomber, I will certainly see that you are given due credit.

Who Was Maggoty Maisie?

When coal man Freddy Harmon dug into Kron's Coal Shed Number Four in downtown Kenora, in the spring of 1964, he wasn't prepared to find an overripe body. His grisly discovery led the police on a search for the identity of the dead woman which has yielded no result to this date. The identity of her killer may never be known.

There weren't many people still using coal in Kenora in 1964. Out of habit and a wish to provide employment for several employees who could do nothing else but shovel coal, Rudy Kron kept the coal sheds open. The sheds were an eyesore and a hangout for drunks and were due to be closed soon. The finding of Maggoty Maisie hastened the day.

It was obvious to the police that Maisie had been raped and murdered. Her underpants were down around her ankles, her dress was up around her chest, and she had been covered with a thin layer of coal. Deciphering of finer clinical details was made impossible by deterioration of the tissues. The ultimate indignity to this poor scrap of flesh and blood is that her identity may never be known.

Peter Pan, the local pathologist, did an open-air postmortem and decided she had been dead for perhaps a few weeks. He sent tissue specimens down to the Center of Forensic Sciences in Toronto.

Later on in the summer, Dr. Pan realized he hadn't seen the hyoid bone—a little bone in the neck which is frequently broken by strangulation during the course of a vicious rape. If the bone were to be found broken it would, of course, add fuel to the rape theory.

By the time they dug her up, Maisie was in even worse shape than when they had buried her. They poked around in what was left of Maisie's neck, but didn't find the hyoid bone. Instead they cut off her head and neck, put it in a lard pail, and Coroner Sam Burris sent it down to the Center of Forensic Sciences.

They can do marvelous things at the Center. As one of the world's outstanding crime laboratories, they can match guns to fired bullets, they can match paint samples, detect poisons and chemicals, tell all sorts of things about spermatozoa and vaginal secretions, and they can match handwriting specimens. But, they couldn't find Maggoty Maisie's hyoid bone. All they could say was the victim was a young North American Indian woman, and that since her demise she had suffered two distinct maggot infestations—thus dating her death at some time before the cold weather set in the fall previous to her being found.

Until this latter opinion as to the time of death, we had thought we had a perfect candidate in Mary Lou Brave, a girl from a reserve some seventy miles distant from Kenora, who had been missing for some time. But Mary Lou was known to be alive and well just a few weeks prior to the finding of the body, so the police went back to search for an identity for the body, and they continued to search for the killer.

Meanwhile, back at the lab, someone got the idea of boiling the flesh off the skull, then building up the features with clay, to try to reconstruct a likeness based on the bone structure. The clay head was then painted a dark skin color, and the eyes and lips appropriately shaded. The result was as grotesque and horrifying an apparition as I have ever seen. It bore little resemblance to a human face, and was totally useless as a means of identification. Chief Jack Pike was handy with tools, and he built a curtained glass case for the head. When Mary Lou Brave's sister came in to make an identification, she took one look at the grisly thing and fainted dead away. After that Chief Pike never showed it to anyone.

Eventually we convened an inquest into the death of the Unknown Female. Our witnesses told of Mary Lou Brave's movements in the days prior to her disappearance. The police, pathologist, and coroner opined that she had been raped and murdered. We had three real prime suspects, including a fellow who the year before had raped and murdered his half-sister and gotten away with it, but all three denied having anything to do with the girl. One name kept cropping up in the testimony of the various witnesses as a woman who should be able to throw light on Mary Lou Brave's demise—we will call her Edna Williams. Everyone said Mary Lou and Edna were in frequent company with each other, prior to Mary Lou's disappearance.

Trouble was, we couldn't find Edna Williams, and the coroner's jury wanted to hear from her. So we adjourned the inquest *sine die*, that is, indefinitely, while the search for Edna Williams continued.

Eventually, the Sheriff of Couchiching County, Minnesota, located her for us, and tried to talk her into going back to Kenora to testify at the inquest, but she wanted no part of it and refused. "Never mind," he said laconically, "I'll let you know the next time she's in the county jail for being drunk." I didn't know how that would help us.

A few weeks later the good sheriff called and asked us how quickly we could reconvene our inquest. A hurried phone call to Coroner Sam Burris and the jurors, and we decided we could do it by one o'clock the following day. I called the Sheriff back and told him. "Good," says he, "have a police car waiting on the Fort Frances side of the International Bridge at exactly nine in the morning. And have her back on my side of the bridge by nine o'clock in the evening, as that is the latest our jail will let her back in."

Precisely at 9 A.M., an OPP cruiser was waiting for Edna. A Couchiching County Sheriff's car pulled up at the other end, and a Sheriff's deputy got out and opened the door for Edna, making it plain she'd damn well better move her ass across the bridge in a hurry. She did, and four hours later found herself on the witness stand in Kenora.

Edna Williams was no help to us at all. She denied knowing anything. I still think she knew all about the death of Maggoty Maisie, and
could have told us who killed her had she been so inclined. Probably she
was scared out of her wits, not so much by her somewhat unorthodox
extradition as by someone who threatened her.

By two in the afternoon Edna was on her way south, and at six
o'clock she made her solitary way across the bridge and into the waiting
Sheriff's car. Fifteen minutes later she was snug in her own little cell in
the Couchiching County Jail.

Inspector Bob MacGarva of the Criminal Investigation Branch of
the OPP was in charge of the Maggoty Maisie case, and never lost
interest in it even though he was promoted to other duties. Years later
Mary Lou Brave's mother got a note from another daughter, who also
happened to be named Mary Lou, in the eastern part of the province,
enclosing a letter from Mary Lou, who said she was married and living
happily in a village in northern Quebec. This was a puzzler, as we were
certain that Maggoty Maisie was Mary Lou in spite of what the Center
of Forensic Sciences had to tell us about the time of death. In any event,
Inspector MacGarva dug out the old file and dispatched "Our Man in
Quebec" to the boonies to find out where Mary Lou had been all these
years. It turned out that Mary Lou was a woman who had known Mary
Lou Brave's sister, Mary Lou, at some time in the past, and wasn't the
missing Mary Lou at all. At least that confirmed that Maggoty Maisie
could be the missing Mary Lou.

But it didn't really. Maggoty Maisie hid discreetly behind the
curtains of her dusty glass box for another ten years before she was
hauled out to have further indignities perpetrated on her in the name of
justice.

Chief Pike was long gone, and was replaced by Chief Webb Engstrom, who, of course, knew the story well. Every morning for years he
looked up at the glass box on the high cupboard in his office and
imagined Maggoty Maisie glaring balefully at him from behind the
curtain. Every morning, he promised himself he was going to get rid of
the box that very day.

In the spring of 1979, Chief Engstrom took a course in forensic
pathology. He learned from Chief Provincial Pathologist, Hillsdon
Smith, that an old method of identification had been revived. Skull
comparison had been experimented with briefly in the 1930s, but was
abandoned decades ago as unsatisfactory. However, Dr. Smith had

revived skull comparison with the aid of a highly innovative electronics technician and his video cameras.

It works like this. The skull to be identified is placed loosely on a pin, in such a manner as to permit it to be rotated and shifted to various positions. A video camera is focused on the skull and the image is cast onto one-half of a video screen. At the same time a second camera is focused on a photograph of the person who (it is hoped) is one and the same as the former owner of the skull, and this image is cast onto the other half of the screen. The skull is then rotated until the first camera views it at precisely the same position as the second camera is viewing the photograph. The apparatus is then adjusted so that the two images are moved one on top of the other. Voila, magic. The two images coincide in every minute detail. An identification is made!

The loathsome glass box was removed from the cupboard in Chief Engstrom's office, and taken to Toronto with two photographs of Mary Lou Brave. This was going to be a triumph of modern science. Webb and I were planning to write it up for the RCMP Gazette. Oh, yes, kudos to the persistent sleuth and the learned Crown attorney! Perhaps even a crumb of recognition to Dr. Smith.

When the report came back it was negative. Maggoty Maisie was not the girl in the photographs. Not only that, but the two photographs were of different girls. Damn Smith and his gadgetry. So much for fleeting fantasies of forensic fame. Back went the glass box to Chief Engstrom's shelf.

Maggoty Maisie stared enigmatically down at Webb Engstrom from behind her curtain for several more years. Sam Burris always said he was going to give her a decent burial in his garden, but he never got around to it. Sam went to glory, and Webb was replaced by Chief Don Munro, who in turn was replaced by Chief Bob Marchant. And still poor Maisie lurks in her box in a dusty storage room in the Kenora Police Office. Her assailant may never be known.

But where is Mary Lou Brave, and who was the girl in the coal bin?

Six

Cultural Divide

I should explain why I have not said more about the Northern Ontario Indians, Canada's First Nations people, up to this point.

While the anthropological study of races is of great interest to me, I believe that centering a race or defined group for some form of action tends to make a special case out of it, which in turn means emphasizing differences. Once you start getting into differences the concept of separateness presents itself, as the two concepts just naturally go hand in hand. Bear in mind that this book is not about anthropology, but about law and order in northwestern Ontario.

In one of the great common-law judgments in history, *Brown versus Board of Education*, 347 U.S. 483 (1954), the Supreme Court of the United States considered a proposal that a midwestern school board should build a separate but equal high school for black students. In a judgment that amounted to high philosophy the court said there could be no such thing as separate but equal schools. The two concepts simply can't coexist. The court was not simply dabbling in semantics, but was expressing a basic ideology that was intended to guide a nation, and with this landmark judgment an errant school board was forced to integrate.

To carry this thinking to its logical conclusion, once you pronounce a human institution to be separate from other similar institutions you are well on the way to saying it is unequal, which is tantamount to saying it is inferior. It is for this reason that I oppose the current brand of government sponsored multiculturalism now prevailing in Canada—it artificially props up small groups and magnifies their differences, thus fragmenting rather than cementing the patchwork of the larger society, thereby weakening a great nation. When carried beyond a commonsensical point, beyond "affirmative action," this type of sponsorship may even diminish the group it proposes to strengthen.

If any minority group within the Canadian mosaic wishes to follow its own customs and beliefs it is free to do so. But when these customs and beliefs become artificially subsidized by government, they assume a stature that is inconsistent with the interests of nationhood.

In my view, the races that make up Canada should be encouraged to mix. I am not talking assimilation, but only a degree of integration. If a minority race is allowed to hive itself off rather than interacting with the mainstream, the contribution to the nation is surely minimized.

And so it is with Canadian Indians. I take great interest in them as a segment of Canadian society, but I do not wish to encourage people, including aboriginal people themselves, to look upon them as a curious race separate and apart from the larger society, from the Canadian nation.

For the most part, with some exceptions, what I have written to this point is not really about Indians. I have written about everyday people. Many of them just happen to be Native Canadian Indians. The substantial exception, which I make in the name of history, is the next chapter, A Long, Hot Summer. The final chapter, On the Coast of Hudson Bay, also happens to be about Indians, but could be about isolated communities anywhere.

A Long, Hot Summer

The spring of 1974 was no different from any other spring. The trees blossomed, the birds nested, and everyone looked forward to the holiday months of July and August, the months when Canadians traditionally take to the lakes, the summer cottages, and the highways of the nation.

Everyone, that is, except a group of disaffected young Indians who had nothing exciting on their horizons. Some of them might have headed back to the somnolent reserves from which they came. Others might have continued to work at their uninteresting jobs, or drawn welfare and hung around the streets of Kenora. They could have done a number of things, but for the most part their activities would not have been as exciting or as much fun as the things the average young white adult in the Kenora area had planned, and that is how the occupation of Anicinabe Park was born. It was the last uprising, or at any rate it was the last uprising prior to Oka in 1990.

To understand why Anicinabe Park was born we have to look generations back into history.

The race of Indians as we know it has occupied Northern Ontario for hundreds of years. At the time of Columbus their numbers were fewer, and they lived a nomadic life unhampered by strongly developed notions of social structure, personal property, or community planning.

191

From generation to generation their lives changed but little, and children could reasonably expect to live the same sort of lives their forefathers did. The coming of the fur trade made things a little better, but one suspects that life was not easy for the nomadic bush Indians of the Canadian Shield. If anything, the coming of whiskey and guns made their lives shorter and more unpleasant.

Certainly the missionaries who accompanied the fur trade did very little for the people. The People—that is what the word Anicinabe means—had a belief in the Great Spirit and they possessed a reverence for life and for nature quite as satisfactory to them as was the white man's religion to him. But the missionaries told them they were wicked and evil, and called them pagans, in a pejorative sense. As late as 1957 the churches and the sectarian teachers they employed told the children they were going to hell, to an eternity of everlasting fire and damnation if they did not adopt the superior Christian religion of the white man. I know this to be so from my own observations over the years, as far back as my early childhood in northern Quebec, when my father was flying in the fur trade.

I will reinforce this generalization with a single anecdote from my days as a student-at-law in the office of Jack K. Doner in Kenora. One day Jack asked me to see the chief from the Whitefish Bay Reserve, a community about equally divided between Roman Catholics, Presbyterians and Animists, the latter being a label I am attaching rather arbitrarily to define the beliefs of the Indians of a former day. Chief Paypompe didn't speak much English, but he was sizzling mad, and I had no difficulty in understanding what his complaint was all about.

The story Chief Paypompe told me was incredible. He said they had a lot of trouble getting rid of a teacher who was bootlegging right out of the teacherage, just a year or so previously. This teacher was replaced by a fanatical lady who was resolved to convert all the Presbyterians to Catholicism, by whatever means was necessary. She left the pagans (the word was common at the time, and did not necessarily have a negative connotation) alone, but she declared a vendetta on the Presbyterians. The chief said that teacher was known to have taken the hand of a child and held it briefly to the hot woodstove, in order to teach it what hell was like, and he gave about a dozen more instances of gross abuse of children in the name of religion. I was able to talk to a few of the children and their parents, but most of them were unwilling to rock the boat, and beyond grudging admissions that certain bad things had happened I got almost no details. The child who had been burned and one other who had received a serious cut to the head at the hands of the new teacher spoke to me about their own cases, but corroboration was not forthcoming. This reluctance to testify is a characteristic of Native people, and while it is commendable in certain circumstances, it can be fatal to a prosecution, and this is as true now as it ever was.

It is worth noting that the police believed these terrible things, or some of them, were happening, but they were not successful in gathering credible evidence of it. The Department of Indian Affairs would not even discuss the matter with me. It was plainly a hot potato. After a few weeks of my asking questions, the local Catholic Church hierarchy took the matter in hand and tacitly admitted to Magistrate Joe Fregeau, a sincere practicing Catholic himself, that the teacher was doing wicked things, and he passed the information on to me. Teacher was said to have been sent to a rest home, and then reassigned to less sensitive duties. Today a young law student with fire in his bowels would probably raise hell and go to the press, and insist on the laying of charges, but I suppose, in retrospect, I figured I had accomplished enough at the time, given that I had at best a very weak case against the teacher.

That is the end of my digression. I assure you it was not for the purpose of telling you what a hero I was, but to convince you there was in truth an element of actual and tangible evil in the attitude of many Whites concerned with bringing religion to the Indians. In spite of all this it must have been tempting to the Indians at the turn of the twentieth century to adopt the ways of the white man. After all, didn't the white man have warm clothing, comfortable houses, healthy children, and an abundance of food?

Of course the Indians wanted the better things in life, and that was only natural. Missionaries of all denominations played upon the unsophisticated native people and let them think that conversion to Christianity was a pre-condition to attainment of the good life. The Indians, however, were not convinced and many stubbornly hung on to their old beliefs, passing them on from generation to generation, possibly even while paying lip service to one or the other of the established Christian religions.

Many of the present-day Ojibway and Cree are devout adherents of one Christian religion or another. Some retain the philosophical concepts which served them well over the centuries. Hard-line Christian theologians may disagree, but in my view there is nothing inconsistent

193

between the ancient Indian beliefs and modern Christian teaching—both advocate a respect for life and adherence to the golden rule. Only the trappings are different. Unfortunately, the missionaries in their zeal for converts took their duties too seriously, and I think it is generally true to say they attempted to exorcise from the mind and psyche of the Indian race all knowledge of self, all folklore, all history and culture, all philosophy, in short, all attributes that made the Indian people a distinct cultural entity and gave them pride. I hope and expect it will be beyond controversy when I say the Canadian government implicitly approved of this policy.

It is not fair to paint the whole Christian clergy with this brush, as many priests and ministers were dedicated, wise, and tolerant, but my perception is that missionaries like this were in the minority. I assert this with some authority, as I lived alongside them from time to time during my formative years. I worked with them during my years in the bush, and during my years as Crown attorney I traveled the North and tried to be of assistance to the Natives in their struggle towards self determination. Over the years I met many missionaries both good and bad, but even some of the best of them seemed to be patronizing in their attitudes.

I don't take a conspiratorial view of history, or of modern affairs, for that matter. I don't believe, for example, that the Catholics and the Anglicans and the Presbyterians and the rest told their people, "Go out and force the Native people to move in and form communities around the churches and trading posts. Give them rations to keep them there. Put yourselves on a pedestal." No one had to articulate such a plan and disseminate such instructions. It all just came about naturally, and it suited the traders and the government people equally well. The wives and families were induced to stay in the villages, and the men were encouraged to go out trapping and bring back the furs. Commercial fishing also became feasible for some.

Everyone benefitted from the new system, which became actual government policy during the 1940s. The missionaries had their souls all wrapped up and accessible. The government administrators had heads to count and paper to push, and the teachers and medical people found it much easier to cope with a stationary population. The benefit to the traders is obvious. Now they got all the furs and every last dollar that came into possession of a family without having to go to the camps in the bush and find it.

There were great benefits to the Indians, too, in moving in and forming communities, chiefly in that they now had access to schooling and medical services. Communication, human companionship, and regular visits by floatplanes or skiplanes all played their part in the new life. Life should have been much better for them, and it probably was, for a while. The children got at least some education, even if it was inferior. Infant mortality decreased, the women had access to some of the amenities from the local store, usually a Hudson's Bay Post, but perhaps a free trader, and when the men were in the village they could work cooperatively at repairing equipment, fishing, or just spend time gossiping.

Frequently whole family groups would uproot and go to hunt and trap in some remote place for weeks or months on end. At these times they returned to a more traditional way of life, and it refreshed their spirits and renewed their pride. As time went by these forays back to their roots became fewer and shorter, and the people began to lose their old skills. This waning of interest in the old ways can be accounted for by a number of factors, only one of which is the necessity for regular schooling of the children. A trapline is a lonely place when there is no family to come home to. By the 1940s most of the older children were in residential schools, and in the 1950s there were day schools on many of the reserves, and the older children were in boarding homes in towns many miles away from the villages. Another factor which caused the decline of the trapping and fishing camps was simply the decreasing value of the product. A man has to work just as hard to trap a beaver today as he did half a century ago, yet the returns in terms of the purchasing power of a pelt are less than a tenth of what it was then.

So why hunt and trap and fish any more? It just isn't worth the trouble. The pickings were slim in bygone days, and now it is impossible to make a living at it. It is tough, lonesome work—freezing cold in the winter, with clouds of blackflies and mosquitoes in the summer. And the loneliness, the constant loneliness. Supposedly we live in an enlightened age, and shouldn't have to live like that any more. To do it occasionally is good for the soul, but to do it permanently is not a reasonable alternative in the 1990s. Perhaps it all comes down to expectations. Modern technology, meaning television and airstrips, has created an expectation of a better life.

In all our enlightenment (or is it pangs of conscience at having misunderstood and ignored the native people for so many generations?)

the larger society has devised a welfare program that keeps body and soul together. Welfare is now automatic to the people of the North. The larger society decided that all who wanted it should have it without question, and thus welfare became an established way of life by the mid-1960s.

The coming of welfare was a blessing to the people of the North, although it was disastrous in the sense that it created a generation of welfare bums and sapped the pride of the people. It accelerated a formerly proud and self-reliant race on a slide to booze, indolence, and a loss of self-respect. The welfare was forced upon them by circumstance and by a lack of the understanding necessary to resist it, and, of course, by the poor economic circumstances in which they found themselves. The extreme extent to which they embraced the grape might be because they had not had generations of exposure to it, or because of some innate racial predilection to a low alcohol tolerance—perhaps science will one day tell us which. But certainly the new lifestyle in which there was very little work to make a man feel useful and necessary contributed strongly to the excessive use of alcohol.

In fairness I have to say that in the 1990s it appears that education and strength of character are asserting themselves both in the villages and on the "outside" and the future looks brighter for the native people than it has in a long time. But such was not yet the case in the 1970s.

The result of the decline of the old way and the coming of the new was that the native people lost their pride and self-reliance, and one frequently hears from uninformed observers that they are indolent and lazy, and have no ambition or sense of responsibility. The other side of the coin is that in this age in prosperous Canada it is surely incumbent on us to see that every citizen has a certain minimum income on which to survive, as well as a reasonable education and good health care. Consequently it can be said that the native people are individually longer lived and better educated than ever before in history.

But they are dreadfully bored and dissatisfied, and this is true whether they live back on the reserves where there is no work or in the cities, in many of which there is a subtle job discrimination and also a shortage of work. In the early 1970s this dissatisfaction reached a peak among the younger Indians of North America, many of whom had acquired good educations, culminating in Wounded Knee in South Dakota, the occupation of the Bureau of Indian Affairs in Washington D.C., and in numerous sit-ins at Indian Affairs offices across Canada.

A focal point for much of the dissatisfaction was the American Indian Movement (AIM).

This is where that loosely knit group of impatient young men and a few women calling themselves the Warriors Society came into the picture. The stage was now set for the occupation of a municipal camping ground on the outskirts of Kenora known as Anicinabe Park —Indian Park, as we might translate it. The word is pronounced ah-nish-in-ah-be, with equal emphasis on each syllable.

Many years before, Anicinabe Park had belonged to the Kenora Indian Agency, which looked after the affairs of about a dozen bands of Indians situated on and north of the Lake of the Woods. It is difficult to know today precisely how this land was held—was it land belonging to one of the bands, and therefore reserve property? Was it trust lands held for the common use of the local bands? Was it simply a property acquisition to be held for business purposes? The legal verities will one day be sorted out by the courts and it will be interesting to see whether there was any breach of trust involved in the subsequent sale. The indisputable fact is that the local bands had an attachment to that piece of land and continued to resort to it for camping and living on when they visited Kenora for business or shopping. This situation prevailed until the late 1950s even though the land had long since passed into private hands and eventually to ownership by the Town of Kenora.

The use of Anicinabe Park declined with the coming of roads to the reserves in the fifties and sixties, making it unnecessary to come to town by boat. The only people to use it were drunks of all races, and many were the beatings, minor robberies, and temporarily abandoned children to be found there. The residents of Kenora tended to avoid the place, as did many Indians who simply wanted to come to town for business or social purposes. As far as anyone in town knew, no native person ever gave it a thought when in the 1960s the municipal authorities decided to build a pavilion on the property and turn part of it into a tourist trailer park and camping area. The new facilities were only second-rate, but they served well enough to travelling summer tourists who wanted to halt their travels on the shore of beautiful Lake of the Woods to let their children rest and swim for a few days.

But let us return to the Warriors Society, that group of restless young men anxious to raise themselves and their people above the paternalism of the Department of Indian Affairs and the larger society, for which read "White" society. In the interests of historical accuracy I

197

should say that there was a large component of mindless adventurism mixed in with the more legitimate purposes of the exercise, but that seemed to be acceptable to the permissive society of the time. The Warriors were really a subgroup affiliated with the Grand Council of Treaty Number Three.

Treaty Three, or the Northwest Angle Treaty was signed with the Indians in 1871. In the 1960s, the adherents were encouraged to organize their own associations in order to stimulate the native people to assume some of the affairs formerly administered by the monolithic and torpid Department of Indian Affairs. In reality, the government hoped that the treaty organizations would become a counterfoil to the moribund civil servants in the Department. On a less cynical note I will point out that many of the more highly motivated politicians, such as local member John Reid, sincerely hoped to foster self-determination among the Indians of Canada when they promoted the development of these new organizations.

Twenty-two chiefs of the Kenora Indian Agency and the Fort Frances Indian Agency were the governing body of Treaty Three and these older men were vaguely distrustful of the Warriors Society. I was told they sensed from the beginning that these young men in a hurry did not necessarily intend to work within the system, although this might have been hindsight.

The Warriors first flexed their muscles in 1973, when they staged a sit-in at the Kenora Indian Agency in the federal post office building. It came as a surprise to the townspeople, but not to the media people. The CBC was tipped off in advance, as was a Winnipeg radio station. What the protest was aimed at slips my memory—what sticks is that it was a rather inept publicity gesture. I recall hearing over my car radio from a Winnipeg station, that there were riot helmeted police breaking the heads of the demonstrators in Kenora. In fact no heads were broken or even thumped, and no one even got charged with trespassing. I have always wondered if the false radio report was as a result of a pay off, or merely dreadfully unethical and incompetent journalism. At the very least the radio station allowed itself to be manipulated in a most improper way.

After a few days the kids in the office went away. The elders had a meeting, then approached Chief of Police, Webb Engstrom, and undertook to keep the young people busy and productive in the future. The chief commented that it was a darned good idea, and in the absence of pressure from local Indian Affairs officials the matter was allowed to drop without charges being filed.

The Warriors Society kept a low profile for about a year. To outward appearances they were productively engaged in legitimate pursuits. One young man became chief of his reserve. Several found employment directly with Treaty Three. Others helped lay plans for a Native Friendship Center. It seemed the decision not to lay charges over the post office incident was a wise one.

In the spring of 1974 we heard from some of the elders of Treaty Three that the Warriors Society wanted to hold a giant cultural rally and powwow some time in the summer, and they wanted to use part of Anicinabe Park for the purpose. I should have noted at the time, but did not, that the elders were not all fired up with enthusiasm for the idea. I discussed it informally with Webb Engstrom, a very tolerant man for a chief of police, and with Mayor Jim Davidson, who had been my home room teacher in grade eleven, and with my old sparring partner T.A. O'Flaherty, Q.C., now the town solicitor. We didn't really like the idea of the rally because of some of the people involved, but felt that it was improper to object on that basis, and in any event the stated aims of the rally were quite legitimate. We held our breaths.

Somewhat later in the spring the elders asked for an official meeting with the town officials and the police. I went along at the specific request of my friend, Chief of Police Webb Engstrom.

What the elders told us was disturbing indeed. The specific plans were not known to the elders, but it was whispered that the rally was going to be a mere cloak for subversive activities. Guns were going to be smuggled into the park, rabble-rousing speakers were to be imported, and goodness knows what trouble would ensue. I was amazed to hear the elders had no concrete knowledge of the real objectives of the rally, and they feared they could not influence their youth. This boded real trouble, as traditionally the Indian people were very respectful of their elders.

The situation was delicate, as most of the elders and chiefs had children and relatives and band members who would be bound to become involved if the situation developed into a confrontation. We told the gathering nothing could be done to stop the rally in the absence of solid information of forbidden mischief. Whispers and speculation were not enough.

There probably were legal means to block the pending cultural rally, but you must remember the year was 1974, and the times were permissive. I would like to be able to say that a conscious decision was made, after carefully weighing the alternatives, to allow the Warriors to go ahead with their rally, but in fact the town fathers stewed and simmered over the decision until it was too late to say no.

The day the rally opened the tourists started to move out of the park. The Ojibway Warriors Society was not great company with their never ceasing loudspeakers and their taped powwows. A few visiting native people who expected a genuine cultural rally moved out right along with the tourists. The aura of vague hostility that hung over the park might have been attributable to paranoia on the part of the townspeople, or to the same unease middle-class people everywhere feel for summer rock concerts, or perhaps even to plain old-fashioned racial prejudice, and no doubt there were elements of all these in the reaction of the town. The fact that the Warriors invited Dennis Banks to open the rally did nothing to ease people's minds.

Dennis Banks was a vice president of AIM, and was widely believed to be an irresponsible militant. In fact he was under indictment back in the States for incidents that arose from the conflict at Wounded Knee, then fresh in everyone's minds. However, fears were allayed when Banks kicked off the rally by telling the Warriors and their adherents that violence was not the way to achieve their ends. The Warriors could not have been listening, because the guns came out the very next day after Banks left. At first the guns were made visible only to news photographers, for obvious reasons, but after a few days and a development of confidence they were visible to the police. The young people in the park announced that they intended to demand the return of Anicinabe Park to the Indians, and that they were incubating a further list of demands which had to be honored in detail.

The reaction of the townspeople, the police, the government, and the elders was one of total confusion. The word redneck was first used in Canada about this time, having been imported from below the Mason-Dixon line, and denoting po' white trash who hoed cotton and corn in the sun and got their necks sunburned. This class of people exists everywhere, and in Kenora, in 1974, they were the ones who advocated spilling the blood of the group in the park. Send the police in with riot guns. Bring in the army if necessary. Wipe 'em out. Fortunately, they were very much in the minority.

At the other end of the spectrum were the do-gooders who would have showered the Warriors with food and encouragement, and who wrung their hands and talked about the idealism of the people in the park. Both the rednecks and the do-gooders were equally unrealistic in what they advocated. The rednecks could be controlled, but the do-gooders were really an ungovernable nuisance. Many of the do-gooders came in from outside, stayed a few days, went to the park to talk to the Warriors, made vague pronouncements about the nature of good and evil, then faded away.

Even the police were divided as to what should be done. Early in the game the Kenora Police called on the OPP for assistance, and ninety or more outside police moved into Kenora to do park duty. This kept the lid on, but later there was the unfortunate consequence that as strangers to the area they were unable to identify the people in the park from the fleeting glimpses they had got. One faction of the police wanted to move in and clean up the park by force. Paradoxically this was the faction that estimated the largest number of guns in the park. The other faction advocated patience. Both factions hoped for cold, rainy weather, which would have emptied the park.

The Government was totally unprepared for the situation, and with a few notable exceptions the politicians and the senior civil servants had no advice to give. The Federal government took a completely hands-off attitude saying, in effect, that law enforcement was strictly a provincial responsibility, which is true under our constitution. Nevertheless, it made it damned awkward for the province to negotiate alone. That left the conduct of business to the police and local government officials, including myself and Mayor Davidson, both in his capacity as mayor and as a member of the police commission.

We were really faced with two possibilities—to urge the police to be patient, or to urge them to move in. The decision was the responsibility of the police, but they were very good about listening to advice. We felt that the consequences either way would result in black disaster, and if such were the case we would be scapegoats for the politicians. Personal consequences didn't really matter to Assistant Deputy Commissioner Eck Miller of the OPP, on loan to assist Chief Engstrom with the police command, as he intended to retire at the end of the summer, anyway. Mayor Jim Davidson was a retired teacher who was answerable to the Town of Kenora, and not the Province of Ontario. But it mattered a lot to me, with the do-gooders on one side advocating placating the Warriors by promising total capitulation to their demands,

201

and promises of no prosecution—and on the other side the rednecks demanding strict enforcement of law and order, tanks, and artillery if necessary. I suppose the initial silence of my political masters created a paranoia in me. The notable exceptions I mentioned above were The Hon. George Kerr, QC, the Solicitor General, and The Hon. Leo Bernier, the member in the Provincial Legislature for the riding, who was then Minister of Natural Resources. George Kerr said, "We don't know what the hell to tell you to do—you guys deal with it on the spot and I promise you we'll back you up." Leo Bernier said, "I'm not a lawyer or a policeman but I've got lots of airplanes and a big budget - they're yours if they'll help. But get those dumb bastards out of the park without killing them if you can." The attorney general of the day had nothing to say.

The elders were more perplexed than anyone by the events in the park. It is to their credit that they almost always spoke with one voice at any one time, but they vacillated in their advice from day to day. On one day the reaction was, "The people in the park are all our children, and as much as we deplore what is going on, our loyalties must be with them. If there is going to be a fight you will have to come over us first." The next day it would be, "Those dumb kids are openly defying law and order, and it is inevitable that the police will have to move in on them. That will start a race war that will set the cause of the Indians back two generations. We will have to go in and clean it up ourselves, using as much force as we have to. At least a race war will be avoided..." The elders really saw the park situation as a slap at themselves as much as a slap at government and the larger society. They realized they should have been moving quicker in their dealings with government, and that the Warriors were telling them to move over and make way for a generation in a hurry.

And so the long, hot summer dragged on, with the people in the park posturing, shooting off the occasional gun, and promising that the list of demands would soon be ready. I had a cot moved into my office. Every morning and every evening the police authorities met with the members of the town police commission and myself and the mayor and any outsiders who felt that they had a solution to the stalemate. It became apparent that the image of the administration of justice was going to suffer, no matter what. The difficulty was articulated by my friend John Reid, the local member of the federal legislature, by avocation a historian and by vocation a politician. He said that crimes are dealt with by the criminal law, political crimes are dealt with by political means. I hoped that he was wrong about the latter, but in retrospect he was mostly right. In the interests of accuracy I have to admit that many decisions made during this time were prompted by political considerations as much as by purely legal considerations.

For the first week or two there was very little contact between the Warriors and the authorities. We really didn't know what they wanted, and had great difficulty in maintaining patience while they formulated their demands. Only the press were welcomed in the park, but not many of them chose to go. The police cordoned the area with some effectiveness, and searched everyone going in. Police intelligence was not good, but the go-get-'em faction felt that sophisticated weapons were filtering in, and the sooner the rats' nest was cleaned out the better. The patient faction was not sure about that, as certainly nothing like an automatic weapon was ever seen near the road or at the barricades. As it turned out my mother, a stringer for *The Thunder Bay Times*, probably had as good information as anyone, and it could be read right in the paper. As a Nokum—a white-haired grandmother, and one who was previously well and favorably known to the local Indians—she was made welcome in the park. In the whole six weeks she saw only one handgun. There were rusty rifles and shotguns, to be sure, but most of the kids and even the Warriors didn't know how to handle their decrepit weapons. Eventually the situation became so unpredictable that she ceased going to the park. In any event, the fact that she was just a Nokum caused the police to doubt the accuracy of her reports, which was unfortunate, because if the police had indeed been forced to storm the park they would probably have gone in with much more armament than was necessary, and the civil rights people would have had a field day hollering about police brutality.

From time to time, visiting government people went into the park, and came back with conflicting opinions. Some said the Warriors were very sincere people who were out to make a point in order to better the lot of their people. Others said they were just a bunch of kids who were relieving their boredom by larking in the park, and basking in the publicity. It was hard to distill the truth. Early in the game a decision was made not to totally seal off the park—a certain amount of coming and going would be permitted, and a phone would be left open for communication. It was intended that the Warriors should not be allowed to develop a siege mentality. The whole group was allowed out to a legitimate powwow one evening. This looked bad for law and order, but it did not give the Warriors the excuse to say that they were besieged, and to become paranoid. We wanted it to be obvious to the Warriors and their hangers-on that it was their choice to hole up in the park and they were not being forced by the police to do so.

As the days wore on, such little communication as there was revealed some of the personalities in the park.

At the core were several, perhaps five, leaders, most in their twenties, and mostly with some education. Not being the final arbiter of truth, I cannot say whether they were genuinely motivated to better their people, or were mindless militants. Certainly they were fantasizers, and I suppose were psyched up to believe their own oration at some point. At some undetermined time in the occupation of the park, I became aware they were zealots, and were creating zealots of their followers, and might be persuaded to die for their cause, whatever it was. This made them all the more dangerous.

Next to the inner ring was a group, perhaps twenty in number, of fairly solid young people who were quite sincerely supportive of their leaders in the initial stages of the park occupation. There were grievances which needed redressing, and they really felt militancy was the way to get them resolved. They were caught up in the hoopla, and intrigued by the sweat lodge ceremonies and the oratory. Initially they may have been personally committed to violence if necessary, and later I suspect they became disillusioned, and would have liked to find a way out without losing face. A number of productive and dedicated citizens emerged from this group when the smoke cleared and the posturing was finished. Twenty years later we still smile at the unspoken memories when we meet. I do not intend to name them or say what the individuals are doing today, as most of them would rather be anonymous.

In the outer ring was a varying number of hangers-on whose motivation I find difficult to assess. From time to time anywhere from twenty to sixty of these people, mostly kids of high school age, might be in the park. It would be too easy to dismiss them all as larkers, and perhaps unfair to their integrity to do so. Nevertheless, I think the fascination of being involved in something big was what gripped most of them, and the nature of the cause was of lesser importance, the cause being so illusory that not even the leaders were able to articulate it. Maybe the cause was really just pride, but if it was they ran some terrible risks to attain it.

Several people in the park didn't really fit in with any of the three groups I have identified. They were not Lake of the Woods people for the most part.

The most significant of these was a chap named Harvey Major who had his origins in the Northwest Angle area of Lake of the Woods but had transplanted to the American Midwest after the Second World War. He was said to have established a string of profitable businesses, but lost everything after receiving head injuries in an accident. When past the usual age for becoming a revolutionary, he joined AIM, and was known there as an irresponsible radical. He came to Kenora with Dennis Banks for the opening of the cultural rally, and stayed on as a sort of elder statesman to the Warriors. Whatever else he might have been, he was a spellbinder of an orator, and he could use words to hypnotize a group of people. This moving oratory was of a type I have only heard from North American Indians, and then only rarely. Apparently Major could turn the golden words on and off at will, and on the one occasion on which I heard him I admit to being extremely moved by it. Major kept the Warriors whipped up to a fever pitch, talking about the glorious days of the old Indians, and the injustices perpetrated by the white man. Eventually we came to know that Major had considerable influence in the park, although it was hard to say whether for good or ill. Interestingly enough Major had a relative employed by Treaty Three, then considered an organization of the elders, and this relative was summarily discharged when the relationship was discovered and it was learned that there had been much communication between them prior to the cultural rally.

Another figure that emerged was an elderly medicine man, a sort of guru to the Warriors. He was lured to the park to lecture the young people on Indian traditions. I was told that he stayed as a virtual captive when things turned bad. He served a positive function in that he made the young people aware of their background, thus assisting in the instilling of pride of race. Perhaps he even kept the lid on to some extent. I never learned his identity.

A western Indian who stayed and became involved was a fellow I will call Lloyd Copperman. He was handy with a rifle, and used it on one occasion to take a random shot at a helicopter full of firefighters taking off from the nearby Ministry of Natural Resources (MNR) base. He missed fortunately, but his stupid action caused a number of his cohorts to reassess their positions. On another occasion he shot over the heads of some carpenters who were removing some material from a home being built nearby. The potshot at the helicopter was never officially reported, but the incident with the carpenters nearly caused the police to move in on the park. Copperman was an unpredictable nut, and thus dangerous to the people both in and out of the park.

Another enigma was a young lawyer from Toronto. I will call him simply George. His was one of many faces, and his real identity was not known until later. George's features were dark and tanned and everyone assumed that he was Indian, or partly Indian, which suited him very well. He had a personal attachment to things native, a sort of idealistic affinity for the underdog cause. He originally came for the cultural rally, but stayed for the excitement. The Warriors knew he was a lawyer and leaned on him heavily for advice, but his situation became precarious when some of them figured he was an RCMP agent. Even so, he stayed on until he decided his gown would be in jeopardy if he remained, by which time he was frightened that some of the Warriors might literally bump him off if he tried to leave. He was one very relieved young man when he finally made his break. Perhaps I should mention that he would have made it sooner, but in common with the other park inhabitants, he had developed a sort of self-induced paranoia from having exposed himself to the hyperbole of the militants and the purple oratory of Harvey Major. He felt the police were waiting to get him if he simply walked out alone, when in fact they didn't know his name or give a damn about him.

So much for the people in the park. You will note that I have deliberately avoided naming most of them, as many of them today are acutely embarrassed by the fact that they were involved at Anicinabe Park.

There were many people on the outside who played a significant part in developments, either because of their own personalities, or simply because they were on the spot and rose to the occasion. Unfortunately, there were others who did not rise to the occasion, preferring to play ostrich or carp from the sidelines.

One of the good guys was Chief Superintendent Eck Miller who headed up the visiting OPP contingent. Because of his paternal attitude towards his constables, all of whom were far from their wives and families, and most of whom had their holidays cancelled, and because of a certain rotundity which resulted from good living I christened him Uncle Bulgy, and the name stuck. Uncle Bulgy never seemed to sleep, but circulated constantly among his men. He was a career officer on his last assignment and could easily have yielded to pressure to send the men in blue to wipe out the park; however, he chose the other path. It was all he could do to keep some of his men from precipitous and potentially calamitous action.

Eck Miller's right hand was Superintendent Bob MacGarva, who had gotten his start in police work right in Kenora, but had long since moved on. He was detailed to Anicinabe Park because of his knowledge of and friendship with the local Indians twenty years earlier. However, Bob was just as baffled as everyone else at the members of the new generation who called themselves the Warriors Society of the Ojibway Nation. As a digression I would say the Ojibway were historically a peaceful people, not given to raiding and fighting just for the fun of it.

Jim Davidson, the mayor, was an outstanding man who, in my opinion, trod the line between left and right with extreme dexterity. He trod that line out of compassion for the youngsters whom he referred to as "those dumb kids." He knew that in an armed confrontation the people in the park would shed blood and probably many would be killed, and in spite of the fact that he knew it would cost him the mayoralty election in the fall, he counseled patience.

Towards the end of the occupation of the park Dr. Douglas Wright arrived on the scene from Toronto. As the deputy minister of Community and Social Services he had authority from Cabinet to do whatever had to be done. When he first appeared Eck Miller and Jim Davidson and I groaned, "Who the hell is this guy? Another bureaucrat who will stick his nose in, muddy the water, and go away again." There had been many such in the initial weeks of the uproar; however, Dr. Wright was different. He was crisp and efficient but never attempted to remove the final decision on law and order from the hands of the police. It was shortly after his arrival that the Warriors began to talk, albeit incoherently, of their true aspirations, and it was fortunate that there was a fresh ear to listen as there was almost no patience left in those of us who had been around since the beginning. I, for one, was about ready to leave it to the police to take whatever action they deemed necessary to end the occupation.

Frank "Big Red" Callaghan, QC, soon joined Doug Wright. Frank was a big blustering man who didn't tolerate fools easily. As Deputy Attorney General (later he became Chief Justice of the Ontario Court of Justice), he had a whole lot of authority, and he, like Doug Wright, was a model civil servant and not at all the stodgy stereotype. When the danger of an actual shootout disappeared he didn't go back to Toronto, but stayed on to help in establishing several programs that government promised to set up to benefit the local native population.

There were some rather remarkable people among the group I have loosely called the elders. Many of the chiefs from the various bands of Treaty Three practically took up residence in Kenora for the summer, but they couldn't all be there all the time, so much of their duty to be responsible spokesmen and arbiters fell on Doug and Madeline Skead of the Rat Portage Reserve, adjacent to Kenora. They had children and other relatives in the park, and although they could not control events and there was some danger to them personally they insisted on going in from time to time to attempt an arbitration process. At the end Madeline became a sort of trustee—in the sense that she was asked by the police to take possession of such firearms as had not been smuggled back out of the park before the finale. The authorities (another loosely applied label, as government people couldn't agree among themselves about who was responsible for what) frequently took counsel from the Skeads.

Two other chiefs who stand out in my mind were Ray Bruyere of Couchiching, adjacent to Fort Frances, and Willie Big George of Morson, at the southeast end of the Lake of the Woods. They were really big men, immensely powerful physically, but fortunately gentle by disposition. Ray's strong point was cool and analytical detachment, but this sometimes gave way to bouts of frustration when he considered his helplessness to end the situation in the park. Willie, though not an educated man, would occasionally turn on his oratorical powers, and when he did his logic and essential goodness transcended his sometimes halting English. Both these men, like the Skeads, were excellent spokesmen for their race, and could always be counted on to speak with a straight tongue.

Peter Kelly was the chief of the Sabaskong Reserve on the east side of the Lake of the Woods. He was mentally tough and had an abrasive tongue which he used to lacerate the Warriors, the authorities, and his fellow chiefs with equal vigor. Peter was not a popular man, but he had the grudging respect of everyone. Like the other chiefs, his was a frustrating lot, and as time dragged on without any articulation of the demands of the people in the park, he was forced to resort to drafting proposals which he would take to the Warriors and ask them to adopt. Most of the time they didn't, although in the end such proposals as were made were in fact largely his, and the Warriors were allowed to say they were theirs, as a face-saving gesture.

Lastly among the people outside the park I have to tell you about Jim Hook. Jim was raised in the tourist business on the English River, north of town, and consequently knew the Indians very well, as his family had employed them as guides and camp help for years. In 1974 he was a young lawyer making a good living at a busy practice. He owned a waterfront lot immediately next to Anicinabe Park, although isolated from the town itself, and he and Marg were building a lovely home on it. A construction trailer and many thousand dollars worth of materials were on the site at the opening of the cultural rally, but at the end of the occupation there was nothing but junk left. If Jim had been a less reasonable person he could have walked in on any day, pounded his fist on the desk, and demanded that his rights be protected and the law be enforced. But he did not. He knew that to do so would cause an armed confrontation, so he and Marg calmly waited it out knowing full well that they would have great difficulty in recovering their losses, and those of the contractors, at a later date. Jim had it in his power to change the course of events, but was wise enough to foresee the consequences, and refused to do it.

I find it impossible, even in retrospect, to explain the extent of the paranoia of some of the townspeople. It is true that the park was out of bounds, but there was never any threat to the town itself. Yet certain individuals took the whole affair as a personal affront and the possibility of vigilante action became very real. The last thing the town needed was for the breach of the peace to spread beyond the park boundaries, or for ordinary citizens to get involved in a shootout with the people in the park.

After several weeks of the standoff we finally got the Warriors to agree to meet us and present their grievances, on Bush Island in the middle of Kenora Bay, which was neutral ground. They were given a safe conduct pass for the occasion. Unfortunately the day was hot, and the island was covered with poison ivy, albeit a mild variety. We seemed to spend as much time looking for a poison ivy free shady spot and sending to town for cold drinks as we did talking business. The talk was fruitless. The Warriors wanted more time to prepare their demands, so we adjourned until another day. Webb Engstrom and I adjourned to my home, just a couple of hundred yards away from the island, to contemplate the events in the park and slake our thirsts.

I want to discuss the role of the media coverage of the park situation. A wise American statesman once opined that in a democratic society he would rather see a good free press than a bad government. Without taking anything away from the government of the day, I think there is a lot of truth to the observation. At any rate I found the media to be thoroughly responsible. They persistently sought information but were understanding when they were told the lid was on.

One evening a group of reporters representing various interests were standing about on the street watching me in my office through the window when one of them discovered an unlocked side door. They decided to pay me a visit, and trooped in to the outer office to wait for me to finish my phone conversation. As bad luck had it, I was engaged in a series of very confidential discussions with my superiors concerning the possibility of cleaning the park out by force—a very juicy tidbit for the media, if they chose to use it. Imagine my dismay when I looked into the outer office and discovered their presence. They had plenty of time to talk it over, and their spokesman said, "Mr. Burton, we've heard every word you've said. We could all leave here and call our stories in, and you'd look like a fool tomorrow, but we think we've only heard a small part of your assessment of the situation in the park. We don't want to be responsible for making a bad situation worse, and triggering bloodshed and loss of life. We think you owe it to us to lay the whole situation out for us. In turn we promise that not a word of what you said on the phone or what you tell us now will be reported in the press, radio, or television. We will only use it as background for our own information."

I asked them to go over to the HoHo Cafe and bring me back a mound of Chinese food, thereby buying a half hour to think the proposition over. When they returned with the food and a bottle of whiskey we sat down and talked.

And talked and talked. I told them every detail about the personalities involved, and the dynamics both inside the park and out, as far as I knew them, much as I have told them here. I even told them of a remote contingency plan to call in the armed forces to root the park out if worst came to worst.

The reporters were as good as their word. Not a whisper of what I told them ever got into the media.

Over the years I've had a few experiences with reporters misquoting me, or mixing rank speculation in with an otherwise legitimate interview, but by and large reporters and the media generally have been pretty ethical, and I never appreciated it more than that night they visited me at the courthouse at the time of Anicinabe Park.

A day or two after the meeting on Bush Island the Warriors indicated that they now had their list of demands formulated, and would like to meet again. A safe conduct was arranged, this time to the lakefront staff house owned by the Boise Cascade Paper Mill. While I don't have much admiration for Boise Cascade, I must say that they have had some first-rate managers in Kenora, and Bob Birch was one of the best. He put the staff house at our disposal, as a neutral meeting ground.

When the meeting opened we expected purple oratory, and we got it. We also expected a concise list of well thought out demands, but we didn't get it. This was a surprise, as a law student had been in and out of the park on behalf of Peter Kelly, the grand chief of Treaty Number Three, and they had by now had several weeks to formulate their demands in detail. When someone from the government asked, "Do you have your list yet?" there was a marked shuffling of feet and gazing at the floor by the Warriors. After a moment one of them spoke up and said, "Yes," just at the precise instant that another said "No." Almost immediately a third spoke up and said, "Give us until this afternoon and we will have it." It is hard to imagine a more disgruntled group, but we finally agreed to another meeting.

On the way out I stopped into the john, and was followed by one of the Warriors. To my great surprise he turned out to be George, the Toronto lawyer I mentioned earlier. His naturally dark skin had been further burned by the summer sun, and like everyone else, I had taken him for a Warrior. In the few moments we had alone he whispered his name, the fact that he was a lawyer, and added that he was frightened out of his wits by what he thought could happen. Specifically, he was afraid for himself, as the rumor had gotten around in the park that George was in reality from the FBI, not the RCMP. We felt that if he were to leave right then and there it might precipitate a scene that would preclude anything useful happening later that afternoon. I told him that I would arrange for him to simply "fade away" that evening.

I was appalled at George's bad judgment in hanging around the park as long as he did. He was a witness to, and perhaps a party to, numerous offenses, and his continued presence in the park was a guarantee that he would lose his gown. Nevertheless, I saw a golden opportunity to find out what was really going on in the park, so I agreed to snake him out after dark. George slipped away with his companions, assuming a suitably truculent air as he passed the police on the way to the waiting cars.

And so we waited for the afternoon session. And waited, and waited throughout the long, hot day of that long, hot summer. The police told us that people, messengers it was assumed, were flying back and forth to the park. It appeared that they would, after all, produce an important document, perhaps a list of grievances. We hoped so. In spite of the fact that the Warriors were very nearly responsible for setting off a race war, the rest of the world, even the rednecks, felt that some good could be salvaged from a bad situation if only the Warriors would speak up and honestly state their grievances.

But it was not to be.

The afternoon session was tense, and hostility was written on every Warrior's face. They were unable to hide the fact that there was dissension within their own ranks and snapped irritably at each other just as readily as they snapped at us, the so-called establishment.

After some initial sparring, Mayor Jim Davidson asked the leaders, and there were about a dozen of them in the room, if they had anything to present us. They wouldn't answer, and quite pointedly refused to answer, each in his turn making some equivocal statement or turning to one of his fellows to make answer. I cannot emphasize too strongly the patience and the basic decency of Jim Davidson who really did his best to coax something constructive out of the Warriors. As I write this I have been reconstructing and analyzing this phenomenal dullness, this lack of ability to seize the moment, and I have no better idea today than I did then as to why the Warriors didn't come through.

But they did not come through, and it was manifestly obvious to all that they could not. I knew that the jig was up then, and that there was no way I could continue to justify advocating the unlawful situation in the park to continue unchecked. I had to maintain my credibility with the elders of Treaty Three as well as with the police. At the same time I didn't want to give the Warriors the opportunity to deliberately misconstrue what I was about to say, so I wrote out my address by hand. Harvey Major, the middle-aged maverick from AIM, got up and orated in notable style as I wrote and I was grateful for the time it allowed me. I had difficulty concentrating on my task, as Major's rising and falling voice kept impinging on me. He was a spellbinder, and he told with great emotion about how he and Louis Cameron's father had scrounged for garbage in the park as starving young men thirty years previously. There may not have been a word of truth in it, but the rhetoric was powerful, and I ruefully observed the Warriors to be psyched up as he spoke.

Bob Birch, the paper mill manager, stood behind me as I wrote, and looked over my shoulder. He wasn't himself a party to the negotiations, but of course was knowledgeable about what was going on. He could see where I was heading, and he idly picked up a chair leg and twirled it between his fingers. I knew I was going to be all right when Bob caught my eye and winked. As Harvey Major droned on, here is what I wrote, mistakes and all:

"So-called amnesty has been stretched out of all proportions. I am authorized to say this. There has been three weeks of negotiations first with Treaty Number Three and then yourselves. Certain proposals came out of the park which we were led to believe were your proposals. You are obviously split among yourselves, and cannot agree on whether or not those proposals are yours, and in the event they are not yours you cannot agree on what proposals you do wish to present. It is further obvious that your leader, Mr. Cameron, is not in control. Yesterday evening, Mr. Cameron gave the contractor on the neighboring building project permission to enter to the building through the park. He went in with two other civilians and two policemen and was in the process of loading. One of your men stepped out of the park and on to the private property and said, "I am going to count to three and then I'm going to shoot." He counted to three and then fired a shot which went over the heads of the two policemen. They did not use their side arms, but beat it into the bush. Two more shots were fired after them. Moments later other policemen did in fact appear with sophisticated rifles, but the man with the gun had disappeared.

This incident illustrates two points: 1) Louis Cameron is not in effective control of his own warriors, 2) The statement that the guns are only for protection of people in the park is not accurate.

I have sat through one meeting with The Warriors on Bush Island, and this is the third meeting we have had on this site. The only thing we know that we didn't know before, is that you appear to want Anicinabe Park for spiritual and not merely financial reasons. I am therefore forced to conclude that you are not negotiating in good faith, but that you only want confrontation.

I therefore tell you this, and I have the authority of the Attorney

General and the Solicitor General, and the approval of the Minister of Natural Resources when I say it.

The so-called amnesty is withdrawn as of noon tomorrow. Any persons committing offenses in the park will be treated as common law-breakers, and will be charged accordingly, and they will be charged with the unlawful occupation of the park as from July 22, and with any firearms offenses which have taken place since that date, in or out of the park. As from the time you people here re-enter the park after leaving this room, I advise you and your followers to keep all arms out of sight, and I suggest you leave the park by this evening, otherwise it will be sealed by whatever means the police think are desirable. Any incidents that take place from this moment to tomorrow noon either on the fringes of the park or in the park, will be treated as criminal offenses, and are not subject to the amnesty."

When I finished reading the statement from my notes there really wasn't as much pandemonium as I expected. Jim Davidson was mildly upset that I had pulled the pin like that, and a few of the Warriors were greatly upset, as indicated by their gesticulations; the "establishment" people were quite impassive. I couldn't really tell who was on my side and who wasn't. The Warriors, however, got the message and quickly filed out the door and headed for their cars. I just barely had time to whisper to George to meet me at 11:30 P.M. by a certain large boulder at the shore of Anicinabe Park.

Taking positive action brought me a great sense of relief. I could not predict what was going to happen, but at least I knew the people in the park had been given every possible consideration, and my con-science was clear. I spent the rest of the day supplying the press and police with photostats of my remarks to the Warriors.

At about 10:30 I picked up Sergeant Carl Hager of the Kenora Town Police and brought him home with me. We waited for full dark, then paddled over to Anicinabe Park to the boulder by the shore, and picked up a very frightened young Toronto lawyer. We paddled very quickly on the way home.

George had eaten only one square meal in the past four days, and he was ravenous. He sucked up food like it was going out of style, and talked as he ate. It is to his credit that he retained some sympathy for the Warriors, and he was certainly concerned about how much he should say. However as the evening progressed he became more voluble, and eventually told me the first really solid news of how the Warriors were organized, if organization was the word. He said there was almost no food in the park and laughed when I told him the police estimate of the number of guns. On the other hand, he did confirm that there was a core of fanatics who had allowed themselves to be psyched up to the point that they could do something really stupid, like starting a shooting war with the police. However, morale had crumbled, and most of the people in the park just wanted to get out and save as much face as possible.

At some time well after midnight Erica mentioned that Dennis Banks had called me, and was expecting me to return his call. I was dubious about it, as I considered him the enemy, but George urged me to make the call saying he was sure Banks would act as a peacemaker, if allowed. I made the call and got a fellow named Doug Durham on the line.

Durham was Banks' lieutenant (lootenant, in the States) and held some sort of office in AIM. When I got to know him later he turned out to be one of the really great con men I have ever met. He claimed to have a string of degrees as long as your arm in various subjects including English and political science. I doubt now if he ever got out of high school, but I believed him at the time, and he certainly was knowledge-able in many fields. His primary vocation was con man, but he knew the Sioux language and customs perfectly, he understood American poli-tics, and was a cracking good pilot. Months after he left Kenora I still talked to him frequently on the telephone, and he told me he in fact worked for the FBI, his only mandate being to root out communist influence in AIM. Otherwise, he was free to support the cause of the Indians. Come to think of it, maybe his avocation was con man, rather than his vocation, if I might make the distinction. He had a really sharp mind, and was devious enough that he might have gone to high places in politics, had his FBI identity not been revealed.

Durham told me the AIM grapevine had it that the Warriors were in serious trouble, having ignored Banks' plea to have a peaceful rally. He knew they were in disarray, and that Harvey Major was keeping them psyched up. He said if we would let Banks come back up he would cool the whole situation out, and urged me to talk to the district attorney, who was then prosecuting Banks in Minneapolis, if I doubted him.

George and I sat up half the night while he filled me in on the almost mystical esteem in which the Warriors held Banks. In the end I agreed to follow up on it. Greatly to my surprise, I found that the district attorney (DA) and the judge both held Banks in high esteem, so I agreed that Banks should indeed come back to straighten the Warriors out.

In making this agreement I had reckoned without the police, my political masters, and the elders. They were all dead against the idea, at first. Eventually, I talked the police into agreeing to it, grudgingly. The elders said they would consent provided they could talk to Banks first, before he met with the Warriors. But the provincial cabinet remained unconvinced.

Within two hours of my conversation with the DA and the Judge in Minneapolis, a white-faced young reporter, a very good friend of mine, appeared at the police office. She had been talking to one of the Warriors at the edge of the park when Harvey Major appeared and announced something to the effect that "...Burton is Kenora's General Custer, and Dennis Banks is on the way up with a .357 magnum to blow him away tonight...." I didn't like the sound of this at all, and the police took it seriously enough to put a policeman with me for the rest of the day.

Evening approached, and the politicians, or those of them who could be found, still had not agreed to my use of Banks as an intermediary. I was having dinner with my morose police friends—I was somewhat morose myself—when a call came for me at the desk. The call was from one of Banks' staff at AIM, saying that the judge had recessed Banks' trial for a day, and Banks was in the air and due to arrive in Kenora late in the evening.

I panicked.

I tried to telephone my own minister, but as usual he wasn't available. George Kerr, the Solicitor General, said he would support whatever I did, but he thought I should try to keep Banks out until the rest of the cabinet had time to get used to the idea. Leo Bernier, then Minister of Natural Resources, said much the same thing, adding the practical offer of a helicopter to get me down to International Falls, Minnesota, where I could intercept Banks. The police wanted no part of the whole thing, as they figured they couldn't help me if indeed it was in Banks' mind to bump me off.

In the end I stuffed a pistol in each back pocket and took off in a giant Bell chopper with several MNR officials who just came for the ride, and with Ben Ratuski, a friend of the minister's, and sometime pal of mine. We were in the air, wobbling and shaking south when the pilot advised us all that he had never been to International Falls, didn't have a map and needed help with the navigation. Ben Ratuski sat up forward and pointed the way through the darkness while I briefed Ray Riley, a personal advisor to the minister, on what I thought might happen, specifically that there was a chance that someone might try to do me in, although I didn't really believe it to be so. I gave him one of my pistols and told him that if anything happened to me to shoot the tires out on Banks' airplane. In retrospect I felt very foolish, as they meant me no harm at all.

Customs and immigration formalities took only a few minutes, and we moved the big chopper over to an isolated part of the field. When the Commander aircraft landed I had no idea what to say or what to expect, except that I knew I had to keep Banks and friends out for a few days until the Kenora elders and the provincial cabinet got used to the idea.

I boarded Banks' Commander and found myself in the lap of one Ellen Movescamp, a very large and strong lady, my arms pinioned. She patted my pistol pocket and chuckled, saying without any hint of malice, "You won't be needing this" as she dropped my favorite heater into the depths of her ample bosom.

I turned my attention to the other passengers.

Doug Durham occupied the left-hand pilot's seat, and Dennis Banks was in the copilot's chair. Behind them were a young reporter, and to my great surprise William Kunstler, the well-known radical lawyer. The double bench seat was fully occupied by Ellen Movescamp with me quivering on her lap, halfway expecting Harvey Major's pronouncement about Dennis Banks and his .357 magnum to come true momentarily.

The odd thing was that I felt nothing but good vibrations from everyone on the plane, from Banks on down. They were extremely disappointed at being told to turn back, but finally agreed to do so when I promised faithfully to do my best to bring the politicians and the Treaty Number Three elders around to a point of agreement.

On parting, my heater now back in my hip pocket, William Kunstler told me I was a "fine public servant." I didn't know whether to take it as a compliment or not, given Kunstler's involvement with the Chicago Seven, a notable group of bad boys whom he had only just finished defending, and which had caused him to fall out with the more conservative elements on the legal scene in the United States. Today I know that it was a compliment, and I take it as such, because all but the most rabid right-wing extremists in the United States are now prepared to admit that Kunstler stood for something strong and good in the American character when he stood against the system on behalf of the unpopular Chicago Seven.

Ray Riley and Benny Ratuski crawled out of the grass where they had been hiding, waiting to blow the tires on Banks' Commander. The blackflies and mosquitoes had taken their toll, and they were as happy as I was to be wobbling back to Kenora in the beat-up MNR chopper. Since Ben was the only one with money in his pocket, he paid the late night customs fee for all of us.

One of the few funny incidents of the summer happened on this night. Because of the threats made, or presumed to be made, a few days earlier, the police sent a young police officer over to my Coney Island residence to be with my family for the night. My mother came over from next door too, just so there wouldn't be any problems.

When I arrived back in the wee hours from International Falls, Constable Joe Beitz was reading in the living room, trying manfully to stay awake, hearing assassins in every little noise in the bush outside the house. I was dead beat, and didn't even go up the stairs to bed, preferring to flop on the couch in the den.

In the morning I was up early and made preparations to hustle over to the office. On passing through the living room, I saw Joe Beitz sound asleep in an easy chair and my friend and neighbor Mel Henley out cold on the couch, in his pajamas. Mel is a good-natured bear of a man, and a very good friend, but not the kind of person you want to cross. His 30-30 carbine was propped in the corner by the fireplace. Joe's service revolver was on the mantlepiece.

Erica told me what had happened.

At sometime after I went to sleep, Mel Henley was awakened by the barking of his dog. He was actually one of my nearest neighbors, being only 200 yards around a point of land from me, in the direction of Anicinabe Park. When Mel got up to check the dog, he saw two canoes full of people ghosting around the shore, in the direction of my menage. I don't have to tell you what conclusion his mind leaped to. Being a man of action he shouted to his wife, "Douse the lights and phone the Burtons that there is trouble on the way." He pulled rubber boots on over his pajama legs, and ran into the bush, poking shells into the magazine of his carbine as he went. He figured he would head them off at the pass, as it were. He was going to perch on a rock where he had a

218

moonlight view of my backyard, my front yard, and my dock, and pick them off when they came out of the darkness.

No one ever saw the canoes again. Probably they were city kids from Kamp Kejeet out for a moonlight lark. In any event, they weren't Indians on the warpath, but Mel had no way of knowing that at the time.

As Mel ran out, his wife, Elaine, called my number. Erica upstairs and Joe Beitz downstairs picked up at the same time. Elaine yelled, "there's Indians coming your way," at which time Joe hung up the phone and beat it out the back door into the bush, gun drawn. He didn't hang on long enough to hear the rest of what Elaine added, "Mel has headed over with his 30-30." Consequently neither Mel nor Joe knew of each other's existence.

My two protectors came within a hair of shooting at each other. They heard each other rustling about in the bush, and heart in mouth they headed for the noise. Mel levered a shell into his rifle. Crick-click, two distinct noises, just what you would expect from a bushman's lever action rifle. Joe thumbed his hammer-click. Definitely a revolver, and not what you'd expect from a bushman.

Joe quavered, "Who the hell is there?"

Mel answered, not very confidently, "Who the hell are you?"

Joe: "I asked you first. I'm a policeman and if you don't show yourself I'll blow your goddamn head off!"

Mel: "Well, I'm a friend of Ted Burton's and if you're not really a policeman I'll fill you so full of holes you'll look like a friggin' sieve!"

By now it was obvious to both that the situation was not serious enough to warrant a shoot-out. It didn't take them long to discover that the tension had created a fierce thirst in them, and after satisfying themselves there were no bad guys in the weeds, they adjourned to my living room, but not before detouring to the liquor cabinet.

And this is how I found them in the morning, catching up on some well earned sleep.

Two intense days of haggling with the police, my political masters, and the elders, followed. It became plain that support for the Banks visit was limited, and if I persisted in bringing him in and the game went wrong, I would be hung out to dry by all concerned. Finally, I got agreement from Solicitor General George Kerr and Minister of Natural Resources Leo Bernier, and I knew I had it made. My own minister, the attorney general, was not communicative. Deputy Attorney General Frank Callaghan said he would support me personally, as did Director of Crown attorneys, Pat Lesage. The elders never did agree, but I was satisfied I was on the right track. I felt that there was a residue of personal good will between myself and the elders and they would not go for my hide if the Banks venture was unsuccessful.

A couple of days later, The Honorable Leo Bernier again loaned me an aircraft, this time a Cessna 310, normally used as a bird dog on fires, and I again flew down to International Falls. This time Banks and Durham came alone, Banks having got a further reprieve from his own continuing trial in Minneapolis.

The next few days are really a blur in my mind. I had not had a full night's sleep in weeks, nor any respite from the Anicinabe Park sit-in, and I was desperately tired. The dynamics of what was going on were quite beyond me, and all these years later I am still not sure why everything happened as it did.

On arrival in Kenora with Banks and Durham the first order of business was to get something to eat, for none of us had eaten that day. I recall that it was exactly midnight, and we were all staggering weary, when the phone rang. It was my friends, the elders, who announced stonily that they were waiting in a church hall to see us. That meant me, too.

The ensuing session was almost more than I could bear, and to prevent me from nodding off, my friend Chief Raymond Bruyere of the Couchiching Reserve kept thumping me on the back, intoning "Stay awake you son-of-a-bitch. You got us into this and you're going to see it through." Much to my surprise, Banks and Durham were cool and collected, even nonchalant, in the way they responded to the hostility of the elders. Looking back on it, I believe that the anger of the elders was really at themselves, and they resented the fact that an outsider presumed to do what they themselves could not. The fact that Banks and his companion, Durham, were Sioux did not help anything, as traditionally the Sioux and the Ojibway were mortal enemies.

The elders eventually came around, and honeyed words flowed. It appeared when the smoke cleared, that they figured Harvey Major, he of the golden tongue, was the chief instigator in the park, and they badly wanted to see the last of him. Since he belonged to AIM they felt he was Banks' problem and he reluctantly agreed to do something about it.

By the following day the park was again in a state of siege. I believe both the police and the Warriors had developed a sense of paranoia, or a sort of fortress mentality. On top of this some of the rednecks in town were demanding action. Banks and Durham had very little freedom of movement, and I fearfully gave them my car keys, my car being known to the police. Reluctantly the police allowed them unimpeded passage in and out of the park.

Almost immediately, things began to improve in the park. The guns were kept out of sight, and many of the third rank people, those whom I have dubbed larkers, were allowed to slip away. Several of the second rank people, the ones I thought to be misguided idealists, also disappeared. The elders became visible again. The volume of the taped tom toms that had been blasting over the public address system in the park day and night was turned down. The tension was still high, but at least it was quieter.

Banks and Durham hurried back and forth between the park, the elders, my office and goodness knows where. They arranged (with police concurrence) that Madeline Skead should take custody of whatever guns were left, and that the elders would take charge of the demands that came out of the park, and negotiate on behalf of the Warriors to have the demands fulfilled. As I said earlier, the demands had been articulated and planted from the outside, as a face-saving mechanism for the Warriors. When they were finally presented, most of them were quite reasonable.

But there was still Harvey Major, who tended to get in the way at every turn.

One day, perhaps two or three days after they arrived, Banks turned up in my office and announced that Durham was guarding Major in my car, and they had to get out of town quick—right now.

A helicopter flight was out of the question, due to high winds and thunderstorms. Fortunately, the MNR Turbo-Beaver from Fort Frances was in town, and pilot Art Colfer agreed to fly us to the border if I could get permission. A phone call to Leo Bernier fixed that up, and we were on our way. Harvey Major was definitely not himself, and when I asked what they had done to him to shut him up, Banks and Durham just smiled.

The plane ride to Fort Frances was extremely bumpy, and it brought Major to his senses. By the time we reached Fort Frances he realized he was being shanghaied, and he resented it, but was too groggy to do anything about it. When we landed, the MNR mechanic handed me a set of keys to an old car, whispering, "There's exactly one gallon of gas in it. It will take you to the airport in International Falls, and back to town.

Just leave it on the street somewhere, with the keys in the ashtray." I could tell that he was mystified, but I could see the hand of my friend Chief Solomon of the Fort Frances Police in the matter, and I gave no explanation.

Durham shoved Major into the back seat, and got in next to him. Banks ran around the other side and sandwiched Major in the middle. I didn't know what I was going to say to U.S. Customs and Immigration, but I didn't have to say anything—the man looked in the window at the trio in the back seat and simply waved me on. When I looked back, Banks and Durham were fingering the beautiful engraved presentation knives I had given them as tokens of Her Majesty's esteem, and poor old Harvey was looking straight ahead, saying nothing. I think that somehow Banks and Durham had a calming effect on Major.

The calming effect, which may or may not have had something to do with the knives, or with whatever they had given him to keep him quiet back in Kenora, lasted through a quick dinner in International Falls. I was petrified that Major would make a run for it, or call for help, or whatever, but he didn't. As a matter of fact he didn't let a peep out until it was time to climb aboard the Commander. Durham and I untied the plane while Banks and Major yelled and gesticulated. People were coming out of various buildings to watch, and I could visualize the arrival of the police at any minute.

Durham didn't check the oil, eyeball the gas tanks, kick the tires, or do any of the usual walk-around checks—he simply grabbed Major by the seat of the pants and the scruff of the neck and chucked him into the aircraft, like a stick of cordwood. He hit the seat so hard it shook the whole airplane, and then he didn't move. Durham swarmed over him and up to the front while Banks tucked Major's legs in and secured the door.

A bystander said, "Did I really see two old-time Indians in buck-skins and pigtails fire a third Indian into that plane?" I could only shake my head, as Durham gunned the aircraft out of its slot on the tarmac and over to the taxiway. He didn't bother with a warm up or exercising the propellers. He opened the taps and took off on the taxiway. No more than five minutes had elapsed since we had stepped out of the car.

I very quickly put distance between me and the airport, abandoning the car near the police station in Fort Frances. I don't remember how I got back to Kenora.

I never saw Banks or Durham again. Banks disappeared for a few years, then gave himself up to do time for offenses arising out of Wounded Knee. I always thought there was a great deal more good than bad in the man, although the FBI might disagree with me on that.

The document finally presented by Treaty Number Three on behalf of its unruly offspring, The Warriors, is of historical interest, and it is set out in full in the appendix.

Basically it demanded from the senior governments that they should be more attentive to the needs of their wards, the Indians, and it listed land claims, economic development, education, policing, and other matters which cried out for attention. For the most part the demands weren't unreasonable. The Warriors left the tedious business of negotiating the implementation of the demands with the various levels of government to Peter Kelly. Some of the Warriors who did not simply fade back into private life went on to further adventures in Ottawa.

It took years, but a surprising number of demands were actually fulfilled. The Anicinabe Park demonstration may not have been the only influence creating pressure for change, but it was by far the strongest, and I believe the action deserves credit for motivating governments to make improvements over a wide spectrum. Consider the following items that have been dealt with after coming to light in the Anicinabe Park Manifesto.

The head office budgets of district Indian Agencies often exceeded 60 percent, leaving only 40 percent to actually benefit the reserves. The federal government may have been planning to allot more operational responsibility to the reserves all along, but the advent of Anicinabe Park certainly hastened the day. District offices are being phased out.

Increasingly, Native people, whom we now also refer to as First Nations people, are being hired at all levels of government, and are being trained to fill responsible positions.

Land claims are being addressed all across Canada, although not as quickly as the First Nations people would like.

The demand for economic development is recognized as imperative. This only means that people think about it a lot. It doesn't mean that marvellous solutions are a reality for most reserves. High unemployment is still the norm.

Educational service to reserves has improved considerably, but this was in the mill before Anicinabe Park. Keeping native youngsters in school is a problem, as the kind of education the larger society presents them with is simply not in their culture or traditions. Native children do somewhat better when taught courses designed by Native educators.

In the interest of satisfying readers who are teachers I will point out that the Indian method of teaching was traditionally by repeated demonstration, and not by discoursing. It is my view that adherence to the demonstrative method of teaching is not effective, and may even be counter productive in this day and age. I say this with all respect, and in the knowledge that traditional teaching methods were quite appropriate in more traditional times. But I defy anyone to teach algebra or history purely by demonstration.

Housing has been generally improving from year to year. The so-called Indian Affairs houses are being phased out in place of better homes. Thefts by private contractors have been allayed by having the Indians build their own homes.

Moving into the provincial field, we find very serious demands with relation to Native Justices of the Peace (JPs) and the administration of justice. Within a year, several appointments were made and training was well under way. The selection and training of Native JPs is now a full time project with the province. Justice of the Peace courts are now held regularly on more than twenty fly-in locations in Northern Ontario, usually with Native JPs presiding, and in many more drive-in satellites. As quickly as individual Indian bands come up with solid plans to look after their own offenders they are taking over functions previously reserved for the mainstream criminal courts. This, too, is an ongoing process, and is only now in its beginning stages.

The inaction on certain complaints against the province, The Dryden Paper Company, and Ontario Hydro was a serious matter. It took another twelve or fourteen years, but a satisfactory arrangement was eventually reached between the parties in the 1980s. Several millions of dollars in compensation to the Grassy Narrows and Whitedog Reserves was awarded, to be paid over a period of time. I understand that very little benefit has accrued to the people it was supposed to help. It would be interesting to see a full accounting.

As requested, cross-cultural training for police and others dealing with First Nations people was instituted, even in the face of considerable resistance. The problem is that you can lead a horse to water, but you can't make him drink.

Better access to northern reserves is now an established fact. Airstrips exist at even the smallest villages. Regular, efficient (but not cheap) flights are scheduled daily. Indian pilots are now accepted without question.

Violent deaths are still a problem in Indian society, and at this writing, suicides have been prevalent for more than a year in the Nishnawbi Aski area. First Nations people are making an effort to address this problem themselves. Similarly, problems of alcohol and sniffing substances like gasoline seem to be more successfully addressed by First Nations people themselves, as opposed to any government agency.

Police brutality was never a serious problem, in my view. In any event I am not aware the Native people got thumped with greater frequency than anyone else, notwithstanding efforts by civil rights proponents to make a case against the police. Apathy and insensitivity are another matter, and most police forces have made diligent efforts to hire minority people, not only natives. This seems to be paying off in terms of improved relations with cultural minorities.

A street patrol was established in Kenora, funded by the province. It still functions on the waterfront and in the back lanes of Kenora every night. Over the years many lives have been saved, and the idea has been copied in other northern communities. The province assisted in establishing a wilderness camp north of Kenora, for the purpose of sheltering Kenora's street people. The camp has turned into a place where alcoholics and sniffers can go to get in touch with their cultural roots. It is operated by the Native people with very little support (or interference) from government agencies.

So much for the issues raised on behalf of The Warriors at Anicinabe Park. The process wasn't tidy, and the fallout is ongoing. The administration of justice looked bad, but it would have looked a lot worse if a real shoot-out had occurred.

But what about the major players?

Harvey Major came back to Canada in a pine box late in the fall. They said he had been involved in an automobile accident, and they intended to bury him at his home reserve at Northwest Angle, but due to the onset of winter, he was buried at Rat Portage adjacent to Kenora. I did not attend the funeral on the advice of the elders.

Doug Durham was really the most interesting of the lot. It was really he who called the shots for Banks. I have always thought it odd that some of the greatest con men, and he was truly magnificent, could rise to any heights they wished if they put their minds to consistent hard work and more or less honest endeavors, but it is not in them.

225

I had many phone conversations with Durham in succeeding months, as he continued to give me good advice on how to wind down the volatile situation in Kenora. He must have dropped my name in Wisconsin and The Dakotas, because, during the following winter I got calls from law enforcement officials asking what I thought they should do to avert brush fires. In particular, the office of the Governor of Wisconsin called to discuss a reasonable way to deal with the seizure by local Indians of a monastery at Gresham. I was able to pave the way for Durham to go to Ottawa to cool out a native demonstration without violence.

The last I heard of Durham was in 1976 or 1977 when he was on the lecture circuit for the John Birch Society, or some such group.

The rest is really anti-climactic. Negotiations took place between the Warriors, elders, the Department of Indian Affairs, and the province to put into effect some of the demands presented in the name of the Warriors.

Deputy Minister Doug Wright, of the Ministry of Community and Social Services, did a lot of the talking, as did Deputy Attorney General Frank Callaghan, who later answered the more tranquil call of the bench.

Peter Kelly and the elders became more vocal as befitted their status as the proper spokesmen of the Indian people.

Louis Cameron and a few of his cohorts of the inner circle moved on to Ottawa to take part in another demonstration later in the fall. After that the inner circle people just faded away. I have already mentioned that the second rank people had begun to fade away even before the end of the occupation of the park, many of them seeking productive jobs.

Jim Davidson went back to running Kenora. He was turfed out by two votes at the next election, but refused to ask for a recount.

Doug and Madeline Skead continued to live on the Rat Portage Reserve until Doug's death from cardiac troubles. Madeline still lives there at the heart of her family, and is known as an activist and a healer among her people.

Willie Big George, who until he died would leave wild rice on my dock, continued to work for his people until his death a few years ago.

Raymond Bruyere of Couchiching is an old man with laugh lines and wisdom etched on his face. He is considered an elder, and is consulted by both races on matters of importance. I still see Ray from time to time.

Eck Miller (Uncle Bulgy) immediately retired and went to Florida. He never did put in a final report on Anicinabe Park. Bob MacGarva went back to his job as a superintendent, in Toronto.

George, the brash young lawyer from Toronto, took a job as counsel to an Indian organization in southern Ontario.

The government did not fire me as suggested on behalf of The Warriors during the negotiations. Nor did it thank me. Judge Nottingham retired the following year for reasons unrelated to Anicinabe Park. The weather finally turned cool. It had been a long, hot summer.

On the Coast of Hudson Bay

Winisk (now Peawanuk) and Fort Severn are so far north they do not appear on Ontario's official highway map, for the rather inadequate reason that they are three or four hundred miles north of the province's highway network. One day, I am sure, the villagers will be able to drive right to their doorsteps, but I don't think within my lifetime it will be possible to get there except by flying. I have been to both villages many times, and have watched them acclimatize to the phenomenon of modern technology.

For a few brief years, in the fifties and sixties, Winisk was an important place, because five miles away to the east, on the other side of the meandering Winisk River delta, stood one of the main bases of the Mid-Canada Early Warning Line. This closer-in twin of the Dew Line was operated by a dozen Royal Canadian Air Force personnel and 200 civilian contractors. The base consisted of a tiny artificial harbor, an airstrip, a self-contained camp, and some highly sophisticated doppler (radar scanning) detection equipment to which only the few air force personnel had access. Several men from the village found employment at the base, but the village was off-limits to all but the commanding officer, the base nurse, and the helicopter pilots. For the rest of the personnel, the base might as well have been 500 miles away.

My first trip to Winisk, in 1962 or thereabouts, was to prosecute a woman who had an unpleasant habit of beating people up if they disagreed with her. This was unusual among the Cree, as they tended to be peaceful people who settled their own troubles without intervention from the police and the courts. This willingness to look after their own problems is still evident in many of the more traditional villages, as the people seem to have an instinctive understanding of the dictum that "the police are the people and the people are the police."

I have said a great deal elsewhere about the violence that people of the northern villages commit upon one another, but nevertheless, it would be a mistake to conclude this is true in all villages. There is as much difference between the various northern villages and the people who live in them, as there is, say, between Thunder Bay and Hamilton. Until the 1960s, Winisk had never known the type of trouble that called for intervention by the larger society. It was therefore a surprise when word filtered out by the Hudson's Bay Company radio network, via the Northern Stores headquarters in Winnipeg, that Maria Shingibis was out of control.

Magistrate J.V. Fregeau, myself, Jack K. Doner for the defense, a young court reporter named Joanne Komorowski, and Corporal Ozzie Corbett of the OPP piled into a chartered Grumman Goose and flew the 575 miles to the gravel strip at RCAF Station Winisk. We were given a rousing welcome by the base personnel, who seldom had outside visitors, particularly not attractive young women like Joanne. Several of the young swains at the evening festivities paid court to her by chugalugging neat whiskey and attempting to dance with her, and promptly passing out. It was truly an evening of glorious revelry, as the mess sported the best booze that could be procured from anywhere in the world. Many of the men had not seen a woman in over a year.

On the following day the RCAF provided us with a big Sikorsky helicopter to fly us over the treacherous Winisk River delta to the little village perched high on the muddy west bank. We left behind the unreality of the base and all its luxuries, and arrived at an equally unreal tundra village which consisted of a cluster of tar paper, canvas, and skin shacks sheltering some 200 souls in what appeared to me to be abject poverty. I later found them to be fairly happy people, because they were still more or less self-sufficient and not reliant on welfare. This very self-sufficiency lent them a dignity that transcended their poverty but this was all to change in a few years.

When the helicopter touched down on the frozen muskeg, Ozzie hit the ground, enlisting the assistance of the first English-speaking person he encountered. Off he went to the bad lady's tent with the rest of the party in hot pursuit. Fortunately Maria was at home, so Ozzie immediately told her through the interpreter that she was being charged with assault. The name of the assaulted party was unknown, as was the nature of the evidence, but those were minor details we could sort out later. The important thing was to get Maria under wraps before she disappeared into the tundra.

We had been told that Maria was capable of living entirely off the land, and that her sister had once jumped off an airplane in Fort Albany and walked 250 miles to Winisk in midwinter, without supplies. It had been autumn when we left Kenora the day before, but on the coast it was winter, and if Maria had escaped she would have been gone for good.

When I looked into Maria's tent it became obvious that she made very few concessions to the white man's way of life. Her bed was a mound of boughs and a rabbit-skin robe. There was a tin airtight space heater in one corner, with one pot and a frying pan on a box. Her prize possession was evidently a little wind-up record player that sat on the ground, together with a dozen 78 rpm records. That was all. No clothes. No furniture.

Maria was true to her reputation. The moment Ozzie relaxed his vigilance she took off through the muskeg like a startled moose. Ozzie took off after her, cussing a blue streak. The rest of us, including the magistrate, cheered Maria on and shouted bad advice to Ozzie. It looked like Ozzie had her when he managed to grab the back of her jacket, but she slipped out of it and continued her dash for freedom through the semi-frozen swamp. She would have gotten clean away if she hadn't run into a clearing of chained dogs that immediately lunged at her, causing her to swerve right back into Ozzie's arms. This time he hung onto her. The rest of us, indeed the whole village, was convulsed with laughter. Neither Ozzie nor Maria thought it was funny.

Court was immediately convened in a heated building that served as a meetinghouse and a school, when there was a teacher. Ozzie had to watch Maria like a mother hen, so I set about putting the case together myself. It wasn't difficult, because everyone except the priest was there. The facts of the case were not serious by my standards. Maria had slapped women on several occassions when they had come to remonstrate with her about keeping their teenagers up late listening to the record player. Now, to most people these slaps were not earth shaking, but consider that these were peace-loving people who, up to that time, were completely self-governing and knew only the natural law that flowed from community consensus. And the consensus was that the community was outraged!

Persuading the judge to convict poor Maria was no problem, but Jack Doner and I got into a serious debate over the appropriate sentence. The helicopter pilot, Bob Connor, was an observant young man with a highly developed sense of social justice as we shall see later. He pointed out that Maria was now an outcast, and if she stayed in the village she would be a pariah. If she were taken out the villagers would see that she was being punished, and would be more apt to accept her back. A stiff lecture would have sufficed in Kenora, but in order that she would not arrive back to a cold, hungry tent in midwinter, His Worship had to give her six months in the District Jail in Kenora. So, from the primitive village the chopper wobbled us back to Station Winisk, a miracle of modern civilization with its gourmet food, fine liquors, and warm beds.

What to do with Maria that night was a matter of some concern. The commanding officer (CO) refused to have her in his cell because that was where they kept the liquor and cigarettes, and he refused to lend us men to guard her; regulations, I suppose. Ozzie installed her in a spare room in one of the dormitories, first being sure to remove her socks and moccasins. He and I took turn about sitting with her and being grateful guests at the officer's mess, which was situated in a large building 200 feet away through a howling blizzard. Even half-time, sitting under Maria's baleful stare, was enough to create a powerful thirst in her guards, Ozzie and me.

I was guarding Maria, if drinking rum and coke and eating sauteed butterfly shrimp can be called guarding, when Ozzie came to relieve me. I, of course, took his place back at the mess. A few minutes later Ozzie appeared and announced that Maria had finally gone to sleep, and if she woke up she could go barefoot in the snow, as far as he was concerned. As an afterthought he mentioned that he had borrowed the CO's command car, which he had found with the engine running, and gotten it stuck while trying to drive it the 200 feet to the mess. That put a damper on the party for all of thirty seconds....air force regulations abruptly changed, and two more or less sober men from the base were detailed to watch Maria for the rest of the night.

The following morning the Goose took off without me, as it could not get airborne with the necessary fuel in the tanks as well as the extra burden of Maria. Martyr that I am, I elected to stay at the base until alternate transportation could be arranged.

I spent four more days at the base, until the Transair DC-4 that ran a weekly schedule between Ottawa and Churchill stopped in to pick me up. I spent the time sleeping, eating, drinking, and hunting ptarmigan with a .22 pistol. Twice, Bob Connor smuggled me over to the village in the big Sikorsky helicopter, giving me a few brief hours in which to learn something about the remarkable people of the village. Looking back on it I would have to say that their most outstanding characteristic was their ability to be self-sustaining in that harsh environment. Welfare was not yet a lifestyle, and for a cash income the people trapped and took in goose hunters. For the rest they hunted, fished, and lived off the land. Life was hard, but satisfying, which is not to say that it was better then than it is now, which, after all, is a judgement only the people themselves can make.

Helen Gull, or Helen Kwiash as she was called in her native Cree, was not, of course, known to me at the time. I never did meet her, because she died the following year. Helen Gull was in her sixties and in failing health. She had been out to the Zone Hospital at Moose Factory on more than one occasion, where her illness had been diagnosed as chronic. The nurse from the base would see her periodically and give her some pills prescribed by the doctors at the Zone Hospital. The chopper pilots or one of the villagers who worked at the base would report on her condition if it got bad. Helen Gull was sick, but not terminally ill by the medical standards of the day.

One day Bob Connor heard that Mrs. Gull had taken a turn for the worse. He looked into her home and found her barely conscious. The nurse flew over and had a look at her, then returned to the base, immediately calling the Zone Hospital at Moose Factory for instructions. The Zone Hospital was indifferent, and told the nurse to continue to administer the same medication. The CO offered to fly Mrs. Gull out in a chopper, all the way to Moose Factory Island, but the Zone Hospital thought it was unnecessary.

The next day Connor phoned me by the complicated system of land lines and radio links that existed at the time. He was frustrated, and the CO and the nurse backed him up. I said regretfully that there was nothing I could do, but asked to be kept posted. The next day Bob and the nurse called me again to say that Mrs. Gull was not expected to live the night. The following day Transair offered to take her to Ottawa on the weekly schedule, but Helen Gull died as they were loading her on the plane.

They chopped a hole in the frozen tundra behind the village and laid Helen Gull to rest. The base personnel raised a howl that was heard in Ottawa and Toronto, and it wasn't long till Dr. Beatty Cotnam, the supervising coroner for the province, was on the phone to find out what the furor was about.

The subject of health care for northern residents was on everybody's mind at the time, so we decided to hold an inquest. Jack Hills from the chief coroner's office chartered an Apache and flew up with Dick Bender of the OPP to do a proper investigation, arriving on a frigid day in early winter. It was too cold for the choppers, so they were pulled across the treacherous river by dog team, which was no doubt a thrill, but a lot less comfortable than a chopper. To their surprise the men found that the people of the village were not as upset as the people at the base. To the people of the village life and death were all a part of a grand design, or continuum, over which man has little control, and Helen Gull's death was but one more event in the great scheme of the unfathomable universe.

An inquest was called for the following spring, and it was to be held at the village. This would be the first inquest ever held in the far northern part of the province. The Zone Hospital officials were of course required to be in attendance to justify their lack of response to Helen Gull's plight.

On June 8 we left Kenora in a Cessna 180 on floats. The pilot was competent but inexperienced, so my father, who was a retired bush pilot, came along to give him moral support. My wife Erica came along to act as court reporter. Our last fuel stop was to be Big Trout Lake, and we were fortunate to find an open strip of water between the shore and the ice edge just big enough to get in and out of. On leaving we flew over still frozen lakes for an hour and a half and landed on the meandering Winisk River just before dark. Chief Coroner Beatty Cotnam and Jack Hills, his exec, came in on another float equipped aircraft out of Timmins, and the head doctor from Moose Factory came in on a Beaver. We all stayed at a house owned by the Forestry Branch, as it was then called, pooling our resources of food and drink.

Preparations for the inquest began first thing in the morning. Jack Hills was to act as coroner's constable, and my father was to help me with the witnesses, some of whom had not previously given statements.

The three pilots were to be on the coroner's jury, together with the Hudson's Bay store manager, and an Indian who spoke good English and had been away from the village all winter and who was not related to the family of the deceased. We also arranged for translation into Cree of all the proceedings. Having an honest to goodness Indian on the jury and interpreting the proceedings were unheard of innovations at the time, although it became standard practice in the 1970s. I assign myself some of the credit for advances of this nature.

The inquest was a madhouse. The Indian agent from Moosonee arrived in unexpectedly to pay treaty, and the two parties had to share the meeting room, the same one in which Maria Shingibis had faced her trial the year before. Every man, woman, child, and loose dog crammed into the room, and at intervals two young men marched back and forth between the coroner's desk (two plywood powdered milk drums) and the Indian agent's desk (a plank across two boxes), carrying the flag. The Union Jack no less!

In spite of the pandemonium, I managed to call the witnesses and get their evidence. We had frequent adjournments while the three pilots on the jury flopped out in their hip waders to move their aircraft to accommodate the exceptionally high spring tide, and the official inter-preters for the two parties conferred on the meaning of words.

The inquest heard from Helen Gull's family, who told how she had suffered for many years from her ailment, and from one of the village elders who said that the people simply didn't know how to deal with the government bureaucracy when it came to solving problems. The nurse and the CO from the base told about their efforts to look after Helen Gull, and how their offers to transport her to the outside world had been rebuffed. Everyone who had anything to say was given the opportunity.

The last witness was, of course, the doctor from the Moose Factory Zone Hospital. He attempted to justify the handling of Helen Gull's case by the health authorities, but no one was in a mood to listen to him. It was quite apparent that Helen Gull could have been saved for many years of productive living had the authorities been willing to make the effort. The jury brought in a verdict which was a scathing attack on the delivery of health services in the North, and it had the effect of changing the way the Zone Hospitals related to the people they served.

Later on the good doctor referred to the Helen Gull inquest as "the time they put me on trial at Winisk."

On the way back south we stopped in at Hawley Lake on the Sutton

River. A large family, the Chookamoolins, who seemed not to be connected with any Indian reserve was living there and running a tourist camp. Some of their people were living in teepees covered with skin and canvas, a practice which has died out since. Erica took the last of our oranges, which we carried as a medium of exchange, and distributed them to the children, who did not seem to know what to do with them. An older child took an orange and showed the younger ones how to peel and eat them, causing sighs of wonder and delight.

I was to go back to Winisk several times in the sixites and seventies. I went in several more times with Chief Coroner Beatty Cotnam on his annual tour, and on trials at the provincial court level.

The life of that oasis of luxury, the base facility, eventually came to an end. The mid-Canada line became obsolete and the government simply shut it down. They dynamited the main antenna and walked away from the base leaving millions of dollars worth of buildings, furnishings, and machinery intact. It was cheaper to abandon it than to fly it out or move it out by sea. An international construction firm bought the base, intending to move it to South America. However, they had moved out only the two giant diesel generators when a storm destroyed the landing barges used as lighters, so the construction firm was forced to abandon the project when the tiny harbor silted in. When I visited the abandoned base in 1977 only the big hangar and the gravel airstrip remained operational, maintained by a caretaker employed by the Ontario government. All the buildings except one used by the villagers to put up goose hunters were in ruins, the windows having been smashed by vandals, permitting the harsh climate to do its work on the interiors. Two dozen trucks, buses, bombardiers, and bulldozers were vandalized, wrecked and left to rust in the salt air. Only the furnishings and portable buildings were put to use, and they can be found as far down the coast as Attawapiskat and as far up the coast as Fort Severn.

And what of the village itself? It did not prosper, its well-being fluctuating with the vagaries of leadership. Booze can be a curse, although the villagers tried to cope with it in a novel way, not by banning it but by encouraging people to drink only in moderation. If Winisk had just gone on and on without some intervening factor it would eventually have sunk into a morass of despondency; however, something else did happen.

In the spring of 1986, a sudden ice jam (the action of the river ice breaking up and piling up on itself) caused the river to overflow its banks. A wall of water and ice blocks rampaged through the village. Within minutes the village was gone, the buildings tumbled about by the ice and washed out onto the tundra. Miraculously only two people were killed; however, all but five buildings were destroyed, and they were filled with mud and rendered useless. The village has been relocated to high ground, seventeen miles south on the banks of the river, with modern insulated houses, plumbing, and sewage disposal. It is now called Peawanuk, "the place from which flint is gathered."

In 1994 leadership is strong, and one hears that the people have become happy in their new environment, but there is almost no useful work for the people to do, and they are mostly on welfare. Government would do well to give serious thought to some means of giving the many hinterland settlements of northern Canada something to do, honest work of some kind, in order that the people might live in dignity. Only in this way can the nation protect its interests by maintaining a strong presence in the North. Even if massive subsidization of some industry is required in each village then the government must do it, otherwise the North will deteriorate into an enclave of hopeless welfare communities, and Canada will no longer be able to say it is effectively occupying the North.

Good use could have been made of the old RCAF Station Winisk if only government, either provincial or federal, had the resolve to do it. It could have been turned into a sort of wilderness prison camp for warehousing that very small percentage of offenders for whom rehabilitation is, in practical terms, a lost cause. Because of its isolation across several hundred miles of tundra and wilderness, escape would have been almost impossible. Large numbers of guards and expensive escape proof technology would have been unnecessary. Service would have been effected by weekly air freight deliveries, the only expensive part of the operation. The villagers would have had real work, and several hundred individuals considered to be incapable of rehabilitation would have had lodging society could afford while serving their sentences.

But it was not to be. Comparisons were made to the notorious French penal colony on Devil's Island and to Alcatraz, thus creating a roadblock to any meaningful consideration of using Station Winisk as a jail facility. Even very recently this same attitude presented itself when the proposal of an island jail in British Columbia was made. And so the old RCAF Station Winisk corrodes in the salt air of the Hudson Bay, and soon will be only a memory.

Appendix

Further to the chapter A Long, Hot Summer, the following is the list of grievances advanced on behalf of the Warriors Society:

Federal Matters

1. The Department of Indian Affairs and its programs should be changed immediately in the following respects.
a.) Unequal and manipulative provision of services to reserves must be ended. No more starving one reserve and force feeding another to drive wedges between the various bands.
b.) Large portions of the Department budget must no longer be absorbed by the department's internal administration. More should be allowed to reach the Indian people themselves.
c.) A youth division of the department should immediately be established to deal with the problems and aspirations of youth.
d.) Senior department officials at the Kenora and Fort Frances agencies should immediately be fired and their replacements should be selected only with the approval of the local Indian people.
e.) Subject to approval by Indians across Canada, the voting age for band matters should be lowered from twenty-one to eighteen years.
2. Immediate attention to Native land claims across the country as well as in the Treaty Number Three area. No more stalling and procrastinating and passing the buck.
3. Medical and dental services equal to those available in urban areas, and with an emphasis on preventative programs must be made available immediately.

4. Experts on economic development must be brought together and instructed to draw up, in consultation with the Indian people, a full and effective plan to make the reserves viable economic units. The government must realize that this will cost money, but it has held back so much in the past that now it must make up for past mistakes.

5. A complete inventory of the quantity and quality of resources and services delivered to the various reserves must be drawn up in order that inequalities and stupidities may be exposed.

6. Educational services to Indians must be improved drastically and immediately. No more closing down of schools without consultation with the people affected. Elementary schools, fully equipped and staffed to be located on all reserves. Indian high schools should be established in the Treaty Number Three area at central locations. Ojibway language and culture should be a large part of the courses of studies for all Indian students.

7. Housing programs for Indians must be improved. No more construction shacks called houses. No more thefts and robberies by private building contractors.

8. The provision of social services and other resources to Indian people must be centered on the reserves and in the Indian settlements, not in the large centers away from the people.

9. Certain aspects of the administration of justice should be turned over to the various bands. There should be Indian Justices of the Peace and summary conviction courts established on the reserves. Such programs should be established with the approval of Native people across Canada.

10. A massive effort to provide permanent jobs for Indians should be undertaken immediately. Indians do not want to be a reserve of unemployed who are kept available only to do temporary, low-paying jobs.

Provincial Matters

1. Provincial Judge Nottingham must be removed from the bench. His sentences are unduly severe and cause misunderstandings and resentment among the Indian people. (A verbal request was later made to consider taking E.C. Burton out of service.)

2. The province must demonstrate that it is willing to bargain in good faith on the question of mercury contamination of the Wabigoon and English River systems. So far its attitude has been evasive and insulting.

3. The government should establish a police college in northwestern Ontario. This college would aid the economy of the area and could

include special courses to train Indian officers and to teach white officers how to deal with Indians.

4. Establish an Ontario Native Council on Alcoholism—controlled by Indians and operating in cooperation with, but not under, the Addiction Research Foundation. Its activities should be based on the reserves, not in the large towns.

5. Access to isolated reserves and settlements should be improved. Subsidized bus services should be set up. Roads should be constructed and properly maintained. Native people, when traveling, should not have to rely on fourth-rate privately owned roads maintained for the use of pulp trucks only. Air access to reserves must be improved and subsidized. Indian pilots must be trained immediately and aircraft made available to them so they no longer have to come hat in hand when they require transportation.

6. Provincial human rights legislation should be toughened and enforcement procedures strengthened.

Quality Hancock House Titles

Fatal Prescription
A Doctor without Remorse
John Griffiths
ISBN 0-88839-369-5

Descent into Madness
The Diary of a Killer
Vernon Frolick
ISBN 0-88839-300-8

Good Lawyer
Bad Lawyer
David Nuttall
ISBN 0-88839-315-6

Jack Mould and the
Curse of Gold
Elizabeth Hawkins
ISBN 0-88839-281-8

Gang Ranch
The Real Story
Judy Alsager
ISBN 0-88839-275-3

The Bootlegger's Lady
Ed Sager & Mike Frye
ISBN 0-88839-976-6

Available from Hancock House Publishers

USA: 1431 Harrison Avenue, Blaine, WA 98230-5005
Canada: 19313 Zero Avenue, Surrey, B.C. V4P 1M7
For orders call: 1-800-938-1114 Fax: 1-800-983-2262
Credit cards accepted. Business line: (604) 538-1114

Unsolicited manuscripts accepted for consideration.